"When Bill Fossett went down the street wearing his gun, I wondered who was at the end of the street—or the county or the territory—that would be brought in."
Elmer Soloman, Kingfisher, Oklahoma

W. D. "Bill" Fossett

Pioneer and Peace Officer

by JIM FULBRIGHT

Mid-South Publications
Goodlettsville, Tennessee

Data:

Fulbright, Jim
W. D. "Bill" Fossett: pioneer and peace officer
Includes maps, illustrations, endnotes, bibliographical
references and index.
ISBN 0-9664039-5-9 (paper)
Subjects: Fossett, William D. "Bill," 1851-1940.
1. Peace officers—Oklahoma—Biography. 2. Peace officers—
Kansas—Biography. 3. Frontier and pioneer life—Kansas and
Oklahoma. 4. Oklahoma—History. 5. Kansas—History.
6. Outlaws—Oklahoma history. 7. Outlaws—Kansas history.
8. Oklahoma—Biography—Anecdotes.

Published by:
Mid-South Publications
PO Box 718
Goodlettsville, Tennessee 37070

Printed in the USA by Print Media, Bowling Green, Kentucky

Contents

List of Illustrations

Preface

William D. "Bill" Fossett was a Western figure that many have heard of but no one knows. Often described as both caring and courageous, he was a towering, handsome figure of a man who stood well over six-feet tall. He fit the romantic image of a cowboy and lawman and worked as both in real life. Put succinctly by a contemporary, Bill Fossett "was a frontiersman of long experience and without fear."

He grew up in Minnesota and became an early settler on the plains of Kansas and Oklahoma where he wore a badge. He lived until well up in years and well down in funds, passing, apparently in peace and contentment, into relative obscurity.

Bill Fossett came to my attention while researching an old revolver that had been passed through the family of a Rock Island Railroad man. It turned out that the pistol was used by one of the bandits during the 1894 attempted train robbery at Pond Creek, Oklahoma. Evidence indicates Fossett probably shot the outlaw. He was there, not as a hero, just a man pursuing his duties as a railroad detective. His relentless determination and calculated method of tracking the remaining outlaws were striking, particularly compared with the wild and often exaggerated tales usually associated with such events. While the train holdup itself is well known, Fossett's involvement as a detective in rounding up the bandits is not. It seemed to be an untold story that begged the telling. And there was more to the man. Finding it was seldom easy and, to be sure, there is much more of the Bill Fossett story yet to be told.

What has emerged so far is a life caught up, like so many in that day, by the great westward movement; a man with a family who came to a new and wild country with the freedom to grasp opportunities and make decisions as he saw fit. He served as a Kansas and Oklahoma lawman in a tempestuous time when that section of the country knew little or no law. His exploits as a frontiersman, pioneer, detective and marshal are significant, but have gone virtually unrecorded because Fossett was a quiet man, not given to talking much about himself. Pulitzer Prize winning author Marquis James, who grew up in Enid following the opening of the Cherokee Outlet, was acquainted with Fossett, remarking in his book *The Cherokee Strip* that "Mr. Fossett was one of the great, though unpublicized, peace officers of the powder-stained Southwest; a man to mention with Wild Bill Hickok and Bat Masterson."

In his book *They Had Their Hour,* James further observed, "No one is better qualified than Bill Fossett to rate Oklahoma outlaws according to their merits. He has been in Oklahoma about as long as any white man, having arrived in 1873. He knows more about the old days and the men who made them, and says less in proportion to his knowledge than any man now living, or, I believe, who ever lived and kept on the side of the law."

The reticent Fossett said little about his exploits until the late 1920s. Perhaps only then because of public interest in the fortieth anniversary of Oklahoma's opening and the release of former U.S. Marshal E. D. Nix's book, *Oklahombres,* concerning outlaws and lawmen of Fossett's time. Then, in his late seventies, he gave an interview to the *American Legion Weekly* magazine. It resulted in two stories entitled "Bad Men," both reprinted in the *Kingfisher Times.* They were his accounts of the attempted Pond Creek train robbery and the successful outcome of the hunt for outlaw Bert Casey.

In 1937 Fossett participated in the Indian-Pioneer History Project conducted by the Works Progress Administration. That forty-page interview provided a few details about his coming to Kansas and Oklahoma, his trail herd days and his years as a law officer, but raised more questions than it answered. In attempting to fill gaps left by that interview, research has uncovered brief snippets of Fossett's life, as well as several stories of his involvement in other important events, but never an unbroken timeline.

While many of his peers penned their memoirs or had others do it for them, Fossett did not, leaving names, dates, places and the details of many events to slip away with time. In recovering as complete an account of his life as possible, original records, first-hand reports and newspapers have been consulted, where they exist. Where these records leave gaps in his life, the lack of information is acknowledged, and in some cases, logical assumptions are offered. The attempt here is to factually establish Fossett's personal deeds as well as recount some of the significant history of his time and place.

What becomes most apparent about Bill Fossett is that, in the tradition of the cowboy life he followed after first coming west, he was independent, resolute and rugged. There was restlessness too, as he never spent more than eight to ten years in one location or job. Fossett was a notional man and his wandering may explain why he was married five times.

As guarded as he was in his personal affairs, he used even more caution as an investigator. One county attorney recalled that Fossett never talked about a case where people could overhear, even to the point of taking the discussion out on the open prairie where no one was around. Fossett, he said, "was intelligent, capable, cautious and gave expression only to the words necessary to convey his meaning."

There was another side too. Close friend and trusted deputy Joe Grimes characterized him as the biggest-hearted man he ever knew. Grimes recalled Fossett once saying, "I'd rather make someone happy and have my pockets empty than to turn down someone who is in need."

Fossett's grave in Kingfisher bears no epitaph, for his gravesite is merely a small, unmarked patch of grass between other monuments in a far corner of the cemetery. Indeed, the taciturn Bill Fossett left it for others to speak about him, and it may be fairly concluded that he was unassuming, introspective and possessed an acute desire for common sense and justice. He was a man whose faith and respect for the law drove him to doggedly and skillfully pursue those who disobeyed it; a man who, although unheralded, was as big a player in taming the frontier as many better known peace officers of the era.

JIM FULBRIGHT

Nashville, Tennessee

Acknowledgements

Several individuals and institutions have provided valuable assistance in the preparation of this book. Mollie Stehno of Shawnee, Oklahoma, spent many hours scanning newspaper microfilm and other documents, as did Deborah Durr of Kingman, Kansas, who also offered insight into Fossett family history.

Firearms collector Thurel Emerton of Goodlettsville, Tennessee, who purchased the old revolver used in the 1894 Pond Creek, Oklahoma, train robbery, was the first to discover its unique history and was a valuable aide in all facets of research. He has since generously donated the pistol to the Chisholm Trail Museum in Bill Fossett's hometown of Kingfisher.

Special thanks to Walt Fossett of Venice, Florida, and Paul D. Fossett, II, of Albuquerque, for sharing family genealogical information and other important leads, and to Albert Stehno of Billings, Oklahoma, who offered exceptional insight into the history of the early cattle industry.

I am indebted to many people whose names appear in the text and notes and owe special gratitude to the following: Robert L. Klemme of Enid, Oklahoma, who has set out markers on every section line of the Chisholm Trail from the Red River to Kansas and knows the trail's history better than anyone else; Norma White, now retired from the Caldwell, Kansas, Carnegie Library; Renee Mitchell and Ginger Murphy of Kingfisher Oklahoma's Chisholm Trail Museum; Della and Melvin Shafer of the Wellington, Kansas, Chisholm Trail Museum; Lawrence Ediger and Don and Gloria White of Caldwell, Kansas; Marvin Bules of Pond Creek, Oklahoma;

Bob and Tammie Chada of Guthrie, Oklahoma; and my editor, Greg Kinman of Pleasant View, Tennessee.

All of us interested in history are, likewise, indebted to the many fine institutions, museums and libraries that collect, protect, organize and display invaluable links to the past. Specifically, I am grateful to: The Oklahoma Historical Society, Oklahoma City; The Oklahoma Territorial Museum, Guthrie; The Chisholm Trail Museum, Kingfisher, Oklahoma; The Kingman, Kansas, Carnegie Library and the Kingman County Museum; The Museum of the Great Plains, Lawton, Oklahoma; The El Reno Oklahoma Carnegie Library; and the Kingfisher, Hennessey and Medford, Oklahoma, Public Libraries.

Chronology
of selected events

1803   Most of the land between the Mississippi River and the Rocky Mountains is transferred from France to the U.S. in the Louisiana Purchase.

1803-1843   The formation of Indian Territory begins by moving the five civilized and other tribes to what becomes Oklahoma, a name derived from two Choctaw words meaning "red people."

1833   John and Susannah Fossett migrate from Ireland to America, settling in New York State.

1851   William D. "Bill" Fossett is born near Watertown, New York.

1856-1862   The Fossett family moves from New York to Wisconsin, then to Minnesota.

1861   Kansas becomes the thirty-fourth state.

1866-1867   The great northern cattle drives begin in large numbers from Texas, across Indian Territory, to Kansas. In 1867, the Chisholm Trail becomes the dominant route.

Oct. 1867   Plains Indians and U.S. representatives meet along the Medicine Lodge River in southern Kansas. Plains tribes are compelled to move into Indian Territory, opening the way for white settlement and railroads throughout much of the West. In return, Indians are to be protected from white hunters invading the buffalo range, given annuities, and provided schools and farm implements. Both sides break the treaty. Some tribes continue widespread raiding, while the army refuses to stop whites from slaughtering buffalo.

1869	The Eastern states and the West are joined by completion of the Trans-Continental railroad.
1870-1873	A new wave of Western migration into Kansas begins.
1871	The town of Caldwell, Kansas, is established.
1872	Bill Fossett marries Elizabeth Footman in Fairbault County, Minnesota.
1873	Lewis D. Fossett is born in Minnesota, and the Fossetts move to Sumner County, Kansas.
1874	Major Andrew Drumm is the first cattle rancher in the Cherokee Outlet.
March 1874	Building the town of Kingman, Kansas, begins.
June 1874	Angry over the slaughter of buffalo in violation of the Medicine Lodge Treaty, Comanche, Cheyenne and Kiowa warriors attack a caravan of hunters, traders and teamsters at Adobe Walls, in the Texas panhandle.
July 1874	Teamster Pat Hennessey is slain by Indians along the Chisholm Trail in Indian Territory, as part of the same outbreak over the killing of buffalo.
1878	Mary Frances "Mamie" Fossett is born in Caldwell.

1880-1883	As more cattlemen use the Cherokee Outlet for grazing, the "Cherokee Strip Live Stock Association" is formed in 1883. This cattlemen's group leases over 6 million acres from the Cherokee Nation to be used by its members.
April 1880	David L. Payne leads the "Boomer Movement" to open Indian Territory for white settlement. He and twenty-one followers enter the Unassigned Lands but are arrested by the army and escorted back to Kansas.
June 1880	Caldwell, Kansas, attains rail service, to begin its peak years as a cattle-shipping center.
1881	Bill Fossett is assistant city marshal in Caldwell during the fight known as the "Talbot Raid."
1883	Bill Fossett and family move to Kingman, Kansas. He becomes city marshal the following year.
1886-1887	The Santa Fe railroad constructs across Indian Territory, adding impetus to the "Boomer Movement."
1889	The Rock Island Railroad extends its line from Caldwell to the Pond Creek Stage Station in the Cherokee Outlet.
Feb. 1889	An amendment to the Indian Appropriations Bill allows settlement in the Unassigned Lands of Indian Territory.
April 1889	On April 22, settlers flood into the Unassigned Lands in Oklahoma's first "Land Run." Bill Fossett is the first to stake a claim in Kingfisher. He becomes a Rock Island Railroad detective.

1890	Oklahoma Territory is formed, apart from Indian Territory, creating the "twin territories." The government forces cattlemen to leave the Cherokee Outlet in preparation for another land opening.
1891	In May, the Dalton brothers, some of whom once served as either deputy marshals or possemen in Kansas and Oklahoma, take up the "outlaw trail," robbing a Santa Fe train in the Cherokee Outlet. The gang includes Bill Doolin, Dick Broadwell, George "Bitter Creek" Newcomb and others, who become well-known outlaws during the next few years.
July 1891	On the run for several crimes, Nathaniel Elsworth Wyatt, alias "Zip" Wyatt, and Dick Yeager, kills a deputy sheriff near Greensburg, Kansas.
1892	The Rock Island line reaches the Texas-Indian Territory border.
Oct. 1892	The Dalton gang attempts to rob two banks at the same time in Coffeyville, Kansas. Four townsmen and four outlaws are killed in a bloody gun battle, including Bob and Grat Dalton. Emmett is seriously wounded.
Nov. 1892	Bill Doolin, "Bitter Creek" Newcomb and Charley Pierce, who had left the Dalton gang prior to Coffeyville, form their own gang and are joined by Bill Dalton and others to begin a series of violent robberies in Kansas, Missouri and Oklahoma. They are known variously as the "Dalton," the "Doolin" and the "Doolin-Dalton" gang.

Sept. 1893	On September 1, the Doolin gang shoots its way out of a trap set by lawmen in the town of Ingalls, Oklahoma Territory. Three deputy U.S. marshals are killed.
1893	The Cherokee Outlet is opened to White settlement on September 16.
1893-1894	The "Railroad War" rages around Enid and Pond Creek when the Rock Island refuses to recognize certain townsites.
April 1894	Bill Fossett prevents a Rock Island railroad robbery at Pond Creek.
June 1894	Bill Dalton is tracked down and killed by officers in Indian Territory.
1895	The Doolin gang robs a Rock Island train near Dover.
July-August 1895	Fossett helps track down outlaw "Zip" Wyatt/Dick Yeager, during a lengthy manhunt across central and western Oklahoma.
Jan. 1896	Bill Doolin is captured by Deputy U.S. Marshal Bill Tilghman at Eureka Springs, Arkansas.
July 1896	Doolin and several other prisoners escape the federal jail at Guthrie.
Aug. 1896	Doolin is killed by a posse led by Deputy U.S. Marshal Heck Thomas near Lawson, Oklahoma Territory.

June 1897	The Al Jennings gang begins its crime spree and is joined by ex-Doolin gang members "Dynamite" Dick Clifton and "Little" Dick West.
Nov. 1897	Fossett becomes chief deputy U.S. marshal under Canada H. "Harry" Thompson. A posse kills "Dynamite" Dick Clifton in the Creek Nation.
Dec. 1897	The Jennings brothers and Pat O'Malley are arrested.
Feb. 1898	Fossett begins a lengthy investigation into the burning death of two Indians in Pottawatomie County.
April 1898	Fossett kills outlaw "Little" Dick West in a brief gunfight when he resists arrest.
1899	Fossett and deputies break up a mail theft ring in western Oklahoma.
March 1901	Fossett's only grandchild, Irene Madaline Miller, is born in Chickasha, to daughter Mamie and husband Richard Miller.
June-Sept. 1901	Fossett heads a small force of deputy U.S. marshals to maintain order at Lawton during the Kiowa-Comanche land lottery.
August 1901	The Bert Casey gang kills 11-year-old Jay Beemblossom enroute to attend the land lottery.
March 1902	President Theodore Roosevelt appoints Fossett U.S. Marshal for Oklahoma Territory.

August 1902   Fossett releases two federal inmates and appoints them deputy marshals in an undercover scheme to capture or kill the notorious Bert Casey.

Oct. 1902   The Casey gang lynches Deputy U.S. Marshal Lute Houston.

Nov. 1902   "Inmate-Officers" Wes Hudson and Ed Lockett kill Bert Casey and his cohort in a gunfight near Cleo. Prior charges against Hudson and Lockett are dropped, and they are freed.

1903   The murderous Martin brothers gang lead Fossett and deputies on a wide-ranging manhunt across Oklahoma. In August, they are finally tracked and killed by deputies Wiley G. Haines and Warren Bennett.

1903   Wes Hudson and Ed Lockett begin new crime sprees in Arkansas.

1904   A Harrison, Arkansas, marshal kills Lockett. Wes Hudson fatally shoots a lawman in Jasper, Arkansas, but is acquitted.

1905   Deputy Marshal Jim Bourland arrests Wes Hudson, wanted in the Lute Houston murder investigation.

1906   Fossett loses reappointment as U.S. marshal to Jack "the wolf catcher" Abernathy in a political fight.

May 1906   Wes Hudson, along with Jim and Ben Hughes, are acquitted of Houston's death during separate trials. Two nights later, Deputy Marshal Bourland and Hudson fatally wound each other in an Anadarko saloon gunfight.

Nov. 1907	The Twin Territories are joined to make Oklahoma the 46th state.
1908	Fossett is city marshal in Waurkia, Oklahoma.
1909	Bill becomes Chief of Police for the Rock Island's Oklahoma Division in El Reno.
1919	Bill is appointed Chief of Police in Kingfisher.
1921-1924	Fossett's last law enforcement positions are as Oklahoma City Police Department jailer and deputy U.S. marshal for the western district under Marshal Alva McDonald.

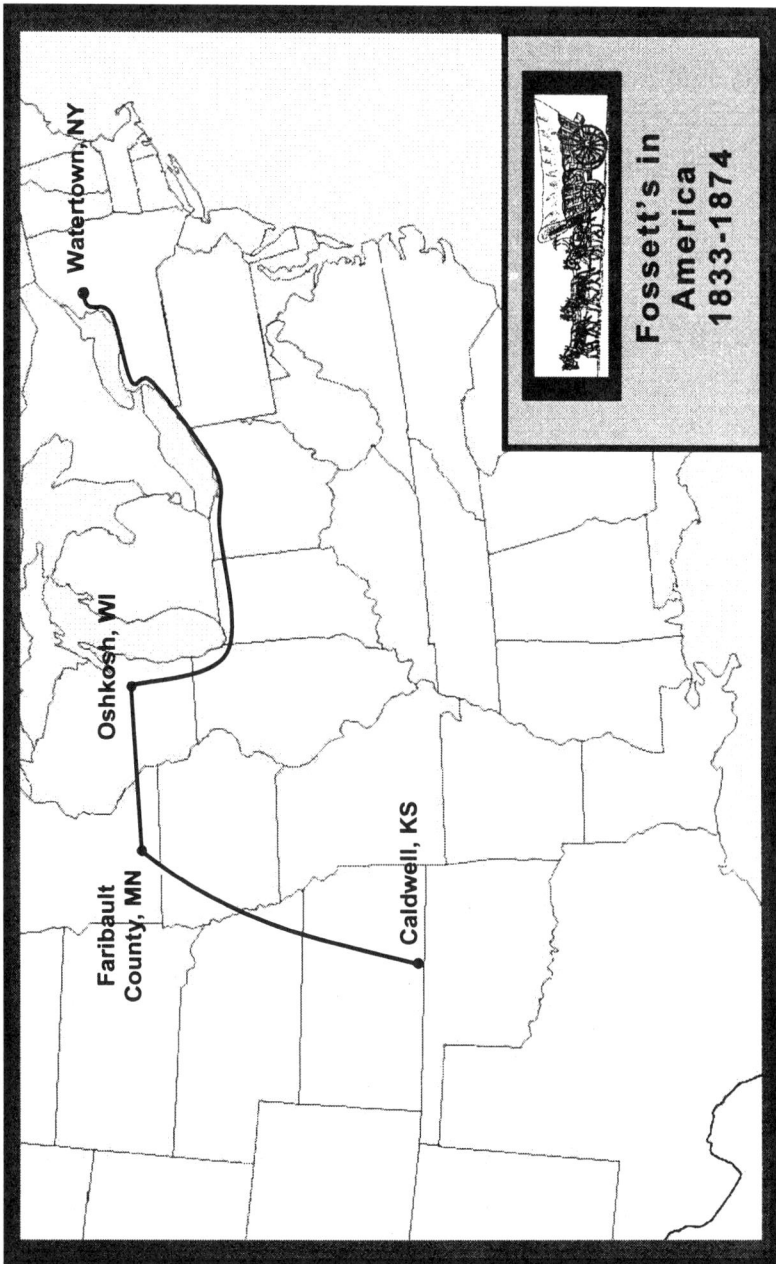

Fossett's in America 1833-1874

Watertown, NY

Oshkosh, WI

Faribault County, MN

Caldwell, KS

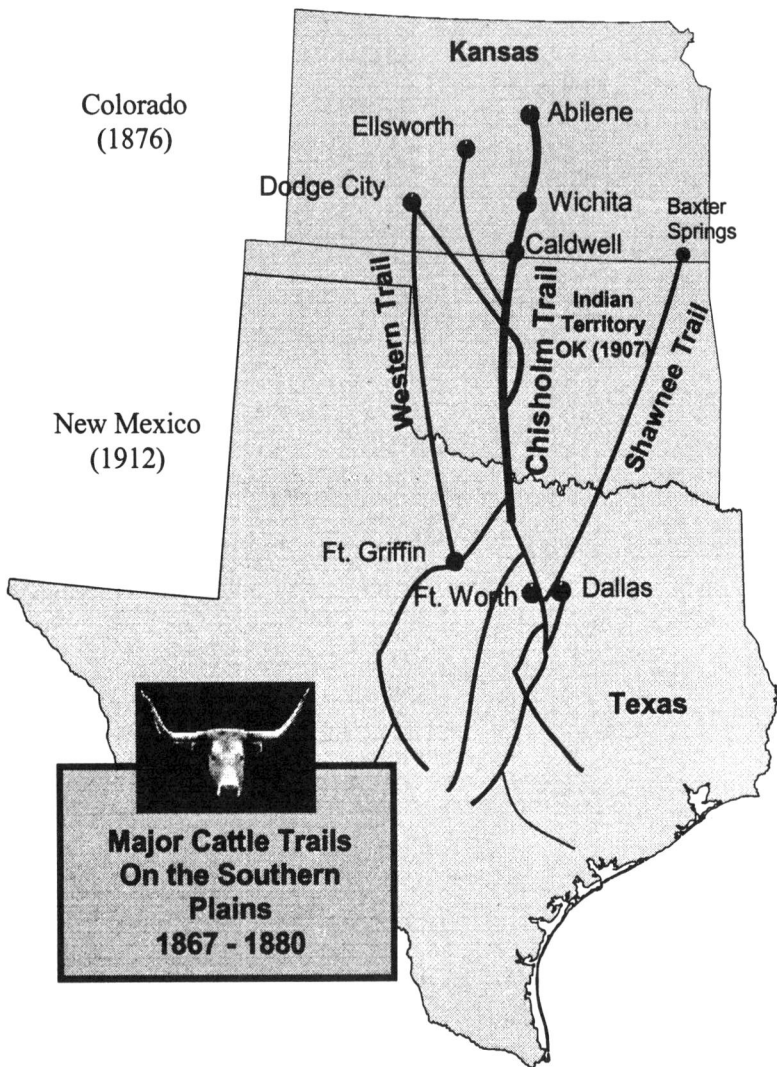

Colorado
(1876)

Kansas

Ellsworth

Abilene

Dodge City

Wichita

Caldwell

Baxter
Springs

Western Trail

Chisholm Trail

Indian
Territory
OK (1907)

Shawnee Trail

New Mexico
(1912)

Ft. Griffin

Ft. Worth

Dallas

Texas

**Major Cattle Trails
On the Southern
Plains
1867 - 1880**

Kansas & Oklahoma
Railroads – 1895
(Selected)

Colorado

U.P. (K.P.)

Topeka

Hays   Salina   Abilene

Ellsworth   Herington

MO. Pac.
(D. M. & A.)   C.R.I. & P.

Hutchinson   McPherson

Dodge City   Newton

Kingman   Wichita

Medicine Lodge   Wellington

Anthony   Oswego

Caldwell

Newkirk

Pond Creek   Vanita

A.T. & S. Fe

Enid   Perry

Kingfisher   Guthrie   Muskogee

El Reno   OK City

Chickasha   McAlester

C.R.I. & P.   M.K. & T.

Waurika
(1902)   Ardmore

A.T. & S. Fe
            Santa Fe R.R.
C. R. I. & P.
            Chicago, Rock Island &
                        Pacific
M. K. & T.
            Missouri, Kansas & Texas
U. P. (K. P.)
                Union Pacific
            (formerly Kansas Pacific)
MO. Pac. (D. M. & A.)
                Missouri Pacific
(formerly Denver, Memphis & Atlantic)

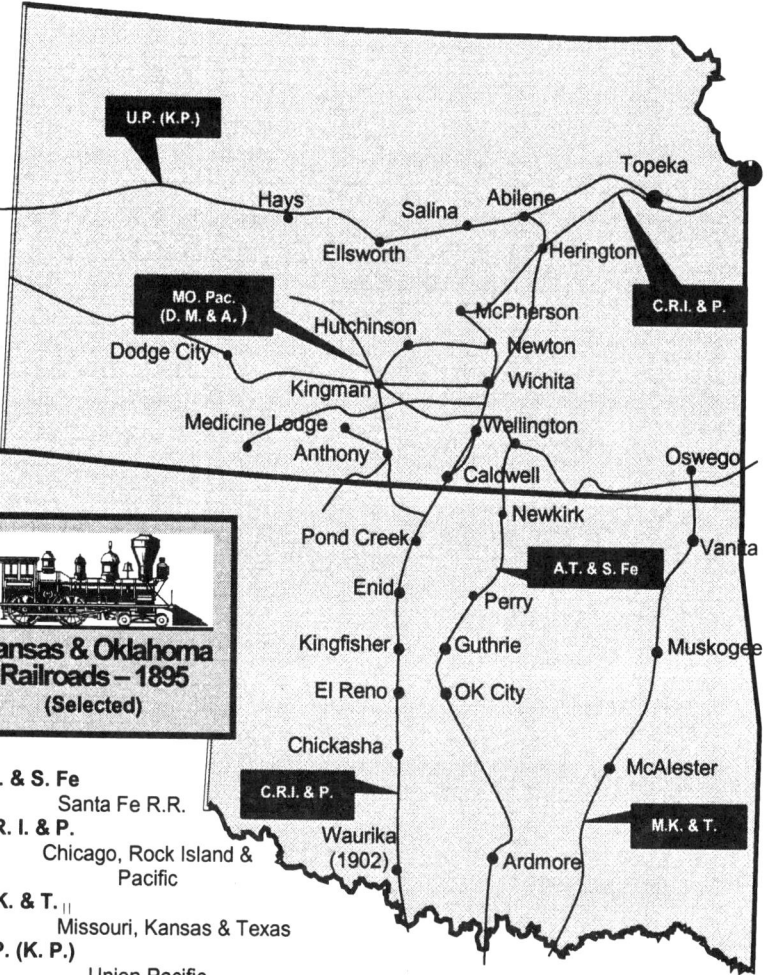

xxiii

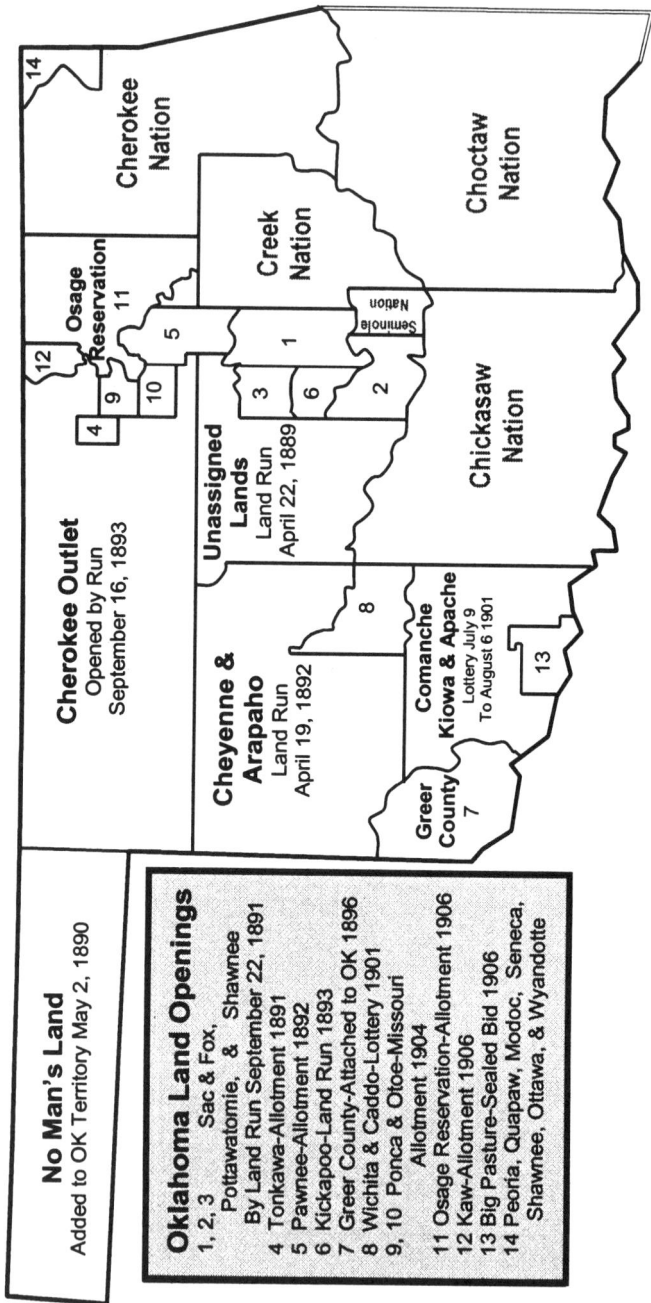

No Man's Land

Added to OK Territory May 2, 1890

Cherokee Outlet

Opened by Run
September 16, 1893

14 Cherokee Nation

12

Osage Reservation

11

4 **9** **10** **5**

Unassigned Lands
Land Run
April 22, 1889

3 **6** **1** **2**

Creek Nation

Seminole Nation

Choctaw Nation

Cheyenne & Arapaho

Land Run
April 19, 1892

8

Chickasaw Nation

Comanche Kiowa & Apache

Lottery July 9
To August 6 1901

13

Greer County

7

Oklahoma Land Openings

1, 2, 3   Sac & Fox,
Pottawatomie, & Shawnee
By Land Run September 22, 1891
4 Tonkawa-Allotment 1891
5 Pawnee-Allotment 1892
6 Kickapoo-Land Run 1893
7 Greer County-Attached to OK 1896
8 Wichita & Caddo-Lottery 1901
9, 10 Ponca & Otoe-Missouri
Allotment 1904
11 Osage Reservation-Allotment 1906
12 Kaw-Allotment 1906
13 Big Pasture-Sealed Bid 1906
14 Peoria, Quapaw, Modoc, Seneca,
Shawnee, Ottawa, & Wyandotte

Kingfisher - Guthrie
& Environs
(1895 U.S. Atlas)

0   25

1

THE WESTWARD MOVEMENT

In the fall and early winter of 1870, "train after train of prairie schooners" sailed through the grass of southern Kansas. This latest stage of the great westward movement centered on new lands recently relinquished through a government treaty with the Osage Indians in which the tribe agreed to move a few miles south to a reservation in Indian Territory.[1]

The tide of immigration brought seemingly endless waves of newcomers from Eastern states, all making their passage to claim privileges under the Homestead Act, the 1862 law giving them the right to settle on a quarter section, or 160 acres, of unappropriated public land. The only requirement was their habitation and the "cultivation" of the property for five years, after which it was theirs for the payment of $1.25 per acre.[2]

For the next two years a steady stream of settlers poured onto the treeless prairies. They discovered a land of harsh extremes where creeks and rivers could change from ankle-deep trickles through sand bars, to churning torrents several hundred feet wide in just a few hours, and where the black and slate-gray clouds of a boiling afternoon rainstorm could drift away to reveal the brilliant hues of an evening's golden sunset.

To those who came from hill and tree country, much less the mountains, judging distance on the open landscape was challenging. The sky and the prairie seemed to merge as one from horizon to horizon, and the tall grasses waved above the flat lands for endless miles. This view was broken only occasionally by small bluffs and sand hills, or where buffalo herds disturbed the vegetation or where, more recently, cattle had rutted trails as they tramped north from Texas. It was stifling hot in the summer and bitterly cold in winter, both conditions aggravated by howling winds.[3]

In the "civilized" and populated East, this new frontier was known as "The Great American Desert."[4] It was mostly a wild country troubled by Indian raids, radical weather, and, very often, widespread lawlessness. It was constantly changing, too. Settlement throughout the West had increased considerably following the Civil War. By 1869 the Union Pacific and Central Pacific Railroads linked the East to the far West, and other rail lines were expanding. The Texas cattle industry had revived on eastern demands for beef at exorbitant prices. Trail drives to newly established Kansas railheads grew bigger and more numerous, and along the way, ranches dotted the range and homesteaders planted roots.[5]

Prior to the Osage Treaty, the Kansas legislature carved out several new counties from the southern tier of the state. Some white settlers had already encroached on the eastern portion of the Osage Reserve before the Indians relinquished it, but once the treaty was finalized, they came in droves, filling the southern counties as they already had "thickly settled" other parts of the state. One of these new counties along the Indian Territory border was Sumner, and among those who settled there was William D. "Bill" Fossett, the youngest son of an Irish immigrant.[6]

Typical of many in that era, Bill Fossett and his family had been stricken with "western fever." The "malady" promised predictable hardships with no certainty of a cure. Many of the "afflicted" new westerners were lured by the reports of early explorers who crossed west from the Arkansas River to return with stories of the soil's "marvelous fertility" and the "abundance of water" in the new Kansas counties.[7] Others simply took the advice to "go west and grow up with the country."[8]

Farmers made up the backbone of the movement. They came first and planned to stay, shaping the country with one sod shanty, one farm, and eventually one town at a time. Although the ability to turn public land into personal property was the key attraction, settlers were driven by a variety of interests. In a time when the flower of the American dream was in full bloom, to "go West" meant more than direction or location. Depending on individuals and their circumstances, the word "West" was interchangeable with opportunity, independence, change, a fresh start, and even escape. For the young, particularly, the prospects for self-betterment by moving West far outweighed any conceivable loss. Thus, there was likely little hesitation when twenty-one-year-old Bill Fossett made up his mind to head for Kansas.

★ ★ ★ ★

W. D. "Bill" Fossett was born in Watertown, Jefferson County, New York, on November 3, 1851. He was the youngest of nine children born to John Fossett of Donegal, Ireland, and Susannah Bee Carrigan of Glasgow, Scotland, who migrated to America in 1833.

The Fossetts were originally Huguenots, French Protestants who fled France at the time of religious persecution in the Seventeenth Century. The French spelling of the name is seen sometimes as *Fossette*. This line of Fossetts anglicized the name by dropping the last *e*. As a group, Huguenots settled in the north of Ireland, Protestant Ulster.

John and Susannah Fossett's first child was Elizabeth, born September 15, 1831. Two years later the family left Donegal for the trip to America. They first settled in the town of Denmark, Lewis County, in upstate New York, a short distance east of Watertown, Jefferson County.

In June 1836, the couple's first son, John, was born, followed by Isaac, Jane, Nell, Susan, Margaret and Christina.[9]

Last came young William in 1851. His sisters considered their young brother a handsome and magnetic boy, giving him the nickname "billet-doux." In later life, William D. "Bill" Fossett almost always signed his name as "William D."[10]

The family engaged in farming in the Jefferson and Lewis county area until about 1856 when John, the eldest son, and his father set out on foot for the Erie Canal, traveling the water route to Wisconsin in preparation for a move west. They eventually settled in Fond du lac County, Wisconsin. First-born son John was married there, and his son, John Francis, was born near Oshkosh in 1859. In 1862, the family moved to Winnebago City in Faribault County, southern Minnesota.[11]

The most memorable event of Bill Fossett's early life came during the carnage of the 1862 Indian uprising in southwestern Minnesota. The Santee Sioux, who occupied the northeastern edge of the Great Plains, had sold off most of their Minnesota land to white settlement in the early 1850s, but the government was slow in making yearly payments to the tribe. Frustrated, angry and starving for lack of money to buy food and other goods from white traders, Chief Little Crow and his warriors went to war in August 1862. They attacked small settlements and trading posts along the Minnesota River killing nearly one thousand settlers.[12]

On the day of the initial attack, ten-year-old Bill and some family members were traveling by wagon to a local trading post, but were detained on the way when a horse became lame. The delay may have saved their lives, for when they finally arrived at the little settlement, Indians had already raided it, leaving behind butchered bodies and burned out cabins.[13]

Two days later the Santee made organized attacks on the lightly defended garrison of Fort Ridgley and the little town of New Ulm before finally withdrawing up river. To fend off the uprising, former Minnesota Governor Henry Sibley was commissioned as colonel and ordered to organize a volunteer army of settlers to replace Minnesota regulars who were engaged in Civil War campaigns far from home. Within weeks of the rampage, Sibley's troops forced the surrender of over 2,000 Sioux. Nearly 400 were tried, and thirty-eight were singled out as proven rapists and murderers of settlers. On the day after Christmas, 1862, the thirty-eight Sioux warriors were led to a specially built gallows in Mankato and hanged, marking the largest mass execution in American History.[14]

By then, General Sibley had mounted a much larger and better-trained army. It included a cavalry regiment known as the Minnesota Rangers, and two of its soldiers were Bill Fossett's older brothers, twenty-seven-year old John and twenty-one-year old Isaac. During 1863, the army pursued and defeated the Santee Sioux in several major battles in the Dakota Territory. In late winter that year, the Fossett brothers' regiment was disbanded at Fort Ripley, Minnesota, where they were mustered out of service.[15]

For the next few years the Fossetts worked their farms in peace, Bill growing into a strong, strapping young man who hunted often and became an expert shot. He traveled as a fur trader for the Hudson's Bay Company for a short time, and somewhere along the way, he met a young woman named Elizabeth Footman, whose family had moved from Ohio to nearby Fillmore County.[16]

In March 1872, Bill and Elizabeth (Lizzie) were married in Faribault County, and on January 10 the following year, their son Lewis was born. In the spring of 1873, when the harsh Midwest winter improved enough to enable travel, Bill loaded his wife and son in a covered wagon and set off down the trail from Minnesota to Kansas.[17]

Over the next several months, Bill's brothers, John and Isaac, and their families, along with his parents and several sisters, also made the move to Kansas.[18]

The trip to the new frontier may not have been the first for Bill Fossett. In later years there is reference to his having "experience . . . as a lawman in Texas" about 1872.[19] Another similarly vague statement says "he turned up as a teenage cowhand riding the cattle trails from Wichita through the Cherokee country as early as 1867...."[20] This may well have occurred, after which he returned to Minnesota to be married in 1872. Fossett himself, however, never mentions such experiences. Instead, he clearly specifies 1873 as the year he went to Kansas, a fact verified by a "paper trail" of property records, newspaper accounts and other documents beginning with that year.[21]

2

ALONG THE CATTLE TRAILS

Bill Fossett's move to Kansas took him first to Salina. He worked the spring and summer there for a rancher named Baker who had a cattle spread on the Smoky Hill River. In the fall of 1873, he took his family on south into Sumner County near the burgeoning little cow town of Caldwell on the Jesse Chisholm Trail, three miles from Indian Territory.[1]

The Fossett family settled on farms in the newly organized Falls Township east of Caldwell. Kansas census records for 1875 show the senior Fossetts, John and Susannah, in the same home as daughter Elizabeth and son Isaac, while Bill, wife Elizabeth and son Lewis lived in their own home a short distance away.[2]

Beginning in the summer of 1875, and for the next four years, Bill and brother Isaac bought, sold and traded several large parcels of property in and near Caldwell. Bill finally settled on and received a government homestead patent for a forty-acre lot immediately west of town, adjacent to the corporate limits. His oldest brother, John, and his family had also moved from Minnesota to Kansas by this time.[3]

Isaac Fossett, better known as "Ike," was in his early thirties when the family arrived in Kansas. Married with no children,[4] he was industrious, outgoing and active in civic affairs. He served on Caldwell's Independence Day Celebration Committee, engaged in a trading expedition to Indian Territory, and was written up in the newspaper as "one of the boss farmers and horse traders of Bluff Creek." He often boasted of good wheat and corn crops and once said he regretted "that he didn't come to Kansas several years ago." According to Elizabeth Fossett Manigold, his widowed sister, Isaac was the main source of support for her and her parents.[5]

John, known as "Jack" or "A. J.," already had six children when he moved to Kansas in 1874. He farmed, was involved in raising his large family and helped care for his aging parents. He lived in the town of Caldwell until his death in 1910.[6]

Of the three boys, Bill was the youngest and most restless. Even though he came from a family of farmers, he was the least likely to stay put and work the land for very long, as evidenced by his future exploits and business ventures. Work-hardened and solid, he struck an imposing figure at six feet, four inches tall and over 200 pounds. His alert eyes, creviced chin and thick, but well-kept mustache, highlighted his strong features. Quiet and somewhat reserved, Bill didn't say much, but was decisive when he took action and was considered a "crack shot" with both rifle and pistol.[7]

Independent and free-spirited, Bill was naturally attracted to work as a cowhand soon after his arrival in Kansas. He made several drives along the Chisholm Trail from Texas into Kansas. On one of his first trips down the trail he remembered:

> Outlaws stole all the horses and mules along the line and started with them toward Wellington [Kansas]. Enroute there, however, the outlaws were captured and the last place they ever hung around after that was a cottonwood limb.[8]

That example of swift, frontier justice was his first introduction to the basics of law enforcement, and it played a major role in his later life.

Bill's earliest and deadliest encounters with bandits occurred in Mexico. In one incident, he and four other men were enroute to buy horses at Monterrey when they stopped at a tiny village south of the border. Fossett's companions began drinking, and he urged them to stay the night and sober up, but they insisted on pushing ahead. By that time, villagers were aware that the American horse buyers carried feed bags stuffed full of silver dollars. Striking out along the trail in darkness, they were followed and fired on. Disoriented and unprepared, Bill's four drunken companions were quickly cut down. He alone escaped the ambush alive, taking cover in the brush until daylight. Bill then picked up the bandits' trail. After overtaking and killing four of the Mexicans in a brief gunfight, he hightailed it across the border for help.

With a posse of eager Texans joining him, Bill led the way back across the Rio Grande to Mexico, finding the bandits where his friends had been gunned down the night before. After a wild shootout "with practically the whole town," he recovered the stolen money and the bodies of his companions.

On another trip below the border, Bill was returning from Monterrey with a herd of newly purchased horses when he and the five cowboys with him were attacked by bandits about twenty miles south of Laredo, Texas. It was dusk and the dim trail they followed led down an arroyo, twisting through a tangle of cactus and mesquite:

> Suddenly my sixth sense warned me that something was wrong, but before I could warn my companions ... we were ambushed by a group of Mexicans. Four of our men went down instantly, riddled with rifle fire, but I and a fellow named Milnee weren't hit. We dived from our horses and began shooting back at the bandits who began running toward us. I killed five of them and Bud got his share also. Our fire scared the rest off and they saddled up and left. We buried our companions and rounded up the horses, losing only two of the ponies that had strayed too far for recovery.[9]

During the winter of 1873, Bill and a friend named Albert Roberts left Caldwell for Ft. Sill in Indian Territory, where they planned to prospect for gold and silver. At that time, the Nation, as it was often called, was still primarily a lawless land.[10]

Not until 1875 did Judge Isaac Parker and his force of marshals begin to rule the region from Ft. Smith, Arkansas. Prior to that, the U.S. Army was the only legal authority in the territory; its efforts primarily directed toward maintaining peace among the Indians. The Indian nations, considered sovereign in the region, were not permitted to enforce their laws against whites, so while the Army spent its efforts dealing solely with the Indians, the territory became a refuge for outlaws or any non-Indian who lived on the fringe of the law.[11]

Even under the Army's near constant supervision, Indians still managed to frequently escape the reservation long enough to steal livestock and mount raids on small settlements across the territory. The army's confiscation of Indian guns and ponies failed to fully thwart this activity because the Indians simply hid their best horses and rifles.[12]

After stocking up with supplies at Ft. Sill, Fossett and Roberts drove their wagon into the Wichita Mountains. A few days out, a snowstorm hit the area and the two men became completely lost. When the storm let up, they began driving toward the sound of some barking dogs, only to discover the dogs were in an Indian camp where the inhabitants were conducting what Bill described as a Sun Dance. The ceremony centered on a young Indian boy who was tied to a tent pole. Fossett related the events in his 1937 *Indian-Pioneer History* interview:

> They had raised the skin on each side of his breast and had run a stick underneath his skin. Then they tied him with rawhide whangs and danced around him making a lot of noise with what they called a tom-tom, which was a sort of drum.

Fossett said Roberts was completely unnerved by the Indians, but was finally persuaded to enter their camp. Bill boldly crawled into the shelter of a teepee. The Indians abruptly stopped the ceremony, sat down in a circle, got out a pipe, lit it and began passing it around. Each man took a puff or two, and when the pipe came to him, Bill did the same:

> The Indians then got up and went ahead with the dance. The young brave who was tied with the rawhide whangs would pull back, apparently with all his strength, trying to tear the stick from his body. They finally hacked it with their knives as they passed by and when it finally gave away they had what they called a young warrior.

The Indians were completely hospitable to the two white strangers. They gathered blankets and buffalo robes and prepared a warm shelter for their visitors. It included two hammocks made of willow branches and rawhide straps that were stretched between stakes in the ground. In the shelter they left Fossett and Roberts in the company of two young squaws:

> I never knew why the Indians left the two young squaws in this tent where they had fixed the hammocks. Roberts was so afraid of the Indians that he took the blankets we had and went to the bushes. I stayed in the tent but never spoke to the squaws during the night. I thought at that time…that these squaws were left in that tent on purpose and if Roberts or I had spoken to them this would have given the Indian braves an excuse to kill us. The next morning they gave us breakfast and directed us the way into [Ft.] Sill.[13]

In midwinter, Bill returned to Caldwell alone, leaving Roberts at the army post and expecting him to follow in a few weeks. Several months passed without a word from him. Finally, in June of 1874, a telegram arrived on the military line from Ft. Sill reporting that Roberts' body had been found about twenty miles southeast of Ft. Sill, along Cache Creek.

The foreman of Laughlin's Bull Train, a freight outfit that transported government supplies from the railroad to the fort, had discovered the body in heavy timber near the creek. Reportedly, Roberts had been dead about a week. His skull had been crushed and his clothing rifled of valuables. His horses were tied to a tree and were almost dead of thirst and hunger when found. The circumstances of Roberts' death were never known but it was suspected that Indians had killed him.[14]

Bill was determined to recover the remains of his friend, and with a wagon and team he began the long journey from Caldwell to Ft. Sill. At the fort he asked the post carpenter to make a wooden coffin lined with tin:

> I got some fellows to go with me and we dug up the body, which had just been rolled in a blanket and buried two weeks before. We took his shoes off and did the best we could to get him in shape, put him in the wooden box and sealed it tight, and I started back with his body to the nearest railroad point at Wichita, Kansas.[15]

He planned to ship the body by rail to the dead man's parents in Iowa, but the journey was trouble-filled from the outset.

On the fifth morning out, Bill awoke to find his horses gone. He was afoot and alone, save for the wagon and the pine box. He began walking, following the tracks, and soon reached a low, timbered hillside:

> Suddenly, he found himself surrounded by Indians—all of them dead. The spot was an Indian burial ground, and in the trees were bodies wrapped in blankets and buffalo robes. He hurried past, and later in the day found his horses grazing beside a little stream.[16]

Two nights later he camped at Nine-Mile Hollow, several miles south of present day Kingfisher. The next morning his horses were missing a second time. The moccasin and pony tracks left a trail that led westward, but he realized it would be futile to follow the Indians again, so he abandoned the wagon and pine box and struck out on foot to Ft. Reno.[17] There the Army loaned him a horse and ordered a squad of cavalrymen to return to the wagon with him and begin pursuit. Far to the west, they finally overtook a marauding band of Cheyenne and recovered the horses.[18]

By the next evening Bill reached the trail crossing at Kingfisher Creek where he spent the "most lonely night" of his life. He camped in the cut along the creek bed, and only half a mile away, on the embankments above both sides of the creek, smoke from a Cheyenne encampment ascended into the evening sky. At dark the dancing began, and the dull sound of beating drums filled the still night air. As the night wore on, Indians from both camps began riding past his wagon shrieking bloodcurdling war whoops: an eerie chorus in the accompaniment of hoot owls and coyotes. Relieved at the coming of dawn, Bill gathered his gear and was thankful to move on.[19]

Exhausted by the long miles and sleepless nights of the depressing and perilous trip, he finally reached Wichita, where he shipped Roberts' remains to Iowa by train. Driving back into Caldwell, he merely nodded his head to acquaintances on the street. He went to a saloon and began drinking and finally dropped into bed, sleeping for two days and ridding his mind of the unfortunate Roberts and the experience of bringing his body back.[20]

During the mid-1870s, Fossett worked on several ranches in southern Kansas. As an itinerant cowhand he drove horses and cattle through Texas and Indian Territory to various points in Kansas. From those many journeys he became exceptionally familiar with the Chisholm Trail, writing and telling of it often through the years.[21]

The trail was born when Texans returned home from the Civil War to find their ranges overflowing with cattle. They had thrived, multiplied, scattered and grown fat during the war and now, with the Texas economy in shambles and Confederate currency worthless, the huge herds promised an obvious solution if the wild, footloose assets could be rounded up and driven to northern markets.

Illinois livestock mogul Joseph G. McCoy was keenly aware of potential profits from Texas cattle, and convinced the Union Pacific Railroad (its Eastern Division became the Kansas Pacific in 1868) that the village of Abilene, Kansas, would be the perfect cattle shipping point. McCoy was to build the cattle pens if the railroad put in a switching yard. They completed the deal and notified Texas cattlemen of the new shipping yards at Abilene. McCoy also described the best route for drovers to use. It was a trail that had been blazed by a half-Cherokee Indian trader and guide named Jesse Chisholm during his earlier trading excursions across parts of Kansas and Indian Territory.

Only a few herds trailed north in 1866 but the following year, word of McCoy's cattle shipping point and the new preferred route that was west of the old Shawnee Trail, spread across Texas. In 1867, the first year the trail was open, only 35,000 cattle were marketed in Abilene, but it began the transformation of the little village to a booming cattle town.[22]

In the following ten years, 5.5 million longhorns were driven north to various Kansas cowtowns and then shipped to packinghouses in Kansas City and Chicago.[23]

Actually, there were several cattle trails in Texas. Prior to the Civil War, most of these led north to Missouri and eastern Kansas.[24] It was after the war that the great cattle drives occurred in increasing numbers, the majority pointing toward the Chisholm Trail and crossing the heart of Indian Territory. Eventually, the entire main trail from southern Texas to Kansas was commonly referred to as the Chisholm Trail. Herds going north varied in size but the average was 2,500 head. The drives began at various points in Texas during the spring and moved north at a pace of about five to fifteen miles a day.[25]

Fossett frequently made the point that the Jesse Chisholm and John Chisum Trails were often confused. He said both trails ran north and south, but the John Chisum Trail was the more westerly of the two:

> The Jesse Chisholm Trail, about which there has been much dispute, ran from Caldwell, Kansas to Wichita [after crossing Indian Territory] but the cattle trail which was the old Chisholm Trail extended to Abilene, Kansas; that was before there was any thought of Dodge City, or the John Chisholm [sic: Chisum] Trail that ran into Dodge City, Kansas from western Texas.
>
> Jesse Chisholm was a post trader but a great many have gotten the two trails of the two men … mixed. [26]

As the first Kansas cow towns became settled and farming encompassed more land around them, the cattle drives moved farther west and south, giving rise to new shipping destinations such as Ellsworth, Russell, Hays, and later, Dodge City, Kansas. In its *1874 Guide Map of the Great Texas Cattle Trail*, the Kansas Pacific Railway, then shipping the majority of Texas cattle, sarcastically made the point that drovers should bring cattle further west to give them "freedom from the petty annoyances of settlers, arising from the cattle trespassing upon cultivated fields."[27]

Another reason for more westerly cattle trails during this period was the Kansas farmer's dread fear of "Texas fever," a tick-born disease sometimes carried by Texas cattle that could wipe out a local herd. This resulted in a series of legally mandated quarantine boundaries outlawing Texas cattle in parts of Kansas. These boundaries moved west, forcing the cattle trails west as more towns were settled. In 1880 drovers and the railroads circumvented the law by pushing cattle into huge holding pens that opened up south of Caldwell at the Indian Territory line. Cattle drives could then technically end at the border where shipment by rail began.[28]

Having crossed Indian Territory many times on trail drives, Fossett became familiar with the old Kingfisher Stage Ranch where, several years later, he would help settle one of the first towns in the "new" Oklahoma Territory.

The stage lines ran practically down the middle of the old cattle trails, and in the early 1870s, the federal government established a mail route between Wichita and Ft. Sill:

> The mail carriers were equipped with Concord Coaches pulled by mules and horses. The coaches did not run every day. They used mules and buckboards and what you might call relay stations [that] were established about every twelve miles along the route.
>
> One station south of Caldwell was called Pole Cat; next was Pond Creek, next Skeleton (where Enid now stands), then Buffalo Springs (Bison now), then Dover (following Bull Foot Station), and then Kingfisher Stage Station which stood one half mile west of where Kingfisher was located.
>
> About twelve miles south from ... Kingfisher,... was a place which used to be known as Nine Mile Hollow, nine miles north of Darlington. These stations were all located on the old Jesse Chisholm Trail.[29]

One of the early stations was known as Bull Foot. It was later named Hennessey, for Pat Hennessey, who was killed there by Indians in July 1874, just a few days after Bill's troublesome journey through the area with the body of Albert Roberts. Hennessey was a well-known and well-liked boss teamster who hauled supplies from Wichita to Ft. Reno and Ft. Sill. On July 1, Hennessey and three[30] other teamsters left Caldwell with four wagons headed for the Kiowa and Comanche Agency. Upon reaching Bull Foot Station at noon on July 4, they "found it in ashes, from which smoke was still rising."[31]

The Cheyennes and Comanches had been raiding all summer, violently aroused by the increased slaughter of buffaloes on the Great Plains. In his book *Wild, Wooly and Wicked*, Harry Sinclair Drago speculated that Hennessey might not have been aware of the recent (June 27) battle at Adobe Walls in the Texas Panhandle. There, a combined force of about 700 Comanche, Cheyenne and Kiowa warriors swooped down on a buffalo hunter's camp near the village of Adobe Walls, intent on wiping them out. After the initial attack, the buffalo hunters were able to keep the Indians at bay, killing scores of the raiders with their long-range Sharps rifles.[32]

It was barely a week after the Adobe Walls fight when Hennessey came across the burned-out Bull Foot Station. The freighters had gone only about 200 yards farther before a band of "screeching Cheyennes" suddenly surrounded them.[33]

Fossett recalled that the stage trail ran a short distance from a deep gulch that could hide hundreds of Indians and their horses. When Pat Hennessey and his comrades rolled by in their wagons that day, the Indians were waiting:

> Pat Hennessey got down under his wagon and fought the Indians as long as his ammunition lasted. The pile of empty shells that were by his body under the wagon showed plainly that he had fought with all his strength.
>
> The Indians captured him and tied him to the wagon wheel and burned him alive. …I have talked with a great many of the old Indians and the most I could ever find out about the Hennessey fight was, the Indian would say, "Heap brave white man", because Pat never even groaned when he was being tortured.
>
> I passed by the place Pat Hennessey was burned a few days afterwards and all there was left were some pieces of iron and some nails from the boxes. Hennessey's body had been rolled in a blanket and buried almost on the Jesse

Chisholm trail. There is still a tombstone where Pat Hennessey was buried at the northwest corner of Hennessey.[34]

W. E. "Billy" Malaley, a deputy U.S. marshal, was escorting Indian Agent J. D. Miles and a small entourage north to Caldwell and safety from the Indian outbreak when he found Hennessey's body. On July 5, Malaley's group reached Red Fork Ranch (today's Dover, eight miles south of Bull Foot Station), where they were told the "Cheyennes are out" and warned not to go farther. They continued north anyway and soon found Hennessey's burned wagons near the main trail. Malaley saw a man's foot protruding from beneath a heap of grain near a wagon wheel. He took hold and pulled out the charred remains of Pat Hennessey. Malaley and the others buried the body on the spot.

It was later learned that two men from the Buffalo Springs Ranch had arrived at the massacre scene earlier in the day and taken the bodies of the other teamsters back to their ranch for burial. They said they "didn't have time" to recover Hennessey's body.[35]

Aside from the temporary interruptions brought on by Indian outbreaks, it was mostly business as usual on the cattle and stage trails. Fossett estimated that millions of cattle and horses were brought up from Old Mexico and Texas and across the Chisholm Trail. He participated in many of those drives, sometimes moving horses to the Colcord Ranch in Kingman County, Kansas. There, Bill recalled, he and other cowboys spent months "bronc-busting" as many as 500 to 1,500 "broncos" a year.[36]

The enterprising William Rogers Colcord, a native of Kentucky and an ex-officer in the Confederacy, began building his cattle empire in Nueces County, Texas, in 1869.[37] He then moved to Comanche County, Kansas, near the mouth of the Red Fork River in the fall of 1876.[38] It was there he

19

helped put together the Jug Cattle Company, so named because the brand depicted a jug with a small looped handle at the neck. The Jug was partially owned by several cattlemen, including R. C. Campbell and Frank Thornton. Colcord's oldest son, Charles Francis, was range boss of the outfit.[39] Charles Colcord recalled that in May 1877, his father went to Caldwell, where he hired a young cowboy named Bill Fossett:

> At the time he was riding a bronco that had its neck pulled down with splints like barrel staves, set around the horse's neck so it couldn't raise its nose over two feet from the ground. This method of forcing down the neck for periods of time was very common practice in breaking wild horses. Released from the splints eventually the neck would come back up all right. Bill Fawcett [sic: Fossett) knew the country well and was great assistance in selling our wild horses.[40]

After he was hired, Bill went with Charles Colcord and a cowboy named Jesse McCartney to an area about ten miles south of Hutchinson, where they found a "pretty thickly settled neighborhood and made arrangements with some man who had a corral where we could pen our horses." Sundays, recalled Colcord, turned into a regular show for the settlers who came from miles around. They took great delight in watching the three young cowboys rope and then ride those wild horses. During the week, the routine was more business-like as the three men paraded the horses around to various farms to sell them. [41]

Jesse McCartney was considered to be a dangerous man with a gun who had already killed five or six men. Colcord was fully aware of that reputation during an incident at the corral one day:

> I had roped a big mare, put on the hackamore and then turned the rope over to McCartney to take her out of

the corral. He got outside of the gate and the boys ran the mare through. McCartney had the rope around his hips to keep it from burning his hands, but the mare came out with such a terrible rush that it jerked him off his feet and he fell flat, face down in the dust, with the mare and the rope gone. Of course, everybody was laughing. When he got up he was the angriest man you ever saw. He grabbed a broken bar from the gate four or five feet long and rushed at me. I saw he was enraged! I waited until he got almost up to me, then drew my six-shooter and fired, but as I leveled my gun, Bill Fawcett [sic] ran between us and knocked my gun up and took the bullet in his hand. McCartney stopped right there and quieted down—though he was a very bad and dangerous man.[42]

Within a couple of years the Colcord operation expanded to include a thoroughbred cattle ranch in southern Kingman County.[43]

Other members of the Fossett family also worked as cowboys in Kansas and the Cherokee Outlet during this period. John Francis Fossett, Bill's oldest nephew, who went by the name "Frank," was foreman of the Blair, Batten and Cooper Ranch, the "Flat S" brand, located in the Outlet south of Caldwell.[44]

Working around cattle, whether on a drive or during branding operations, was clearly more dangerous than is often portrayed, especially when it came to branding Longhorns. Laban S. Records, in his book, *Cherokee Outlet Cowboy,* recounted many of the hazards. Records was working with a branding crew on the open prairie during the roundup of 1881 when a cowhand named Pete Gallagher was badly gored:

> As a cow fell to her side on the ground, it was usual for the man that was to hold her to grab the tail, pull it through between her hind legs and up through her flank in

front of the hip bone, then place his knees on the center of her back, and pull with his weight and strength. This prevented the cow from catching her toes in the turf and getting on her feet.[45]

Gallagher was in that position when another cow ran out of the herd and charged. When someone "hollered," he turned just in time to be struck by the horn, which ran in his mouth through the cheek, below the cheekbone. Records said the incident made the boys so mad that they "roped the cow which had done the hooking and 'throwed' her with the branded side up." They then burned her on every available space from neck to hip with the LU ranch brand.

The following year a similar mishap befell Samuel Robert Fossett, Bill's nephew. Sam, barely twenty years old at the time, was holding a cow in the same way as Gallagher, when another cow "on the prod" ferociously charged without warning. The horn struck, penetrating his "vital parts," eventually resulting in his death.[46]

During the late 1870s, Bill made another foray out of Kansas, taking a herd of mules and horses to Leadville, Colorado, where new gold and silver discoveries created a demand for pack animals.[47]

In 1876 tragedy struck Bill's young family. A July edition of the *Sumner County Press* reported that "Mr. and Mrs. Wm. Fossett's little boy died last Saturday." The reference to their second child was in a brief personal item without further explanation.[48] Eighteen months later, on February 28, 1878, the same newspaper announced the birth of a daughter to Bill and Elizabeth. Her name was Mary Frances, better known in later years as Mamie. In the 1880 census, she was listed as two years old and her brother Lewis, seven.[49]

Mealtime for a range crew in the Cherokee Outlet, circa 1888.

W. D. "BILL" FOSSETT

In 1879 Bill worked the fall roundup for the Montague and Manning Cattle Company, southwest of Caldwell. Both men were locally referred to as "cattle kings." Montague was sort of an absent partner in the operation, occasionally visiting from his home in Matoon, Illinois, while C. H. Manning lived in Caldwell.[50]

Bill recalled that while working that roundup he was asked to take the job of assistant city marshal in Caldwell.[51] The absence of city records for that period make it difficult to confirm that he became assistant marshal in 1879, but he did have that post in 1881 when the infamous "Talbot Raid" occurred, an event discussed in the following chapter.

At the time of Caldwell's incorporation as a city of the third class in July 1879, John Wilson served as deputy constable under W. C. Kelly, and in August, George W. Flatt was appointed city marshal. Flatt reportedly had a succession of deputies or assistants, one of whom may have been Bill Fossett.[52] The positions of assistant constable or assistant marshal were not necessarily full time, thus an "assistant," if Bill was one, would likely have pursued a more reliable means of making a living in town. Whether it was because of temporary work, or other reasons, Bill apparently began spending more time around Caldwell. The November 18, 1879, edition of the *Caldwell Post* noted that "William Fossett has opened a restaurant."[53] The following month, he was advertising:

FOSSETT'S RESTAURANT,
WM FOSSETT, PROPRIETOR,
Caldwell   Kansas
Board by day or week. Meals served at all hours.
Remember the place - -
first door north of the Pacific House.[54]

By January 1880, the *Post* reported that Bill was in the grocery business:

> WILLIAM FOSSETT is at present, proprietor of the Cash Grocery Store, having lately bought out Mr. Beeson & Griffith's interest in that business. This is also a first class establishment and keeps thoroughly up with the times. He has a large and well-selected stock of family groceries. His motto is 'Live and let live.' Mr. Fossett has had considerable experience in the grocery trade. He watches and takes advantage of the fluctuating market, pays cash and gives his customers advantage of low prices.[55]

From trail rider and cowhand to restaurateur and grocer, Bill seemed never to stay at any one job for long. If it was restlessness for something new and different that kept him moving about, he wouldn't have to wait much longer. Up until this point, life in Caldwell had been relatively peaceful, but all that was about to change, especially for those wearing a badge.

The "Jug" brand of
W.R. Colcord
Medicine Lodge, Kansas

The "Flat S" of
Blair, Batten & Cooper
Caldwell, Kansas

"M" of Montague &
Manning
Caldwell, Kansas

3

LAW IN THE BORDER QUEEN

A welcome sight on the furrowed and dusty trail across Indian Territory came when cowhands reached the crest of a long, gentle up slope in the prairie that gradually fell away toward two tree-lined creeks about a mile off. There lay Caldwell, Kansas, a town with two personalities.

The "Queen of the Border" was the first place a cowboy could get a drink, at least legally, after crossing the Red River from Texas.[1] Before her heyday, the scruffy little settlement contained a few saloons and a couple of hotel-casinos with all their trappings. This stood in stark contrast to more customary businesses that were patronized by the stoic men and women, mostly farmers, who lived in its environs. It was both a farm town, supporting settlers who worked the land across the southern tier of Sumner County, and a trail town where lonesome cowboys briefly stopped to spend a few hard-earned dollars on supplies and revelry.[2] There, in the fall of 1873, a few years before Caldwell earned its reputation as a roaring, rough and bawdy cowtown, the Fossetts settled on the rich, nearby farmlands.[3]

Caldwell was the brainchild of merchants and real estate men in Wichita. They sought a place on the Chisholm Trail to capitalize on passing Texas drovers, a location where they could sell whiskey, a little merchandise and eventually town lots, with the vision of someday creating a cattle-shipping center.

In late 1870, cattle speculator Charles Stone and liquor wholesaler James H. Dagner rode from Wichita to the southern most reaches of Sumner County, near the Indian Territory border. The two men found what they were looking for on a slope north of Fall and Bluff Creeks, which were deeply channeled through a lightly timbered meadow. A townsite of 113 acres was staked off north of Fall Creek in January 1871, and cottonwood and hackberry trees were felled. Stone and Dagner built a log house next to the trail and sold groceries "with liquid groceries predominating." The location also served as Caldwell's first post office. The town was named in honor of U.S. Senator Alexander Caldwell of Leavenworth.[4]

The going was slow at first, but with seasonal trade provided by herds passing north to Abilene and Wichita, Caldwell evolved to a small assortment of saloons and supply stores. Amid constant hope that a railroad would soon be put through, the town struggled, yet prospered.[5]

Public land available for homesteading lured the Fossetts and most everyone else to the region. In the late 1870s, Bill Fossett, his brothers and their families, moved from Falls Township into, or immediately west of, Caldwell. In the years to come they would be among the town's most respected citizens, operating grocery and dry goods stores, restaurants and saddle shops.[6]

While Caldwell was slow to flourish as a cattle town, its standing as one was not. In the early years, a variety of "whiskey peddlers, cattle rustlers and other riffraff" were drawn there. These vagrant troublemakers were at the center of several murders and lynchings that gave Caldwell the same reputation for violence as Ellsworth and Dodge City.[7]

Caldwell blacksmith George D. Freeman, among the town's first residents, documented much of the early violent history in his 1890 book, *Midnight and Noonday.* He understood why frontier towns such as his attracted the sometimes less than desirable:

> As the tide of civilization crowded west, and men of integrity, ability, and of a determined character immigrated to western towns and became enterprising citizens, the rougher element could not prevail, hence they too must immigrate west to the frontier towns. It has been said that on these conditions, the crowded cities of Emporia, Newton and Wichita gave up their most reckless citizens to make up a band of rustlers, horse thieves, and bad characters to populate Caldwell.[8]

Rumors of a railroad to Caldwell persisted, but were dashed several times through the early 1870s. Finally, in the winter of 1874-75, Caldwellites initiated their own rail project, but it never materialized. In 1877 the quarantine line for Texas cattle was moved west of town, virtually closing the Chisholm Trail to cattle from the south. Caldwell languished on a cattle trail with no cows until two railroads, the Burlington and Southwestern and the Santa Fe, offered extension lines from the north. The Santa Fe's Cowley, Sumner and Ft. Smith branch was to extend south from Wichita, and with the backing of the newly founded *Caldwell Post* newspaper, it won the county-wide bond proposal. This sent Caldwell's real estate prices soaring by the end of 1879.

After the Santa Fe tracks reached Wellington in September, the railroad's main construction efforts shifted toward Arkansas City in the east. Seeing their boom was about to fizzle, Caldwell citizens tried to entice the Kansas City, Lawrence and Southern (K.C.L. & S.) railroad to extend its line from Wellington to Caldwell. For a time it looked as if the K.C.L. & S. would build that direction, but the railroad switched gears and formed a branch line called the Sumner County Railroad. In May 1880, the new branch started track laying straight south from Wellington to the state line, where it planned to operate its own cattle-shipping center.

This move prodded the Santa Fe to act quickly with its Cowley, Sumner & Ft. Smith branch line into Caldwell. It reached town on June 1, 1880, and by the middle of the month, Caldwell was finally shipping cattle by rail. On June 16, the Sumner County Railroad arrived at the state line where it created the town of Hunnewell, named for the railroad's president.

The competing lines were soon engaged in a shipping rate war that was quickly ended when the Santa Fe bought out the line to Hunnewell to control shipments all along the Kansas-Indian Territory border.[9]

During the summer of 1879, the mere anticipation of a railroad had spurred Caldwell's growth. A forty-acre tract was added to the town, and on July 22, Caldwell incorporated as a city of the third class. The following month, a mayor and councilmen were elected, and the office of city marshal was created. The marshal was to serve on appointment by the mayor and, according to city ordinance No. 3:

> He [the marshal] may appoint any number of assistants, or deputies, for whose official acts he shall be

liable, but they shall have no claim against the city for services.

The marshal, or any assistant, or deputy, or other officer of the city empowered to make arrests, is hereby authorized to call upon any male inhabitant of the city to assist him in making an arrest, or quelling a disturbance of the public peace. Whoever neglects or refuses in said case, when called upon to assist said officer, shall be liable to a fine of not less than five dollars, and not exceeding ten dollars.

...The marshal shall receive for his services, $33 1/2 dollars per month, and in addition thereto the following fees, viz: For making an arrest authorized by law, two dollars; for serving legal process, the same fee as Sheriffs in like cases; provided, however, that in no case shall the city be liable for said fees....[10]

Named to the position created by this ordinance was sometimes saloonkeeper and gun-hand, George W. Flatt. Only a few days before his appointment, Flatt had proved fearless when Constable W. C. Kelly and Deputy John Wilson enlisted his aid in quelling a disturbance by a group of cowboys who were shooting up the town. They confronted the troublemakers in the Occidental Saloon, and Flatt allowed himself to be backed out the front door by two cowboys who held cocked six-shooters inches from his face. When they reached the boardwalk, the cowboys demanded Flatt raise his hands. He replied, "I'll die first," and drew his own two pistols, setting off a point-blank shootout. For the next few seconds, muzzles flashed and roared amid clouds of smoke at the doorway of the Occidental. One startled cowboy fired first but missed. Flatt didn't. He downed the closest man with his right-hand revolver and put a shot through the side of the other cowboy with his left. Deputy Constable Wilson then joined the fray, killing the man with two quick shots before he was wounded in the thigh.[11]

The affair in the Occidental Saloon was evidence enough that Caldwell was becoming a wild and wooly frontier town. It became even more so after the railroad arrived. Until then, Caldwell was on a trail that cowboys and herds passed along enroute to final destinations beyond. The railroad, however, made it a shipping point at the end of the drive where cowboys acted out a ritual of rowdiness. The formula for cowtown troubles was simple enough. Take a group of young men who are looking for the most exciting time possible after spending weeks of trailing cattle up a dusty trail; place them in a situation where they try to outdo each other in the excesses of drinking, gambling, brawling and reveling with dance hall girls; add the fact that most of the men are armed, and you have a recipe for disaster.

Although cowboys could create plenty of trouble, blacksmith and early resident George Freeman knew them well enough to see a balance in their character, concluding that not all of those young men were hell raisers:

> The reader must not picture the cowboy as a desperado.... The majority of cowboys are a drinking, carousing set of young men, and are rough when under the influence of liquor, but take them when they are sober and you will not find any one that will help you in a time of trouble more than this class of young men.[12]

The physical appearance of Caldwell, meanwhile, was another issue with no interpretation required. Newcomers, unaccustomed to cattle towns, were left with a less than inspiring first impression of the bustling border city:

> The inhabitants were . . . housed in a collection of frame, mostly rough shacks of various types, strung out an

eighth of a mile along one street, which ran south, a continuation of the stage road named Reno trail. There were no sidewalks. The town pump, a half-hogshead watering trough and hitching rack, stood in front of the hotel making it a town center. Here the stagecoaches discharged and assumed the care of passengers and mail. Two or three trading stores, many saloons and gambling houses, flanked the Leland House on either side. More saloons and livery stables sprawled on the opposite side of the road. Hogs, chickens, dogs roamed at will. Garbage, tin cans, litter of the trail lay about, all thickly coated with dust.[13]

George Flatt served as city marshal until the election of April 1880, when Mike Meagher became the new mayor. Meagher, an ex-city marshal of Wichita, who came to Caldwell to open a saloon, fired Flatt and appointed William Horseman to the post. Dan Jones, who had served in the capacity under Flatt, was retained as assistant marshal.[14]

On June 19, 1880, just a few days after the beginning of railroad operations in Caldwell, ex-marshal George Flatt was assassinated on a city street while walking with citizen C. L. Spear and policeman Samuel Rogers. Six or seven shots were fired about 1:00 a.m., and arriving quickly on the scene were Mayor Meagher, Marshal William Horseman and officers Dan Jones, Frank Hunt and James Johnson. All testified they did not see Flatt's assailant.[15] Meagher and the officers who arrived after the shooting, along with C. L. Spear and Samuel Rogers, were arrested for complicity in the killing of Flatt, but in each case the charges were either dropped or the suspect acquitted.[16]

Caldwell seemed to take the shooting affair with an amazing lack if indignation. It was as if the town was saying good-riddance to Flatt who had become a vicious drunk and bully since his fiery shootout at the Occidental Saloon the previous year.[17] So embarrassing was the investigation into

Flatt's death that the *Caldwell Commercial* blamed officials in the county seat of Wellington for trying to profit from the arrests and trials of Caldwell's police force.[18]

Flatt's death was not quickly forgotten, however, for on October 8, 1880, Frank Hunt, who had since been discharged as a policeman, was killed by a single shot through an open window as he sat in the Red Light Saloon. With rumors rampant as to why Flatt was murdered, the *Caldwell Post* muddied the water further by asserting, "George Flatt was killed to satisfy a grudge. Frank Hunt was killed for the same reason." Adding a new twist to the plot was the arrest of David Spear, who was charged with Hunt's death. David was the seventeen-year-old son of C. L. Spear, one of the men walking with Flatt the night he was killed. His older brother, George, operated the Red Light Saloon. Charges against David Spear were dropped after a preliminary hearing. The murders of both Flatt and Hunt were never conclusively solved.[19]

Mike Meagher did not run for re-election in 1881, but on July 18, he was nominated for city marshal. City Council rejected the bid, and Meagher said he didn't want the job anyway. A few days later he reconsidered and accepted Mayor W. N. Hubbel's appointment to be marshal "for the present." He served for only five days when council placed the name of James Roberts in nomination for the position. Roberts won in a three-to-one vote.[20] Mayor Hubbel resigned in the squabble over police force leadership and Cass Burrus became mayor. Wanting his own marshal, Burrus named John Rowan, reducing Roberts to assistant marshal and adding John Wilson as policeman.[21] The political turmoil continued through late October when Rowan resigned, and city fathers made John Wilson marshal. It was Wilson, a bartender, sign painter and former constable, who had backed George Flatt in the

Occidental Saloon shootout. Wilson appointed Bill Fossett as his assistant marshal and James Sharpe as policeman.[22]

It appeared that Caldwell could now stabilize under a new police force. The *Caldwell Commercial* urged peace and civility through a crackdown on concealed weapons:

> Now that the new police force has been installed and entered upon their duties, it is hoped that the first work they undertake will be to enforce the law against carrying concealed weapons. There is no reason why a man should go armed in Caldwell any more than in any other place, and certainly there is no reason why mere boys should be allowed to make walking arsenals of themselves. A secretly armed man is a constant menace to the peace and safety of the community and should not be tolerated in any place laying the smallest claim to being civilized.[23]

Then, as now, the well-intended law didn't prevent mayhem and left only law-abiding citizens without arms. Caldwell's calm lasted less than two months. On December 17, 1881, Mike Meagher was cut down by an assassin's bullet during a wild shootout that became known as the Talbot Raid.

Jim Talbot, whose real name was James Sherman, arrived in Caldwell about November as the town settled down after the busy cattle-trading season. He and his wife moved into a house near the corner of Chisholm and Fifth Streets, one block east of the main street. Talbot, claiming he was a Texas cowboy, was soon joined by three other Texans named Jim Martin, Bob Munson and Bob Bigtree. They, too, settled in the same vicinity of town with women purported to be their wives. This close-knit little group spent most days and nights in revelry at the nearby Red Light Saloon, as well as other Caldwell dance halls and dives in the same area. They were often joined in their carousing by Dick Eddleman, Doug Hill, Tom Love, and George Spear, the proprietor of the Red Light

Saloon. Wherever they were, "drunk or sober, they went out of their way to show their contempt for the police," using obscene language on the street in front of women, crowding men off the sidewalk, and firing their pistols in an apparent attempt "to cow the town."[24]

On Friday night, December 16, Talbot and company reportedly exhibited "bad and obscene" behavior during a performance of *Uncle Tom's Cabin* at the Opera House. When *Caldwell Post* editor Tell Walton, who was in attendance, attempted to quell the disturbance, they threatened him and became louder. The shouting match carried into the streets after the play where Talbot's gang declared, "they would fix [Mike] Meagher and that editor."[25] At the time, there appeared to be no connection between Talbot and ex-mayor Meagher.

Talbot and his friends drunkenly stumbled about the saloons all night, while Meagher, obviously agitated by the threats, refused advice from his friends to go home. At daybreak, Meagher went to the house of City Marshal John Wilson, apparently telling Wilson there was a riot downtown and that Talbot and his gang were trying to kill him.[26]

At about the same time, Talbot's gang took to the streets and began shooting their revolvers, "George Spear leading the performance." When Wilson and Meagher arrived downtown they found the cowboys in the Moores Brothers' Saloon where Wilson arrested Tom Love for firing his pistol. Talbot, Munson, Eddleman and a local man named "Comanche Bill" Mankin, were also there, all armed. When Wilson tried to take Love to jail, the other cowboys intervened. Meagher came to Wilson's aid, and as they started up the street with Love, the cowboys rushed them. Meagher ran up the Opera House steps, and Wilson told the troublemakers he would shoot the first man who tried to kill Meagher. The cowboys dispersed, including Love, whom Wilson could not keep in custody during the face off.[27]

There was gunplay and general sniping for the next couple of hours. Talbot's gang took shots at almost any possible target while lawmen and townspeople sought cover and prepared for a siege. By this time, citizens were taking up firing positions and arming themselves with borrowed guns from hardware and supply stores.[28]

About 1:00 p.m., a pitched battle erupted between townspeople and the Talbot gang, and "the bullets were flying thick down the street and singing like bees." The shooting began a short time after Wilson and Assistant Marshal Bill Fossett arrested Jim Martin for carrying a concealed weapon and resisting an officer. Martin was taken before a judge and fined. As Bill crossed Main Street with Martin in custody, Talbot, Love, Munson and Eddleman approached to rescue their comrade, saying there was no need for Martin to pay his fine. In the tense moments of that brief standoff, Bill held his ground with "drawn revolvers." Wilson, who was nearby, ordered Talbot and his men to give up their weapons. They refused, and all of them, including Jim Martin, ran back down the street behind a crowd of spectators. According to Fossett:

> Talbot ran down the street, turned and fired two shots at Wilson, ran between the building east, yelling at the boys to get their Winchesters. He ran to his residence, got his gun, came up fifth street to the rear of the Opera House, and began firing at me. I was then at the rear of Hockaday's Store. Meagher and [Ed] Rathbun were near me. Doug Hill and [Bob] Bigtree were firing at me from the east, and Talbot from the north.[29]

As the shooting continued, news of the street fighting was relayed by telegraph to Wellington and Wichita. The events prompted an editor of the *Wichita Times* to write the now famous line, "As we go the press, hell is in session in Caldwell."[30]

At some point in the fighting, Meagher and Ed Rathbun joined Wilson in the alley behind Pulaski's store. Talbot, armed with a Winchester, began firing at them from the boardwalk near the Opera House. Meagher, with a revolver in his hand and a rifle under his arm, was returning fire when he suddenly sank to his knees saying, "I'm hit and hit hard." Wilson helped the dying man to cover behind a box.[31]

Sam P. Rdings, a young boy who lived in Caldwell at the time, later recalled the shooting in his book *The Chisholm Trail*. He says Meagher and Talbot engaged in a one-on-one rifle duel from around corners of two buildings on opposite sides of the alley. According to Ridings, Meagher then tried to circle around the Opera House and surprise Talbot by coming up behind him. Talbot apparently figured out Meagher's plan and was waiting, killing him with one rifle shot when the ex-mayor reappeared south of the Opera House.[32] This later recollection of how Meagher was trying to circle behind Talbot when fatally shot does not square with testimony from witnesses immediately following the shootout.

After Meagher fell, Wilson, Fossett and the townspeople continued firing at Talbot and the others as they ran for horses at a livery stable. According to Freeman, "bullets fired by the citizens flew thick around them." As the gang saddled horses in the stable, George Spear ran toward the Red Light Saloon where Talbot's horse was picketed. Just as Spear raised the saddle to the horse, he was killed by a rifle shot through the heart, and then the horse was shot. The entire gang, except Eddleman and Love, finally secured saddled horses and rode from the stable at a dead run. Talbot's horse was shot from beneath him, and he quickly doubled up with another rider. The cowboys all escaped, leaving town across the Santa Fe tracks to the east.[33]

Lawmen arrested Eddleman and Love at the stable and quickly formed a posse to pursue the others. After a hot chase to about ten miles southeast of Caldwell, the posse closed the distance, and the gang took refuge in a ravine near a ranch along Deer Creek in Indian Territory. They dismounted and took cover, exchanging shots with the posse for the remainder of the afternoon. When night came, Talbot and his men mounted up and slipped away in the darkness.[34]

The Talbot raid was another example of how Caldwell seemed never to lack for unsolved and un-prosecuted crimes committed for unknown reasons. Even so, speculation came fast and furious.

Blacksmith George Freeman, who witnessed the events, says in *Midnight and Noonday* there were rumors that Talbot came to Caldwell to kill Meagher because as marshal of Wichita Meagher had killed Talbot's cousin. Freeman reported a second rumor that "Talbot and George Flatt were half brothers" and Talbot was out for revenge.[35]

Talbot refuted both claims. He and his gang signed an unusual letter written to the editor of the *Kansas City Sunday Times*, dated January 12, 1882. They claimed to have been law-abiding men while in Caldwell. They went on to impugn Meagher's character, calling him "nothing more than a saloon keeper" and gambler. Meagher was shot, Talbot claimed, because he shot at them. He added that the death of George Flatt "never entered our minds." The letter said Spear was shot by the town mob and that he had "no hand in the fight." The "row," as the Talbot gang termed it, erupted because Marshal John Wilson was on a "protracted drunk" and had given orders to kill them. Talbot further claimed that "the assistant marshal (Fossett) acknowledged that Wilson was drunk, and that if he (Wilson) had let things alone, everything would have been all right...."[36] There is no record that Fossett actually made this alleged remark.

In 1894, Talbot was arrested in California, brought to Kansas and jailed in the county seat of Wellington, where a series of trials began in April 1895. Witnesses included Bill Fossett, his brother A. J. "Jack" Fossett and newspaper editor Tell Walton. The first trial ended in a hung jury and the second in a verdict of acquittal. Talbot returned to his home in Ukiah, California, where in 1896 he was killed by an unknown assassin. Of the other members of Talbot's gang who escaped from Caldwell on horseback that day fourteen years earlier, only Doug Hill was caught and tried. He served six months for manslaughter in the Wellington jail. The others were never heard from again.[37]

Despite citizen outrage over the killings surrounding the Jim Talbot affair, violence continued in Caldwell. On June 22, 1882, George S. Brown, the town's ninth marshal, was fatally shot by two Texas cowboys in the infamous Red Light Saloon.[38]

Caldwell was convinced it had the right man for the job when Henry Newton Brown (no relation to George S. Brown) became marshal in late 1882. He kept order, took no nonsense, and was "quick on the trigger." So appreciative were citizens that they presented him with a customized Winchester rifle with gold and silver inlay and ornate engraving. What the town didn't know was that a few years earlier, Brown had ridden with Billy the Kid and fled New Mexico to avoid murder charges.

In April 1884, Brown returned to his old ways. With his assistant marshal and two hard-case cowboys, he tried to rob a bank in Medicine Lodge, Kansas. The bank's president and vice president were killed in the process and after a brief chase on horseback, Brown's gang was captured. That night a lynch mob stormed the jail and Brown was fatally shot trying to escape. His cronies were hanged from an elm tree.[39]

During the era in which Caldwell dealt with the difficulties of keeping its lawmen alive and in line, it realized its full potential as a cattle-shipping center. In 1882 over 64,000 head of cattle left Caldwell by rail, and in the following two seasons more than 85,000 were shipped north.

Dodge City faired even better, attaining a new dominance in the shipment of Texas cattle, but at the end of the 1884 season, the Chisholm Trail was playing out. Civilization and barbed wire forced some drovers to more westerly trails, while others took advantage of new rail lines laid directly into Texas range country.[40]

The days of cowherds strung out across the lush prairies in a seemingly endless wave were soon at an end. Caldwell, through no special effort of its own, finally became the peaceful town so many wanted it to be.

Looking north along Main Street in Caldwell filled with settlers for the "Run" into the Cherokee Outlet in 1893. On the northwest corner of Sixth (today's First St.) and Main is the Leland Hotel.

4

KINGMAN

While Caldwell experienced its most successful years as a cattle-shipping center, Bill made plans for new ventures in another part of Kansas. His length of term as assistant city marshal is unclear, but he and police officer James Sharpe were apparently still on the job when George S. Brown became the new marshal of Caldwell in April 1882.[1]

Either shortly before or after George Brown was gunned down in the Red Light Saloon, in June 1882,[2] Bill resigned to begin a partnership in the cattle business with his former boss C. H. Manning of the Montague and Manning Cattle Company. On August 2, 1882, a story in the *Kingman Mercury* noted that "W. D. Fossett and Mr. Manning have opened a ranch on the Chikaskia where they intend to raise fine horses and cattle."[3]

"Mr. Manning" was C. H. Manning, who owned a cattle operation with T. W. Montague. Bill had worked for the two men during the fall roundup of 1879. The Caldwell-based outfit used range land in the Cherokee Outlet, southwest of

43

town.[4] This new ranch, known as Red Stone, was located northwest of Caldwell in Kingman County on the south side of the Chikaskia River, near what later became the town of Spivey.[5]

For the time being, Bill's family continued to live immediately west of Caldwell on the forty-acre farm where he had filed a homestead claim a few years earlier.[6] It wasn't until December of 1883 that Bill, Elizabeth, and their children, Lewis and Mamie, moved to Kingman and temporary residence at the Laclede House, one of the town's first hotels. The *Kingman Mercury* noted they "would go to housekeeping as soon as a building can be secured."[7]

Kingman provided a slightly different setting from Caldwell. The high rolling prairies of the region had once been life itself to vast herds of buffalo. From horizon to horizon, the "monarchs of the plains" grazed on the rich grasslands and drank the clear waters of the Ninnescah and Chikaskia Rivers, which ran west to east through fertile valleys. The buffalo, in turn, were a life source for Indians of the Great Plains in terms of both food and clothing.

In 1872 a township company from Hutchinson began what was hoped to be a city where the Hutchinson-Medicine Lodge Trail crossed the Ninnescah River. A house was hauled in from Reno County and rebuilt at the crossing in anticipation of a town that the backers called Sherman. The site, however, was abandoned when the township company failed to obtain property deeds. The following year, J. K. and F. S. Fical, brothers, showed up and made proper claims to the land. A townsite was platted in 1874, and the building of Kingman began as the county seat. The little village consisted of a hotel, store, schoolhouse, a very small courthouse and three residences. The county and town were named for Samuel A. Kingman, an early president of the Kansas Bar Association and chief justice of the State Supreme Court.

A few early settlers to the county located claims along the Chikaskia River, but most of the newcomers chose to live along the Ninnescah River near Kingman. The rich land throughout the region was ideal for grain farming as well as livestock. It is notable that during the earliest years of farming in Kingman County, corn acreage outnumbered that of wheat about two to one. During this period of increased settler migration and growing farm acreage, the great buffalo herds, by then already drastically depleted by hunters, moved on.

In 1878 a new town site company began building directly across from Kingman on the south side of the Ninnescah River in hopes of eventually absorbing the north town. The south town prospered for about a year until it became evident that well water was almost inaccessible there. At that point, the north town prospered quickly as south townspeople moved themselves and even buildings to the north side.[8]

Although not known as a cow town, Kingman was located near a major cattle trail. Beginning about 1873, the Kansas Pacific Railway surveyed a new cattle route from Indian Territory to Ellsworth. This trail branched off the Chisholm Trail at Pond Creek, then swung west of Caldwell and Wichita by way of Kingman and Ellinwood, to Ellsworth. It was known as Cox's Trail, or the Ellsworth Trail, and it crossed the Ninnescah River only a mile and one-half east of Kingman. At that crossing, E. C. Manning, Kingman's first mercantile dealer, operated a supply store.[9]

In 1881 Kingman retained its position as county seat following an election challenge from another town about seven miles south. By then there were several stores, along with a newspaper, a lumberyard, a bakery, a private bank and a flourmill. The flourmill, the first of two in Kingman, was built by Starling Turner and began operating in January 1880. Its power was derived from a millrace cut parallel to and south of the Ninnescah River. The race parted the river west of town and rejoined the main channel on the east.[10]

In the Summer of 1883, local businessmen petitioned the courts to declare Kingman "a city of the third class." Judges approved the request on August 14 and ordered elections by the end of the month.[11]

H. H. Patten was Kingman's first mayor. The native of Indiana had been studying law when the Civil War broke out. He entered service as a private with the Army of the Cumberland in Tennessee, received a commission as first lieutenant and was assigned to lead a unit of the U.S. Colored Infantry, which fought at the battle of Nashville. After an accidental wound yielded him unfit for field duty, Patten became Post Treasurer and later the Provost Marshal of Nashville during the Union occupation. Following the war he completed his law studies in Kansas, and in March 1883, he moved to Kingman, where citizens favored his leadership and Republican politics by electing him their first mayor.[12]

Serving with Mayor Patten were city councilmen A. G. Bowron, R. D. Faught, H. S. Godown, Ethan Waite and B. F. Frazier. Kingman's first city clerk was E. H. Andres, and John P. Jones was city treasurer.[13]

One of the first orders of business for a newly incorporated town was the establishment of a law enforcement mechanism. This meant creating the post of city marshal and specifying his duties. In so doing, Kingman followed the example of other Kansas towns.

The romantic image of a city marshal as a fast-drawing, steely-eyed loner, whose only job is to prowl the streets and keep law and order is far from reality. Local ordinances drafted in Abilene and Wichita, among other towns, placed the marshal in charge of the city jail, police records, and other police force members or deputies. Added to these duties was the inglorious job of looking after city streets, a task that entailed investigating complaints of street obstructions, defects and nuisances, the latter of the type requiring removal by shovel.[14] Kingman's city records are rife with bills submitted by marshals for street work, ranging from removing dead animals to cleanups and improvements.[15] W. A. Liggett was the first to serve in this capacity at Kingman.[16]

When the town incorporated in the summer of 1883, Kingman's entire population was about 350 persons. During the year, ten homes were constructed and new businesses added, including two blacksmith shops, two store buildings and a post office.[17]

Prospects for Kingman's immediate growth centered on the fact that a rail line was under construction west from Wichita, with the promise of reaching town by December first. The Wichita and Western Railroad Company, chartered in Wichita, had completed a bridge across the Arkansas River in October and was laying track on its forty-five-mile run to Kingman, and eventually to Pratt. Grading was completed by the end of 1883, but the much-anticipated event of rail service was still several months away.[18]

Local newspapers kept up a steady stream of progress reports on the line's construction. The *Kingman Courier* of April 18, 1884, reported that track had been laid to "within sixteen miles of the city on the east, and the road is graded west of the city...." The newspaper added that Kingman was not yet a railroad town and required travel by private conveyance or stages:

> For this reason livery stables are numerous and all doing a flourishing business. Will Fossett, proprietor of the Stone Livery Stable on Sherman Street, keeps a good supply of desirable rigs—carriages, buggies, wagons, etc., with a well-equipped stable and many excellent roadsters....[19]

The Stone Livery was one of the structures moved from south of the river when earlier attempts to build a town there failed. It was relocated to the north side of Sherman Street (Avenue) facing south in the block immediately west of Main Street.[20]

By the time Bill began managing the livery stable, he had started construction of his home on North Main Street, just two blocks from the center of town.[21] He may also have maintained his cattle ranching interests with C. H. Manning in Chikaskia Township during this period, probably as an absentee partner.[22]

In May, Bill rode to Caldwell for what was termed, "business." This trip occurred just a few days after Caldwell City Marshal Henry Brown, his deputy and two cowboys died at the hands of a mob after holding up a bank at Medicine Lodge. On returning to Kingman, Bill told the *Courier* that "the people of that town [Caldwell] are not likely to go into mourning on account of the death of their marshal." He said Brown had few friends and that people respected him out of fear alone. The *Courier* concluded, "no one ventures to question the propriety of the mob's work."[23]

In the nineteenth century West, few ventures could rival a railroad when it came to the promise of prosperity. For that reason, on June 1, 1884, the people of Kingman anxiously watched as Wichita and Western railroad track crews reached the eastern outskirts of town. The enthusiasm of citizenry was matched by the *Courier's* vivid report of the event:

> As it advanced mile after mile up the valley, the excitement heightened and increased until last Sunday the workmen came within hailing distance of the corporate limits and the greater part of the population turned out to witness the process of construction. The old and young, the pious and the ungodly, all went out to the deep cut just east of town where the men were at work, totally oblivious to the

sanctity of the blessed Sabbath. Of the crowd of four or five hundred that assembled to witness the work, none were so pious as to condemn it—all were ready to recognize it as a matter of extreme necessity.[24]

By nightfall the rails were laid about halfway through the cut, and when work resumed Monday, the track reached the city limits:

> During the afternoon the crowd of spectators increased, and by the time the laying, and leveling and spiking had reached Main street, nearly one thousand people crowded around to see the first engine make its passage across the principal thoroughfare of the city. The Kingman Cornet Band was out discoursing enlivening music and the spikes sank into the ties to the measure of sweet strains. Engine No. 90, Engineer Tom Banks at the throttle, with his good-looking fireman, "Bennie" Watkins, gazing out upon the sea of faces was the first to make the crossing. While the engine slowly pulled across, the people noiselessly watched its progress and when it had completed the crossing, a simultaneous shout of joy burst from the thousand throats…then someone proposed "three cheers for engine No. 90, the first locomotive to cross Main street." It was given with a will, there being scarcely a male hat that was not swung in the air.[25]

Following the train's 6:00 p.m. crossing of Main Street between Sherman and the river, the townspeople treated over 200 railroad employees to an outdoor supper. For the next several days, rail traffic to Kingman was limited to construction, freight and special excursion trains to Wichita. One evening, according to the *Courier*, a local man named Jim Smyth "flung his grip aboard the train and then monkeyed around with the boys…." The train and grip finally departed without Smyth, who had "the distinction of being the first man to miss a train in Kingman."[26]

On the Monday following the arrival of Kingman's first train, city council accepted the resignation of William Armstrong, the third city marshal to serve in **less** than one year. Armstrong was said to have "resigned for **cause**"[27] on the morning of June 9. It's evident that council members already had considered a new appointee when they met in special session that night. Bill Fossett was chosen by unanimous consent, the *Kingman Courier* noting:

> Mr. Fawcett [sic] has all the requirements of a good officer, courage, prudence and appreciation of the dignity and duties of the position. While he may be classified as "one of the boys" the rest of the young people of the male gender need not expect that he will violate either law or duty in their interest.[28]

The next week the *Courier* commented on Bill's job performance by observing that police court activity was increasing as a result of more fines and arrests:

> A good marshal is a blessing to any town. Will Fossett has been marshal now for less than two weeks and the fines that he has been instrumental in having assessed, will swell the city's exchequer to something near $200.[29]

Bill received only twenty dollars per month for the job until late the following year when the pay was increased to seventy-five dollars. The salary was anything but generous, even for the time, but Bill, like his predecessors, engaged in other pursuits, such as operating a livery stable.[30]

Kingman grew rapidly after the coming of the railroad. Along with an increased population came new roads and schools across the entire county.[31] As a community where life centered on farming, Kingman was never as wild as Caldwell, but the town did have a special set of problems that came with its growth. In December 1884, the *Southern Kansas Democrat* lamented about the lairs of local vice:

> The gambling dens of this town are getting to be more bold every week. At first they were all run in rooms on alleys and other out-of-the-way places. The next step brought them upstairs on the main streets, wherever they could get in. The last move, they secured rooms on the first floor of all the thoroughfares.... There is where our sons are enticed. It is there the demon places his chain around the necks of so many of our promising young men. They are led from one vice to another and finally land in a drunkard's grave or a felon's cell.... The young men are not alone in frequenting these dens—heads whose hair is as gray as the frosts of many winters can be seen there.[32]

Bill's prior experiences in Caldwell contributed to the way he handled law enforcement matters in Kingman. He took decisive action when confronting trouble, so it was not surprising that he chose men of a similar mind as deputies. One was Bedford B. Wood of Caldwell.[33] Wood was an old acquaintance and a cowboy in the early days of Indian Territory. He was at the Pond Creek Stage Ranch during an Indian uprising in1872 when Kiowas killed fellow rider Tom Best. Wood later farmed and ranched near the Fossetts in Falls Township and eventually succeeded him as assistant marshal of Caldwell. Whether it was through the efforts of Fossett and the officers he chose, or simply a matter pure happenstance, the fact is that Kingman experienced a minimal amount of criminal activity compared with other Kansas towns of the era.[34]

One of Kingman's most colorful characters during the town's boom years was Donald Robertson Green, better known as D. R., or "Cannonball," Green. Prior to Green's arrival in Kingman, where he opened a livery stable, the native of Kentucky had explored California and driven stage coaches in Montana.[35] When the Wichita and Western Railroad arrived in town, Green saw an opportunity to provide continuing passenger service via stagecoach to Pratt, Kansas, and points west. Using matched teams of horses that were changed every eight to fifteen miles, Green's line took passengers from Kingman to Coldwater, a distance of 100 miles, in just one day. His stages were so fast, Green said, "even Father Time could not keep up." He likened the speed to that of the Wabash Cannonball express train, and called his company the "Cannonball Stage Line" earning him the moniker, "Cannonball."[36]

Green usually employed drivers but often took the reins himself. Passengers lucky enough to ride beside him as his coach rumbled west, soon learned he was a proverbial "prairie textbook." He explained how to survive on the treeless plains by twisting grass into stove length logs if no buffalo chips, or what cowhands called "surface coal," could be found for a fire. Newcomers were also taught the art of building dugouts and sod shanties, as well as methods for living through blizzards and grass fires.

As the railroads moved west, Green moved with them. He teamed with land speculators in the founding of Greensburg, Kansas. His flourishing line expanded to operate seventy Concord coaches with nearly one thousand horses, and in 1886 he was elected to the state legislature from Kiowa County.

In 1889, when the Rock Island Railway had built only as far as Pond Creek, Indian Territory, Green's line was contracted to take settlers from the rail terminus, south to the "new" Oklahoma towns of Hennessey and Kingfisher. With the opening of the Cherokee Outlet in 1893, Green took a claim near Pond Creek. By then the days of stage travel were almost over, but Cannonball Green's legacy lived on. He made his mark during the heydays of Kingman's growth by creating the very routes the railroads and settlers followed west.[37]

In November of 1884, Bill returned from an "extended trip" through Texas where he and a friend named Jack Betz purchased horses. This trip would not have been remarkable except that the train "on which he took passage was mangled in a wreck." Fossett related what the *Kingman Courier* called a "blood curdling story," including:

> ...the killing of the engineer, the breaking of the brakeman's leg and his own narrow escape from the blessed privilege of having a harp placed in his hands and wings tied to his back. He got through all right, however, neither himself nor his horses having suffered the slightest injury.[38]

As 1884 ended, Kingman could look back on an exceptionally prosperous year. Notable events included the opening of a new county court house; the establishment of two new newspapers, the *Courier* and the *Leader*; the arrival of the Wichita and Western, the town's first railroad; the beginning of the Cannonball Stage Line; the operation of a brick making plant east of town; the opening of a Wells Fargo Express Company office; organization of the Kingman County Teachers Association; and the letting of contracts for a new brick school house.[39]

Among numerous listings in Kingman's business directory were eight doctors and five druggists; ten hardware and general merchandise stores; six attorneys; nine grocers; six restaurants; three newspapers; two banks; two jewelers; and eight livery stables, including a brand new one operated by Edgar Mead and Bill Fossett.[40]

The town's landmark year was also reflected in a population that approached five thousand people[41] as well as the construction of 110 buildings, eighty-six of them new dwellings. One of these, in the southeast portion of town, belonged to Peter Miller, Kingman's first watchmaker and jeweler.[42]

Peter Miller arrived in Kingman from Pennsylvania in August 1883 and opened his shop on Main Street. His wife Louisa and children Minnie, Fred and Richard soon came west to join him. When the Wichita and Western established headquarters in Kingman, Miller was named the line's watch inspector. As the railroad expanded service to towns in western Kansas, he frequently traveled the route as part of his watch inspection job, eventually opening jewelry stores in those towns, thus starting one of the country's first systems of chain stores. Active in the Kingman community and known as a man who "was the very soul of honor," he served on city council and was secretary of the Kingman County Democratic Committee. The Miller children attended school with Lewis and Mamie Fossett, the marshal's children, a matter of significance in the years that followed.[43]

The year 1885 proved to be an eventful one for both Kingman and the Fossett family. The state census, taken in March, listed thirty-two-year-old William Fossett, along with his thirty-one-year-old wife Elizabeth, and children "Louis" (Lewis) and "Mary" (Mary Frances), eleven and seven years old.[44] Within days of that census, Bill sued for and was granted a divorce from Elizabeth, no reason or other details were recorded.[45]

On the night of April 20, 1885, a raging rainstorm moved across Kansas sending the "usually mild waters of the Ninnescah" rising well above flood stage. By the following morning, the river, "normally fifty-feet from shore to shore," had overflowed its banks and stretched away to a quarter of a mile in width. The waters inundated part of the business district along Main Street on the north side of the river, but it was Kingman's southside of the Ninnescah where the flood did its greatest damage.[46] On that relatively low ground addition to the city, "eleven houses with their contents" were carried down the stream." At the height of the flooding, William Crupper, a horse dealer, tried to rescue his stock from waist-deep water when the current suddenly swept him off his feet. He made a desperate grab for the wall of a barn, clung to it, and then managed to clamor atop it, before it floated away:

> The building still continued to turn but he continued to remain on top. Just as it floated down past a tree growing on an island in the stream—a small cottonwood—the barn fell to pieces beneath him. When the pieces floated past he was seen clinging to the tree and … was greeted with cheers from the shore.[47]

As hundreds of people crowded the riverbanks to view the drama, some men launched a boat. On their first attempt they were swept past Crupper's tree out of reach, but on the second try, he was finally hauled in from his midstream perch where he had been stranded for two hours.

The *Kingman Courier* reported that several homes, along with "pig pens, out houses, coal sheds, old boxes, barrels and other trumpery were veing [sic] with each other in the mad race down the stream." Some people "took to the hills" south of town, but others hesitated too long and were trapped by the current.[48] The *Southern Kansas Democrat* added that, "men left their stores and work shops to save the lives of women and children that were struggling in their own door yards with the wild waters."[49]

As the river raged from its banks that day, Bill and several other men made a number of rescues in the vicinity of the Main Street bridge:

> A rope was stretched across the end of the bridge to the store of W. W. Reese, a boat was procured and manned by City Marshal Fossett and George Keyes, a crossing was effected by holding the rope. In this manner Marshal Fossett rescued a number from their perilous position, among them two women who were too ill to sit up. The boat foundered once but fortunately at the time it contained no one but the rescuing patty. It was righted, right speedily and did some good services afterward. Marshal Fossett is entitled to much praise for the courage, persistence and good judgement which he dispalyed.[50]

By nightfall, "the flood sank as rapidly as it had risen." Kingman had experienced its worst flood to that time with an estimated $50,000 in damages but without the loss of life.[51]

On May 10, 1885, barely two months after his divorce from Elizabeth, Bill married twenty-two-year-old Laura L. Kelso in Elvon, McPherson County, Kansas. Laura was born in Iowa and raised in Newton, Kansas. It's not known where the two had met and how long they had been acquainted.[52]

In June, Bill capably handled a couple of scrapes with so-called "roughs" who soon saw the error of their way. These incidents apparently typify Kingman's level of lawlessness during the era, as records do not reveal cases of robbery, murder and mayhem often associated with other western towns.

In one case, a pair of "drunken bummers" from Argonia tried to break up a church social at gunpoint. Learning of their threats, Bill intercepted the two near the doorway of the gathering where he identified himself and politely inquired of their intentions. "With numerous oaths and a display of firearms," the drunks demanded entry. Bill simply slugged one man, who fell in a heap on the sidewalk, a sight that took the fight out of his comrade, who hastily surrendered. The marshal relieved them of two pistols and a dagger before escorting them to a boarding house where they "peaceably retired" to sleep it off. A couple of days later the two "ruffians" wrote Bill a post card from Argonia, "commanding" him, on threat to his life, to send them the "hardware and cutlery he had taken." The *Courier* quipped, "it is needless to say that the murderous weapons have not yet been returned and that the Marshall [sic] still lives." [53]

The following week, a "tough from Texas" named Lewis Carey was on a extended drunk when he "began beating one of his horses and his wife remonstrated." Carey turned his wrath on his wife, trying to spear her with a pitchfork. She retaliated by "procuring a pistol and emptied one chamber at him," settling the dispute for the time. Later that day the couple clashed again at a public horse stable. Carey knocked his wife down and "jumping on her prostrate form," he "horribly" beat her before passers-by could pull him off.

As the woman was attended to, Carey saw his chance to escape:

> He immediately sprang upon a horse and galloped in the direction of Harper. Marshal Fosset [sic] seeing the haste of his departure pressed the first horse he encountered into service and followed. Carey was overtaken some three miles in the country and brought back after having been fired upon once. [54]

That night an outraged group of citizens organized a lynch mob, promising that "should the woman die, daylight would witness the body of Lewis C. Carey hanging from the Ninnescah bridge." Sheriff S. S. Baker secretly escorted his prisoner to the "open prairie in the east of town," away from possible mob vengeance. Carey's wife eventually recovered and Carey was jailed in Wichita.[55]

As the soggy spring gave way to summer's heat, city council decided on a street building program to keep pace with the town's growing population. By unanimous vote, they passed city ordinance No. 38:

> All male persons between the ages of 21 and 45 years, who have resided in the state of Kansas for 30 days and in the city of Kingman 10 days and who are capable of performing labor on the streets, shall be liable each year to perform two days work of eight hours each in the public streets of Kingman under the direction of the street commissioner, or furnish a substitute to do the same....[56]

Even before council's new emphasis on streets, Bill and livery business partner Edgar A. Mead devised a way to deal with the dust clouds constantly kicked up by wagons, and horses. The two men already had a stake in street work; Mead as a building contractor and city street commissioner,[57] and Bill, whose job as marshal included street repairs and cleanups.[58] They built a street sprinkling apparatus on a wagon with a tank on it. Its water supply came from two large tanks behind the Laclede Hotel "where they have erected a wind pump." The *Southern Kansas Democrat* promised the rig would "be ready for sprinkling by the time the 'long six weeks in August' get here."[59]

In July, Bill took up another part-time job, that as manager of the recently opened Ball Hotel on the corner of Sherman and Spruce.[60] He also announced his candidacy for county sheriff in the fall elections. The *Kingman Courier* backed his bid with an unequivocal endorsement as a "trustworthy, reliable and fearless officer." He failed, however, to be nominated at the Republican Convention in September.[61]

Kingman County's summer of 1885 became the most memorable for fear of an Indian uprising. From the southern part of the county, word spread like a prairie fire that "Indians jumped the reservation and headed north on the warpath." The report brought a jam of people who fled to Kingman, their wagons and buggies lining almost every road, as settlers sought refuge from an impending massacre.[62]

Bill organized a scouting expedition to locate the warring renegades. The heavily armed party set out south where they met even more frantic settlers fleeing toward town. Confident they would encounter the Indians somewhere along the Chikaskia River, Bill ordered his men to ride cautiously through the tall bluestem to keep out of sight while "he rode out front a mile or so to spot the savages." On reaching the Chikaskia, no Indians were in sight but "everywhere he saw deserted homesteads."[63]

Riding farther south, Bill's group spotted three lone riders in the distance. They, at the same time, caught sight of his party, and for the next few hours the two groups played cat and mouse with each other; narrowing the distance until close enough to see that everyone rode saddled horses. It turned out to be another scouting party of white men from the southern part of the county.

The two groups joined forces and rode most of the night into Barber County, finding more deserted homesteads along the way. After making camp, they heard shots in the distance and "thought it queer that Indians would be raiding at night." They cautiously moved in the direction of the gunfire, finally locating some homesteaders who were barricaded in a ranch house. Someone had shot a cow during the night, thinking it was an Indian, setting off a volley firing at imaginary foes.[64]

After continued searching revealed no sign of Indians, the circumstances were pieced together. Some settlers recalled that "a saddle tramp came up from the territory," stopping here and there at various homes to tell of "burning and ravaging" by Indians who rode north. The "saddle tramp" was no where to be found. In southeastern Kingman County, meanwhile, a man remembered that recently "some white men dressed as Indians rode into Norwich one night, whopping and yelling" to scare people from their homes.[65] The hoax was finally traced to its source. Some ranchers in Comanche County had spread the false report in an attempt to drive settlers from open grazing land. The days of free range were gone, but some cattlemen would try almost any scheme to get it back.[66] It was not the last Indian scare in Kingman County. The following year, Bill led another contingent of Indian fighters, before a similar report also proved groundless.[67]

The remainder of 1885 passed peacefully. Bill and his wife took in the fair in nearby Harper County, where he entered his "little gray mare" in the races. His penchant for fast horses and racing events were to serve him well in the years ahead.[68] Back home, meanwhile, twelve-year-old son, Lew, broke his collarbone in a fall from his horse.[69]

January 1886 began with a blast of cold air sweeping southward over the plains. A series of snowfalls piled up in drifts of six feet or more, and temperatures dropped to thirty degrees below zero in some places. The worst weather in the memory of Kingman County, and most of Kansas, came on the night of January 6, with fierce winds and heavy, blowing snow. When the wind and snow stopped after thirty-six hours, extreme cold weather set in for several more days. Settlers in hastily built prairie homes were ill prepared for the blizzard. Nearly 100 Kansans died in the storm. Cattle drifted south across the range until they dropped from hunger and exhaustion, many huddling up against barbed wire fences where they froze to death. From Kingman County, west into eastern Colorado, and south across the plains to Texas, herd losses reached seventy-five percent, bankrupting many large cattle companies.[70]

With the turn of the new year, Bill was completing an investigation into the "mysterious disappearance" of a local man. Sherman Crumley had vanished during the previous summer. He reportedly carried about $100 cash when last seen in town in the company of four men. His sudden disappearance raised questions, but the marshal's initial interrogation of potential suspects yielded no answers. Three of the suspects soon left for their homes in Barry County, Missouri, referred to by the *Kingman Courier* as "one of the most miserable regions of the miserable state." Bill questioned the fourth suspect, "an old man, but something of a sport," several more times.

With grand jury murder warrants in hand Bill traveled to Jefferson City, where "a requisition was obtained from the Governor of Missouri" for the arrest of the three men who had left Kingman. Bill finally located the trio and shipped them back to Kingman. At their trials in late January, the cases against them were dismissed for lack of evidence, primarily because the "victim," who disappeared, was never found, dead or alive.[71]

In the spring of 1886, there was renewed concern about Kingman gaining an unsavory reputation. Illegal liquor traffic was on the rise, and city fathers believed that citizens were "anxious for an expression as to what the policy of the government would be regarding morals in the city."

The *Kingman Courier* reported city council's view of the matter:

> There were men in the occupation of selling liquors who made an honest endeavor to live up to the law, while others did not. The liquor traffic was sometimes a source of revenue, and again it was far more of an expense. He [the

mayor] believed in taking a business view of the situation and suppressing immorality. Kingman . . . has a very unenviable reputation abroad—worse than she should have. Some steps should be taken to redeem the good name of the city. Little crime has taken place here, but the free and easy style of living practiced by some should be stopped.[72]

Council ordered Fossett, recently appointed for another term as city marshal, to enforce the new crackdown by seeing that "all saloons, gambling houses and houses of prostitution be closed and kept closed."[73] The order apparently was executed successfully and met with full compliance, as there is no record of any incidents connected with the closings.

In June, Samuel Fossett, one of Bill's nephews, died at his uncle's home. The young cowboy had been gored by a longhorn during a branding operation a few years earlier. It was said the accident "gradually, but surely took his life away." Sam died a few days short of his twenty-fifth birthday and was buried in Kingman. He was survived by his wife and young child.[74]

In spite of cattle industry setbacks from the blizzard early in the year, the attitude in Kingman was as optimistic as ever, and now the town looked forward to the coming of another railroad. The Denver, Memphis & Atlantic Railway (D. M. & A.) had been chartered in Winfield, Cowley County, Kansas, in early 1885. Kingman offered construction bonds to lure the line through Sumner and into Kingman County, instead of it building to Wichita. The new venture promised a saving in freight costs and a direct route for transporting wheat to Memphis and southern markets. After several setbacks, including a lawsuit by the Santa Fe Railway, the tracks were nearing town in the summer of 1886.[75]

Built in several segments, the D. M. & A. was to run from Coffeyville, Kansas, west to Sedan, and Winfield, then into Sumner County through Oxford, north around Wellington to Belle Plaine, and west through Conway Springs and Milton. Entering Kingman County, it progressed through Norwich and Belmont, then to Kingman, and on northwest into Reno County, at Olcott.[76] This building activity afforded Fossett a new career while continuing to serve as city marshal. Bill and Edgar Mead, already partners in performing some of Kingman's street work, formed a railroad construction company and began grading for the first five miles of D. M. & A. track west of Kingman in the late summer of 1886.[77]

At the time, the D. M. & A. was one of many railroads building new lines across southern Kansas. Competition between companies was fierce, and work crews were not above skullduggery and outright theft when it came to meeting deadlines. During the spring, high waters on the Ninnescah River washed out the D. M. & A.'s bridge west of Belle Plaine. When the line's general manager arrived at the location, he ordered the bridge repaired by the next evening. With few materials at hand, the task appeared impossible until a bold, Irish construction boss took charge.

This man and his gang ran a pile driver to the bridge and began working. They drove piles all night, but ran out of material before finishing the job. At dawn, the boss and his men rode the construction engine back to Belle Plaine, where several carloads of bridge and heavy timbers sat on the sidetrack of the Santa Fe, the D. M. & A.'s archrival. Without a question as to ownership, they threw the switch, backed the engine to the siding, and hooked on to the cars. They steamed back down the line to the bridge and continued their project using the freshly liberated bridge material.

At six o'clock that evening, the general manager's car "crossed the break and went to the front." The hastily built, makeshift bridge stood for three months before the D. M. & A. replaced it with a conventional truss structure.[78]

A similar obstacle was overcome when the rails finally approached Kingman from the southeast. Initial grading had been completed in April,[79] but late spring rains had washed out much of it. With a sizeable payment in construction bonds riding the rails to the deadline, and the payoff only three days away, the end of the track was still a mile and a half east of Kingman, where crews found the remainder of the grading unfinished. Now it was raining again, and the oozing mud made it impossible to work the grade.

This time, ingenuity, instead of theft, saved the day for the D. M. & A. The line's assistant secretary was on the scene and averse to explaining the loss of bond money to his superiors. He conferred with his foreman, mounted his buggy and then drove to every farm within a radius of several miles, where he bought up all the straw and haystacks he could purchase. Paying for the immediate delivery of these goods, he returned to the end of track.

He and the foreman then went forward to check the terrain toward Kingman. It was comparatively level except where there were ruts and low "swales" or hollows, which contained soggy ground. They were confident the rails could be laid on the ground and the train run over it, except where the track would sag into the low spots. Into those low places he ordered the foreman to dump the hay and straw. The track crew set to work on orders to place the ties without regard to spacing and to spike the rails only at the ends and centers. As the track work proceeded, the construction train crawled along behind the iron gang. On Wednesday evening, September 8, in the final hours of the allotted time, a blast of a whistle announced that the Denver, Memphis and Atlantic had reached Kingman.

The legal requirement for granting bonds was to have track to Kingman and a train running over it by the deadline. This had been accomplished, and the bonds were delivered to the D. M. & A., even though it took several more days to properly finish the road and open it for scheduled traffic.[80]

Bill spent the remainder of the year with his work crews grading the new rail line northwest of Kingman into Reno and Stafford County. Following a trip to Nebraska with wife Laura during the holidays, he returned to Kingman in early January and submitted his resignation as city marshal, apparently to devote more attention to his growing railroad construction business. The *Courier* said simply that the resignation was accepted, and until a new appointment "our efficient deputies, Bedford Wood and J. S. Wrenchy, will keep guard over the city."[81]

For the next two years, Bill was in and out of Kingman while involved in several railroad projects. In May 1887, when the D. M. & A. was bought out by the Missouri Pacific, he was one of the "principal contractors" for the line in Winfield, Kansas, and for several months, beginning in September, his work took him to Memphis for both railroad grading and levee construction along the Mississippi River.[82] This latter project apparently brought about his financial undoing, as he and "many other contractors at the time lost heavily owing to bad weather and high water that winter."[83]

Bill's construction losses coincided with a general economic downturn across much of southern Kansas in 1887 and 1888. Just as the great blizzard of 1886 had damaged the cattle industry, a drought in 1887 dealt a financial thrashing to farmers.[84] Based on its population growth, Kingman had attained city of the second class status in early 1887, but by the following year, half the farms in the county were tied up by mortgage companies. Next, the Kingman County Bank failed and, even among those not directly affected by farm and bank losses, there was concern that the town had reached its zenith.[85]

By then, Bill was employed part time as a detective for the Chicago, Rock Island and Pacific Railway, which had built across Kansas and into Indian Territory, south of Caldwell.[86] Not only was the railroad crossing territory that was familiar to him, some of it was about to be opened for settlement. The time seemed right for the ever-restless Bill Fossett to move on again.

Looking south on Main Street in Kingman, Kansas, circa 1900.

5

THE RUN

By the mid-1880s, homesteaders occupied the best lands in Missouri, Kansas and Texas, and the U.S. Congress was under added pressure to open parts of Indian Territory for settlement. For years, settlers moving west were obliged to bypass the territory, which was assigned exclusively for Indian use and occupation. It had been so since before the Civil War when, by treaty, several tribes were forcibly relocated from southeastern states to the territory. In the years that followed, a few tribes from eastern states and many from the Great Plains were also settled in the territory. Whites had invaded the Indian's domain too, but they had no title to the land and, in effect, were non-citizens, without rights.[1]

After the Civil War, northern cattle drives brought cowmen to the territory, where they paused to fatten their herds before moving on to market. Most of the grazing occurred in the Cherokee Outlet where, beginning in 1879, the Cherokees sought payment for these rights. In 1883 cattlemen met in Caldwell and formed the Cherokee Strip Livestock

Association to stop rustling and illegal grazing, and to negotiate a favorable contract with the Cherokee Nation, assuring cattlemen of continued use and control of the grassland. An initial charge of ten cents per head eventually rose to a dollar. It was a small price to pay for grazing on the rich prairie, and while the arrangement was satisfactory to the Indians, prospective settlers became even more angry about the privileges of land use.[2]

For the thousands of land seekers, the practice of keeping vast expanses of Indian Territory off-limits to everyone but Indians and cattle barons was infuriating. As early as 1870, the insatiable public appetite for homesteading in Indian Territory was widely proclaimed in political circles by so-called "boomers." They took their case to congress, and emerging from the debate was the Oklahoma Bill, allowing a portion of the territory to be opened for white settlement. Following several weeks of discussion and deal-making, congressional backers used the Indian Appropriations Bill as a means to pay for the rights to 2.3 million acres of land previously ceded by the Seminoles and Creeks.[3]

These Unassigned Lands, in the heart of the territory, were bordered on the south by the Canadian River and on the other three sides by nine Indian reservations. Most tribes, as well as big cattlemen, who had built ranches, corrals and line camps to support cattle drives and grazing lands in the territory, opposed opening the country to the public. But on March 2, 1889, congress approved legislation that placed the Unassigned Lands under the Homestead Law, giving settlers the right to claim 160-acre farms. On March 23, President Benjamin Harrison set the date of April 22 as opening day and high noon as the hour for the land rush to begin.[4]

As the "Opening" neared, thousands of people trekked to the border towns in Kansas and Texas, and on into Indian

Territory, gathering along the borders of the unassigned district. People of every description and social standing, vocation and background came. Businessman, farmer, rich and poor, all lined up to await the sound of bugles and rifles that would signal the start. [5]

This crowd of land seekers included a motley collection of camp followers and hangers-on. Colonel D. F. McMartin vividly described the masses waiting to claim property:

> The spectacular array included the Kansas Jayhawker, the Arkansas Rueben Glue,... the Missouri puke, the Texas ranger, the Illinois sucker, et al. There were nesters, horsethieves, train robbers, hijackers, bank raiders, yeggmen, ragmuffins and vagabonds, brand blotters, broncho busters, sheep herders, cow punchers, spoofers, bull whackers, range riders, minute jacks, wildcatters, four-flushers . . . fire eaters, tenderfeet land whales, butterfly-chasers, blue-sky promoters, sour-doughs, ticket-of-leavers, fellows with nicked reputations, geezers who had just been liberated from the hulks and had ugly corners of their lives to live down.... [6]

The Army was out in force to prevent people from sneaking in and staking claims before the official start. These "sooners" were to be ejected, never to have an opportunity to stake a claim, but not all of them were discovered. [7]

Land seeker Cassius Cade described events as the crowds waited to start the run near Kingfisher on April 22, 1889:

> Ten thousand . . . mostly poor people . . . gathered along Kingfisher Creek, a mile and a quarter west of

Kingfisher. While we were loafing we had nothing better to do except get information and visit. We took an invoice of Democrats and Republicans from the states, and No Man's Land [what later became Oklahoma's panhandle] showed up with no party but what they called Presbyterians and sons-of-bitches. We rode up and down asking the Republicans to get on a certain line or street. Pat Nagle unhitched one of his mules and rode bareback up and down the line, asking all Democrats to line up. The Republicans lined up and outnumbered the others about three to one. Then Fatty Smith went up and down the line, asking all the sons-of-bitches to line up, and Dr. Overstreet . . . asked the Presbyterians from No Man's Land to line up on his side. There were about three sons-of-bitches and one Presbyterian.[8]

Bill Fossett was also there that day, arriving barely in time. Due to the illness of a brother-in-law, he was detained at his home in Kingman until the evening of April 20. He rode to Harper, Kansas, and into the territory, finally arriving at the starting line west of Kingfisher "about fifteen minutes before the crack of the gun unloosed the horde of home-seekers." He could see that most people had been lined up all day, mounted on horses or in their conveyances, fearful of losing their place in line. They were "fatigued and restless from the long wait" and when the gun sounded, Bill led the field, riding the "best horse on the west side"[9]

Jacob V. Admire, the receiver of the Kingfisher Land Office, watched the masses rush in on horses, in wagons and buggies, and on foot:

> I have seen and heard this mad rush compared to the charge of an army. It bore no resemblance whatever to

such a charge. It was more like the wild rush of an excited mob in pursuit of their victim. I saw Bill Fossett jump off his horse about 200 yards west of the Land Office and on the same quarter section, jerk his saddle off, throw it down, and wave his blanket as notice of his claim to be the first settler upon this tract of land.[10]

Bill's knowing choice of the northwest quarter section of Section 15 was easily the most picturesque of the area. Kingfisher Creek, lined with cottonwood, oak and elm trees, carved a full s-turn through the land. On his claim, a short distance west of where he dismounted, was the Kingfisher Stage Station.[11] He recalled his dash for land that day in his *Indian-Pioneer History* interview:

> I had been so familiar with all the Oklahoma country and the trails that I made the run for the hundred and sixty acres that the land office was located on at Kingfisher. Although there were thousands of people who lined up for the race, I beat them all to the hundred and sixty acres I had started out to try and win. I was so far ahead that there was no question or dispute as to who was on the claim first.[12]

Had the land rush been planned in detail, there would have been no dispute, but confusion marked the day. For one thing, the land office in Kingfisher could not open the day of the run. The building was not yet completed, shelves and other fixtures were not installed, and the wagon carrying land office forms for filing claims did not arrive until late in the morning. This forced those filing claims to wait and even camp in line overnight until the land office became fully functional the following day.[13] Adding to the confusion was the fact that most people who dashed in from the west starting line had already agreed to make the south half of section 15, which adjoined Fossett's northwest quarter section, as a townsite named Lisbon. [14]

Within an hour of Bill's arrival, dozens of people, unable to secure townsite lots in the south half of the section, moved to the north section. By then he had already started digging a dugout. Before long, land seekers arriving from the northern starting line began staking claims on Bill's northwest quarter section as well as the northeast quarter section claimed by John C. Wood. These "northliners" chose the name of Kingfisher for their townsite.[15]

Amid the confusion the crowd became restless and unruly. For a time, it looked as if the masses would attempt to make a run on Bill's claim. Fully prepared to make a stand, he ran a barbed wire fence around the east and south boundaries of his land. The townsite settlers countered by cutting a portion of the fence and made "threatening demonstrations" against him.[16] According to close friend Joe Grimes, "Fossett was the coolest-headed man I ever saw...." He drew a line on the ground and holding his Winchester, he told the crowd that the first man to cross it would have to be "carried away." Jacob Admire added, "The crowd, probably a hundred strong, was wildly yelling and threatening him with vengeance. He stood there immovable, determined, and white as a ghost, never batting an eye. I expected him to be shot dead in his tracks...." Admire walked over to Bill and told him he was "foolishly endangering his life," and that by doing so, his case could not be made any stronger. Bill finally relented and accompanied Admire to the Land Office where he deposited his firearms. The gesture apparently quieted the crowd, which eventually dispersed.[17]

One claimant, however, was not satisfied. He made the mistake of confronting Bill, declaring he would either throw him off the claim "dead or alive, or come away dead himself." He then had the audacity to complain that the six-foot, four-inch Fossett was bigger than he was. Bill calmly pulled out his knife and handed it to his prospective assailant remarking, "Here's my knife, trim me down to your size." As the man reached for the knife, Bill "hit him so hard that he lost all notion of fighting."[18]

There were several disputes over claims, and Bill stood up for other settlers who faced claim-jumpers. J. E. Hancock, who was seven years old at the time of the run, recalled, "some fellows tried to scare my father off the town lots and had it not been for Bill Fossett they would have succeeded."[19]

By evening on April 22, about 500 people had encroached on the northern half of Bill's claim, as well as on the adjoining northeast quarter section of Section 15. By homestead law standards, the population was sufficient to warrant making the entire tract a townsite, and settlers were claiming the northern half section to be the townsite of Kingfisher. However, another oversight in the opening of the Unassigned Lands was that the government made no provisions for townsites as is did in later openings. The only laws on the books at the time, provided that townsite lot applications be filed at the land office by "authorities of the town, or by the county judge." Since authorities had not been elected at the time of the land run, there was no way for a legal town to be created in a territory that had just been opened. This lack of governmental guidance created the confusion, hard feelings, and eventually lawsuits, over claims in Kingfisher.[20]

On the night of April 22, a mass meeting was held at the intersection of Main and Robberts Avenues. Robberts Avenue then became the dividing line of the "twin cities," with Kingfisher on the north and Lisbon on the south. John D. Miles, former Indian agent for the Cheyenne and Arapaho tribes at the Darlington Agency, was quickly elected mayor of Lisbon, but Cassius Cade was selected as acting mayor because Miles spent most of his time at Darlington.

On the Kingfisher side of the boundary, the process took longer. Several candidates were rejected because they wore "a good suit of clothes and a white collar." A man named J. W. Creech noted this and cleverly stooped down, picked up a handful of dust and spread it over his suit, taking special care to smear his white collar. When he stepped up on a pile of lumber that served as a stage, the crowd was pleased and yelled, "He'll do! He's all right, he's no dandy." Creech was unanimously chosen as the first mayor of Kingfisher, but served only until April 24, when citizens elected George E. Hubbard their mayor.[21]

Although the two towns of Lisbon and Kingfisher existed side-by-side for several months, they were often referred to as North Kingfisher (Kingfisher) and South Kingfisher (Lisbon). Most people, however, preferred calling it all Kingfisher, because that was the most widely-known name in the area. The designation came from an early day ranchman named King David Fisher. His range and cattle camps were along the stream named for him, and he later operated the stage station there that also bore his name. The town's settlers simply joined the names King and Fisher together as one word.[22] On June 14, 1890, Kingfisher County commissioners formally merged the towns of Lisbon and Kingfisher by passing a resolution calling it all the "Village of Kingfisher City."[23]

Looking south on Kingfisher's Main Street, circa 1895.

While the legal wrangling over townsite and individual claims continued for some time, the building of the town waited for no one. Conservative estimates are that from 12,000 to 15,000 people were gathered in and around the two towns of Lisbon and Kingfisher during the first week. From this initial population, the town of Kingfisher developed from a crowded cluster of about 300 makeshift tents, to a small city of wood-framed buildings.[24] On May 18, 1889, less than thirty days after the opening, the city's first newspaper, *The New World,* later the *Kingfisher Free Press,* reported, "115 frame buildings completed, 50 more under construction, and 126 foundations which were started."[25]

Bill Fossett not only was the first to arrive in Kingfisher, he hauled the first load of lumber from Caldwell that was used to build Kingfisher's first home.[26] Bill also built a livery stable as his own business, on the west side of Main Street, in the second block north of Robberts Avenue.[27] Other firsts included an institution that became the Bank of Kingfisher. It began operating in a tent on April 22, 1889, and was said to have done "a nice business from the very start." Similarly, the first café was opened on April 22, in a tent erected by Marion Blair, where the price of a meal was $1. Two days later, J. R. Chamberlin opened "quite a commodious short order café" from a tent located west of the land office, near where William Grimes, future U.S. marshal, conducted a real estate office from his tent. The first hotel in town was called the Rock Island, and the first child born in the city was Admire Oklahoma Lewis, a name offered by Land Office Receiver Jacob Admire, who won the right of naming in a spirited auction contest.[28]

It took just over three years for Bill to finally win his court case as the first land claimant in Kingfisher. U.S. Land Patent records indicate he was awarded nearly the entire northwest quarter section in the summer of 1892. Only two small parcels in the very southeast corner of his claim were not included. One acre was set aside at the corner of Main and Robberts for the land office, later the post office, and two and a half acres north of Kingfisher Creek, immediately west of Main Street, became a park.[29]

It was "suggested," however, "that forty acres of the quarter be turned into a townsite." Bill agreed to the idea, and that corner of his property was platted "as an addition to Kingfisher,"[30] which was characterized by Jacob Admire:

> ...[Fossett] entered the SE 40 acres of his tract for townsite purposes at $10 per acre, and treated the occupying lot claimants with generosity and fairness.[31]

Evidence of Bill's inclination to solve the dispute over town lots was reported as early as March 26, 1890, when the *Kingfisher Daily World* noted, "that Mr. Fossett is willing to do more for the people than the people are for him."[32]

In the final settlement of Bill's land claim, Secretary of Interior John W. Noble concluded: "...Among these citizens there was complete confidence in and reliance upon the strength of government to protect them from imposition and fraud."[33]

During the time the lawsuit was dragged through the courts, Bill wasted no time in "proving up" his claim as required by law. He busied himself by building his home on a portion of the property that was not under contention by other settlers. It was located on the northeast portion of his quarter section where the "pure, sparkling water"[34] of Kingfisher Creek made a lazy, 180-degree turn, or half circle to the west before it turned back east, to flow away from his property. His home faced, but was set back from, what is today U.S. Highway 81.[35]

This property also served as his farm, about which the *New World* boasted, in April 1891:

> W.D. Fossett has brought to town from his hog ranch a dressed hog that weighed 538 lbs., now who says Oklahoma is not a country for hog industry [?][36]

While the legal niceties of Bill's claim were ironed out in the years prior to 1893, some of Kingfisher's entrepreneurs put a small piece of his disputed property to use. They built a dance hall in the bend of Kingfisher Creek that was known as Sandy Point, so named for the mounds of sand that piled up there. This enterprise became the town's "red light" district, a well-established tradition in frontier towns.

For a time, the patrons of Sandy Point had to ford the creek until Bill built a "rickety bridge" to accommodate them. Sandy Point was technically outside the town's corporate limits, so each week the "chief of police crossed the bridge to collect fines from the girls, such fines thus becoming licenses to ply their trade." For a short time after 1893, Sandy Point continued to operate in what by then had become Fossett's Addition to the city.[37]

In the months prior to the opening of Oklahoma, Bill worked part-time as a special agent, or detective, in the claims department of the Rock Island Railroad. In the fall of 1889, the Rock Island's subsidiary line into Oklahoma, known as the Chicago, Kansas and Nebraska Railway, extended its tracks through to Kingfisher and progressed toward El Reno. As a resident of Kingfisher, Bill became the natural choice for appointment as a full-time special agent, as the Rock Island expanded across territory he knew so well. Bill worked all lines west of the Missouri River, reporting to the chief special agent in Chicago about once a month.[38]

On May 2, 1890, the passage of the Organic Act, signed by President Benjamin Harrison, organized the Unassigned Lands into Oklahoma Territory, thereby providing for incorporated cities and a territorial government with its capital at Guthrie. This act also created six counties in the newly opened lands and extended the territory to include all of former Indian Territory, except the reservations of the Five Civilized Tribes, some small reservations, and the unoccupied portion of the Cherokee Outlet, which remained as Indian Territory. The new Oklahoma Territory also took in the Public Land Strip (No Man's Land or the Oklahoma panhandle) and Greer County (in the extreme southwest area), which was in dispute between the United States and Texas.[39]

On May 22, a special census was taken in the six counties of the new Oklahoma Territory. It recorded Logan County with 14,254 people; Oklahoma County, 12,794; Cleveland County, 7,011; Canadian County, 7,703; Kingfisher County, 8,837; and Payne County, 6,836. The initial land rush resulted in Guthrie becoming the largest city, with 5,884 residents, and Oklahoma City was second, with 5,086.[40]

Before daybreak on May 23, 1890, George Steele, appointed as the first territorial governor by President Harrison, stepped from the train at Guthrie's Santa Fe station and immediately repaired to his temporary housing quarters in the Noble Hotel. At 2:00 p.m., a large crowd greeted the governor's procession with a parade that crawled along Oklahoma Avenue. Military troops, several bands, fire companies and carriages lead the way in a festive parade to the welcoming ceremonies at Capital Square.[41]

While Guthrie eventually became the permanent territorial capital, it was not without a fight. Kingfisher claimed third place in population after the first census, and it "battled on even terms for first place in political leadership, along with Guthrie and Oklahoma City." In the fall of 1890, Kingfisher's leading citizens exerted enough influence for the territorial legislature to pass a bill naming their town the capital, but the prize was lost when the governor vetoed it.

Citizen's of Kingfisher who played prominent roles in Oklahoma politics at that time, and in ensuing years, included: Abraham J. Seay, second territorial governor; William Grimes, U.S. marshal under President Harrison and territorial secretary under President McKinley; Patrick S. Nagle, U.S. marshal under President Cleveland; Matthew J. Kane, chief deputy marshal under Nagle, member of the state constitutional convention and justice of the first supreme court; Jacob V. Admire, receiver of the land office under President Harrison and editor of the *Kingfisher Free-Press*; Jacob C. Robberts, registrar of the land office under President Harrison and territorial attorney general under President McKinley; Harry Thompson, U.S. marshal under President McKinley; and William D. Fossett, chief deputy marshal under Thompson and U.S. marshal under President Theodore Roosevelt.[42]

Other '89ers who made the run to Kingfisher, as well as a mark in Oklahoma history, were of a family named Dalton. Charles and Ben Dalton brought family matriarch Adeline to the territory and helped her establish a claim near Kingfisher. Living with Ma Dalton were thirteen and fourteen-year-old daughters Nancy May and Leona.[43]

Three better-known Daltons, Bob, Grat and Emmett, were already in the territory, Bob and Grat serving as deputy marshals and Emmett as a posseman. They followed in the footsteps of older brother Frank, who was killed in the line of duty in 1887. By 1891 these three Dalton boys had taken up the outlaw trail, Bob and Grat dying in the famous Coffeyville, Kansas, raid on October 5, 1892, and Emmet suffering near fatal wounds there. A sister, Eva Dalton, had joined the family after the 1889 land rush. She had married John N. Whipple in Meade, Kansas, in 1887. Whipple opened a combination butcher shop and farm implement store on Robberts Avenue in Kingfisher.[44]

This couple lived on property near the center of town that was owned by Bill Fossett. As their landlord, and through the natural associations in a close-knit community, Bill became well acquainted with the Dalton clan. In later years, Bill speculated that his familiarity with the family, "might be one of the reasons the Daltons never tried to rob a Rock Island train."[45]

Kingfisher's Rock Island Depot.

6

FORTY MILES THROUGH HELL TO HENNESSEY

In 1886 and '87 the Southern Kansas Railway Company and the Gulf, Colorado and Santa Fe Railway constructed a line from Arkansas City, Kansas, across Indian Territory, to Texas. The railroad built small stations, water tanks and switching yards at Guthrie and Oklahoma Station (later Oklahoma City).[1] This was the second railroad to traverse southward across Oklahoma, the Missouri, Kansas and Texas, better known as the "Katy," having crossed the very eastern part of the territory in 1873.[2]

By the time the Unassigned Lands were opened in 1889, the Chicago, Rock Island and Pacific Railroad had formed a subsidiary, called the Chicago, Kansas and Nebraska Railway. It was constructing a north-south line from Kansas to Texas that would run west of the Santa Fe Railway. In 1889, this track extended from Caldwell, Kansas, "the last outpost of white man's country," to Pond Creek, Indian Territory, in the Cherokee Outlet.[3]

By late 1892, the Rock Island's line was in place all the way to the Indian Territory-Texas border at Terral. Construction crews then began working north from Ft. Worth, completing the entire line on July 30, 1893. It was not coincidental that the Rock Island placed its route parallel to, and directly on, the famed Chisholm Trail. It put the Rock Island squarely in the midst of cattle and farm country, offering another line for moving beef and grain to market.[4]

Having the new line operational by midsummer 1893 made for perfect timing because the Cherokee Outlet was soon to open for settlement, becoming the largest land offering of all. The Outlet was originally designed by the government as a travelway for Cherokee Indians, leading from their reservation in the northeastern part of the territory, to the prime buffalo hunting country in the west. The concept of a hunting travelway likely was surprising to the Cherokees who, for the most part, were civilized and educated by white man's standards, having been farmers and landholders prior to their forcible removal from Tennessee and Georgia. Nonetheless, this band, or "strip" of land, as it came to be called, was created. It was fifty-eight miles wide and about 226 miles long with its northern boundary along the Kansas border. The overall length of the Outlet had been slightly reduced in 1866 when the Cherokees agreed to allow the Osage, Pawnee and other friendly tribes to settle in the eastern portion of it.[5]

Preparation for opening the Outlet began in October 1890 when cattlemen were ordered to clear the grazing land of all stock.[6] By the summer of 1893, Secretary of Interior Hoke Smith made the opening official, setting the date for high noon on September 16.[7]

In anticipation of the opening, the Rock Island Railroad had already built stations along its line in the Outlet, and in doing so, construction boss Hilon Parker decided to bring a little culture to the wild frontier when he placed names on the depots. At the small stage outpost of Polecat, about eight miles south of Caldwell, Parker's crew put the name Renfrow on the station signboard.[8]

About twenty-two miles farther south, the rail station was at the Pond Creek stage ranch, north of the Salt Fork of the Arkansas River. The railroad approved of this designation, so it stayed. It's notable that this particular spot on the Chisholm Trail was known by several different names over the years. It was at this location in 1866 that James R. Mead, one of the founders of the trading post that became Wichita, Kansas, established a trading post along the little stream known as Round Pond Creek. About 1870, the post was taken over by a cattle company owned by Ely Sewell, at which time it became Sewell's Stockade, so designated as a place of protection for travelers of the Chisholm and Black Dog Trails. As stagecoach lines developed along the Chisholm Trail, the stockade also served as a stage ranch, and it was then variously known as Pond, Round Pond and Pond Creek. When the railroad arrived, the tracks and station were placed about 200 feet directly west of the stage ranch.[9]

Farther south in the Outlet, along the Chisholm Trail, was a way station known as Skeleton Stage Ranch, also named for a nearby creek. Railroad executives thought the location worthy of a townsite, so a depot was built at the tracks, about one quarter of a mile due west of the stage station. The name Skeleton didn't sound civilized, so the railroad changed the name to Enid.[10]

Townsite locations were supposed to be an Interior Department secret until opening day, but Secretary Hoke Smith had already decided, privately, to develop townsites around railroad stations previously built at Pond Creek (the location of the stage ranch north of the Salt Fork) and Enid.[11] Secretary Smith also had authority to lay out seven counties, which he lettered "K" through "Q," as well as to designate the county seats of each. [12]

In writing his company's history, *Iron Road to Empire,* Rock Island publicist William Edward Hayes stated, "The records are silent as to the identity of the bright intellect in Rock Island management that laid the groundwork for the skullduggery...." The reference was to someone who, with the cooperation of several Indian leaders, attempted to assure there would be townsite booms at the Pond Creek and Enid rail stations, with the railroad in full control of them. This plan was set in motion when sixty-seven Cherokee tribal leaders sold their pre-selected land allotments to the railroad. Those allotments just happened to adjoin the planned townsites at Pond Creek, which the government called Round Pond, and Enid.[13]

The Interior Department learned of the devious plan on the eve of opening day. Secretary Hoke Smith, who at one time had made a law career out of pursuing damage suits against railroads, ordered his agents to move the planned county seat locations of Round Pond (Pond Creek station) and Enid, three miles south of where the railroad had built depots. This set the stage for eleven months of confusion, anger, and destruction that become known as the "Railroad War."[14]

On opening day, tens of thousands of land-seekers formed a human border around the boundaries of the Outlet. Unlike previous land openings, each person planning to enter the Outlet held a registration card he had obtained at special "border booths" during the four days prior to the September 16 opening. This was supposed to prevent "soonerism" but failed, because anyone with a card could slip into the Outlet under cover of darkness and present the card at the land office when filing for property. A second, unique part of opening the Outlet was that claimants were to pay $1.00 to $2.50 per acre to help the government defray the cost of purchasing land from the Cherokees.[15]

As the noon hour approached, would-be settlers anxiously awaited the starting gun. At the territorial border south of Caldwell, thousands of people packed into open cattle cars on a special Rock Island train that would take them south to the "promised land." Others prepared to make the dash in just about "every conveyance known to man." Most people on the Outlet's northern border had their eyes on the townsite of Round Pond. On the south border, the masses waiting to plunge north from the starting point at Hennessey hoped to find land around Enid.[16]

At the appointed hour, soldiers, stationed about 200 yards inside the Outlet, fired their pistols. "The smoke of the pistol was seen," said land seeker George Rainey, "but its sound was lost in the thunder of hoofs and the rattle of wheels."[17] Eyewitness accounts in the *Guthrie Daily Leader* were graphic:

> The mobs plunged forward as if some great force had impelled them from behind.... Men knocked each other down as they rushed onward. Horsemen tumbled on to the ground, women shrieked and fell, fainting.... Vehicles of all kinds were smashed and made useless. Men, women and horses were lying all over the prairie. Here and there men were fighting to the death over claims which each maintained he was first to reach. Knives and guns were drawn—it was a terrible and unforgettable scene; no pen can do it justice....[18]

The chaos was just beginning. Within days, new towns in the Outlet were teeming cities, but "they weren't teeming around the Rock Island stations."[19] The people of Enid were building on the government-designated townsite, three miles south of the Rock Island's Enid station. The Enid townsite was the county seat of "O" county (later Garfield County). The 6,000 new settlers living there referred to the railroad station site, where about 1,000 residents also constructed a little town, as "North Enid," or the "tank," because trains took on water at the location. The North Enid people, meanwhile, retaliated by calling the government townsite South Enid.[20]

There was similar confusion at Round Pond. About 2,000 people occupied the new government townsite, located south of the Salt Fork River, about three miles from the Pond Creek railroad station on the north side of the river. At the rail station itself, meanwhile, about 400 residents built their own town, calling it Pond Creek. The government had already named the south town Round Pond, county seat of "L" (later Grant County), but most of the citizens didn't like the name, and they incorporated it as Pond Creek, making for two towns of the same name only three miles apart.[21]

Local newspapers went into action, declaring that confusion over town names must end. In a testy editorial, the fiery editor of the *Enid Wave*, J. L. Isenberg, proclaimed:

> There is but one ENID. The Post Office address of the city is simply Enid. The Post office in the addition is called North Enid, but there is positively no South Enid. You uneducated scapegoats, can't you understand that?[22]

It was even more confusing at the government-named townsite of Round Pond. Even though the government considered the south townsite Round Pond, most people living there called it Pond Creek following the opening, and for months, both names were used at the south town. This resulted, in part, from the fact that Round Pond was a name used by many territorial and Kansas newspapers to designate the south town. These same newspapers also referred to the north town as Pond Creek.[23]

A partial solution came at Pond Creek Station when the new postmaster, W. J. Hicks, formerly of Jefferson, Texas, was asked to choose a name for the post office. Hicks chose the name of his old hometown; thus, on January 12, 1894, the town of Jefferson was born at the site of the Pond Creek railroad station north of the Salt Fork River. Even this distinction did not soothe many of the residents, who continued calling the town either Pond Creek Station, or North Pond Creek.[24]

The Cherokee Sentinel, published in the government-designated townsite of Round Pond, persisted in referring to the south town as Pond Creek and attempted to clarify matters for its readers:

> Pond Creek is the government townsite of "L" county, is situated three miles south of Jefferson (Pond Creek Station), and between the towns flows the Salt Fork of the Arkansas River, which at times is impassible. Pond Creek has a larger population than all the other towns in the county combined.[25]

Undoubtedly, people felt the name confusion was minor compared with the other growing problems created by the townsite mess. Whether it was lumber, store goods, farm supplies or personal belongings, it had to be dragged or hauled to and from the rail stations, three miles from each town. The economic necessity for having a railroad station in town was obvious, so civic leaders of Enid and Pond Creek appealed to the railroad. "No depots," said the railroad. "You got depots north of you three miles. That's what you'll use. We're not spending any money to build new stations at your new townsites."[26]

A Rock Island train, with settlers loaded on cattle cars, awaits the signal for the "run" into the Cherokee Outlet from the Kansas border south of Caldwell.

Round Pond (Pond Creek), January 1894.

The railroad passed down orders for all train crews to ignore government townsites and their four-mph posted speed limits. Stops would be at Rock Island stations only.[27] Occasionally, a brave passenger tried getting off the train anyway. Ned Sisson, an Enid real estate agent who later served as a deputy U.S. marshal, jumped from the train at Enid's E Street one day. The *Daily Wave* commented, "he now has a growth of bark on the exterior of his stomach." According to Sisson:

> A man realizes a curious sensation sliding on his stomach over the uncultivated soil at the rate of thirty miles per hour.[28]

Such annoyances soon gave way to a fury, and the townspeople of Enid and Pond Creek declared war on the Rock Island.

Rail passengers soon became accustomed to the sound of gunfire as they rode the line. F. J. Callahan remembers that "passengers got so they would get down on the floor of the cars when they came near town. No one was ever hurt as the people shot over the cars in order to scare the trainmen."[29] It made for an interesting train ride through the Cherokee Outlet. So commonplace were the attacks that as southbound trains progressed into Oklahoma from Kansas, porters passed through the cars announcing, "forty miles through hell to Hennessey."[30]

In spite of the numerous and imaginative scare tactics, the trains continued to roar through the government townsites, throttles wide open and whistles shrieking in defiance of the settlers. People poured soft soap on the tracks, but the engines had sandboxes, nullifying any slipping effect.[31] They tried placing dynamite caps on the rails and waving red flags and lanterns at the engineers, but the trains sped on.[32]

W. D. "BILL" FOSSETT

Residents in the north towns of Pond Creek Station (Jefferson) and North Enid took the Rock Island's side in the war, and when citizens of the other towns came to the stations to pick up goods or passengers, they overturned wagons and buggies and cut harnesses. If they couldn't have train stations, the people of Enid and Pond Creek at least wanted mail service, and they pleaded to the government. Washington responded by ordering the Rock Island to deliver mail directly to each town. The railroad complied by erecting cranes so the mailbags could be hooked and hauled in without even slowing down. More than once the pouches were ripped apart as the train roared by, scattering mail all along the right-of-way. [33]

While some people considered it sport to occasionally shoot at a passing train, others were bent on the outright destruction of railroad property. During the spring and summer of 1894, there was trouble almost daily along the railway near the county seat towns. Bridges were dynamited and burned, and everything from wagons to houses placed on the tracks. In Pond Creek the railroad crossed the main street near the center of town, and every few days someone would be unable to get his conveyance off the tracks just as a train came through. The trains never even slowed up, scattering wagons, buggy parts and wooden splinters all over that part of town.[34]

On the night of June 6, Pond Creekers moved a heavy freight wagon on the tracks, and a Rock Island engineer dutifully blasted it to bits as his train raced on across the prairie. As soon as it passed, a determined crowd gathered sledgehammers and crowbars and began knocking the spikes from the rails. Just south of where the tracks crossed the main street, about 200 men, by sheer strength, lifted over 900 feet, or about two blocks, of the disjointed track on its edge. A man was sent running south to flag down a northbound stock train with thirty cars of cattle as it came swinging up the line from

Texas. As usual, the flagman was ignored, and the engineer peered out his side window to glimpse what new obstruction had been placed on the tracks this time. He saw the rails on edge, with ties sticking up and declared to the fireman, "This time they're trying a windmill." Once again the throttle was opened, and the train steamed on. With a mighty roar and clouds of dust, the engine hit the torn up roadbed and plowed through the dirt. It didn't turn over but the cars did, most of them breaking open and scattering cattle everywhere. A Rock Island train had finally stopped in the government townsite of Pond Creek.[35]

Over 100 steers were crippled or killed but, miraculously, the train crew was uninjured. They were arrested by the city marshal and jailed, but released on bond by a railroad attorney the next day. The government acted quickly by sending a deputy U.S. marshal and fifty armed men down from Kansas as guards for a rail crew that worked overnight to repair the track. The following day, about forty Pond Creek residents were named in federal warrants. They were rounded up and taken to Kingfisher, ostensibly to appear before an unprejudiced court. The sheriff refused to jail them without proper local warrants, so the "prisoners" were held under guard in a hotel. It was finally agreed to return the prisoners to Grant County for trial before a Pond Creek magistrate. To no one's surprise, a grand jury could find no evidence to indict, and all those held were freed.[36]

Railroad haters in Enid were not about to be out done by their Pond Creek neighbors. Under the cover of darkness on the night of July 12, some men sawed through several key timbers on the bridge over Boggy Creek, south of town. At dawn, a northbound Rock Island train thundered on to the bridge, and about half way across the engineer felt the structure begin to sway. The engine and tender barely made it across before the timbers collapsed, sending freight cars tumbling into the ravine. The trailing cars then pulled the engine and tender down into the wreckage. Two oil tankers and six cars loaded with wheat were spilled into the dry creek bottom. When news reached Enid, "thousands of people flocked to the scene."[37] As the engineer came crawling up from the wreckage, he told townsfolk, "Yuh done a damn good job of sawing that trestle."[38]

Rock Island attorneys in Topeka were incredulous. They wired Governor William Renfrow to again ask for protection of railroad property. Officials in Guthrie consulted with the Territorial Supreme Court and marshal's office. They wired Washington requesting federal troops be sent to Enid and Pond Creek The troops came with a show of force, leading to several confrontations with angry mobs in both towns, but resulting in only a few arrests. Once guards were posted along bridges and other key locations in and around the two towns, railroad property destruction ended, but the anger of citizenry did not subside. They wanted depots in their towns.[39]

In the months prior to the escalation of destructive violence against the railroad, Pond Creek and Enid officials had traveled to Washington to help draft a bill requiring depots at all townsites in the territory wherever a railroad right-of-way had been obtained under an act of Congress. The House approved the legislation, but there was intense opposition in the Senate, mostly from railroad lawyers, who tied up the bill in conference committee. Following the Enid bridge fiasco, Governor Renfrow made a personal plea in Washington. He then returned to Pond Creek and Enid to assure citizens that Congress would help if they would pledge to cease further hostilities.[40]

With a temporary truce in hand, the governor then went to Chicago for a meeting with Rock Island officials. He was successful in persuading railroad president Ransom Cable to back off his hard line, but Cable had the last word, saying the Rock Island would abide by any law approved by Congress, but "it will never surrender to a mob." Cable then wired his attorneys, telling them to cease all opposition to the bill requiring the construction of depots. On August 1, 1894, the Senate approved the legislation, bringing the bitter "Railroad War" to an end.

The news brought huge celebrations in Enid and Pond Creek. Bonfires flamed in the streets as cheering crowds soaked up free drinks offered by local saloons. Within days, work crews arrived, and in a startling tone of civility, mayors of both towns were told, "If you will kindly drive a stake on our right-of-way showing where you want the depot we will build it just as soon as the materials can be moved in."[41]

Enid opted for a station where the line crossed E Street (today's Broadway). The Rock Island first stopped at the crossing on September 16, 1894, the one-year anniversary of opening the Cherokee Outlet. The railroad moved in an old freight car and built a platform around it until a permanent structure went up.[42]

Once the sign "Pond Creek" went on the new depot in that town, the name gained widespread favor and use, and it remains as Pond Creek today. The railroad site of Pond Creek Station, meanwhile, had already been using the post office name of Jefferson for several months, and it was eventually incorporated as such.[43] Pond Creek, however, ultimately lost its county seat status. On January 9, 1908, following statehood, a special election was held in which Medford became the new county seat of Grant County.[44]

On June 6, 1894, local citizens made sure that a Rock Island train finally stopped in Pond Creek.

July 13, 1894, the morning after railroad "warriors" in Enid partially sawed through supporting timbers of the Rock Island bridge over Boggy Creek.

7

RAID ON THE ROCK ISLAND

While Oklahoma's land openings brought new opportunities for settlers, they greatly changed the lives of the men who once freely rode the trails and grazing lands of the territory. Throughout the West, the coming of civilization turned the cowboy's open-range culture askew. Following the four successive land openings from April 1889, to September 1893, thousands of new home seekers divided much of the old territory into farms, small ranches and towns. Rangeland was diminished, and barbed wire, termed the "devil's hatband" by cowboys, created an unfriendly barrier across the once open country.[1]

Not unexpectedly, their loss freedom provoked ranchers and range riders to regard the newcomers with contempt and suspicion "not unmixed with active hostility." At the very least, cowboys most surely were perplexed, viewing the settlers as small-minded. Not only did they jealously stake a paltry 160-acre claim, they would then set out to plow up the soil, which cowmen figured was already "right side up" in the first place. Then, too, on the open range there was a standing invitation for any rider passing through to "light and fill up" (step down and eat), but many settlers never seemed to warm to the concept. The farmers fed chickens, milked cows and mounted a horse like a man going up a ladder. As far as cowboys were concerned, the intruders, derisively called "nesters," had funny ideas about freedom, independence and the wide-open spaces. For the most part, the range riders disliked the newcomers, who returned that dislike in full measure, as the settlers considered the cowboy a wild and reckless being who "feared neither God nor man."[2]

These first settlers were but the "advance agents" of a great population soon to follow. In the decade from 1890 to 1900, the population of Oklahoma Territory grew from about sixty-one thousand people to over four hundred thousand. As the settlers poured into cow country to take up homesteads, it forced some cattle ranching toward the rougher uplands, where water and grass were sparse. In effect, the land openings created a mixture of cultures not easily joined, and while eventually they were, cowmen faced the most difficult adjustment.[3]

Cowboys who became unemployed, or were otherwise affected by the changes, had options. Some drifted north with migrating herds, others became small ranchers or went to work in town. Legend has it that many out-of-work cowboys became outlaws, but the notion that they were the central forces of Oklahoma outlawry has essentially been debunked.[4]

While some western writers contend that former cowboys, driven from the freedom of the open range, used their saddles, guns and daring, the tools of their previous occupation, to work outside the law,[5] others find evidence to the contrary. Harry Sinclair Drago, in *Outlaws on Horseback*, asserts that very few outlaws were ever "working" cowboys, with exceptions such as Bill Doolin and some of his gang. Glenn Shirley, in *West of Hell's Fringe,* maintains that horse and cattle thieves, and the daring gunman who infested Indian Territory from the early days, remained in the same class of shiftless no-accounts after Oklahoma Territory was opened to settlement.[6]

The history of all cultures reveals a nucleus of troublemakers existing in every society, in every era. In contemporary terms, it is sometimes characterized as class warfare, where the "have-nots" are always at odds with those who "have." In today's society, as then, this criminal class would rather take from others instead of working for it themselves.

It was no different in early Oklahoma, where a class of men preyed on pioneers, rather than doing their share of backbreaking labor. Elmer Peterson, who made the run in 1889, called them "lousy loafers," and "the scum of civilization."[7]

> They lived by stealing from those who did the real work, murdering them if they resisted. The real building . . . was done by obscure, leather-faced, toil-bent men and women who never dreamed of notoriety or whiskey-crazed gun-fights, except to uphold the marshals and sheriffs who stood off those criminal camp followers.[8]

At the same time, a few previously honest, out-of-work cowboys were lured to the lifestyle of easy money and glorified reputations.[9] One man who noted that trend was Harry P. Fox, superintendent for the Rock Island Lines in Kansas and Oklahoma in 1894. Fox blamed several robberies and acts of violence against his railroad on the proverbial "out-of-work" cowboy, and he believed that was the make-up of one gang in particular, that attacked the Rock Island on the night of April 9, 1894.[10]

As the Rock Island's special agent, Bill Fossett was "looking after business" at the depot in North Enid, Oklahoma Territory, that day. It was during the height of the "Railroad War" and Bill, who lived in Kingfisher, was required to spend much of his time in North Enid, where the railroad nearly always experienced trouble.[11]

Late in the afternoon, he was completing a report to the railroad's chief special agent in Chicago, when the door to the small office behind the ticket counter opened. In walked Lew Humphrey, an old friend from Kingfisher. Bill finished his work and the two men chatted for awhile, talking of the trouble the railroad was having with the townspeople in Enid and Pond Creek.[12]

At about 5:00 p.m., Bill invited Humphrey to accompany him on the northbound train to Caldwell, Kansas, recalling, "There was no place in the Strip where you could get as good a meal as they put up at the Harvey House (railroad station restaurant), so Lew was glad to go." They planned to return that evening on the southbound express.[13]

After their meal that night, Bill and Lew Humphrey boarded the No. 1 Express. As the train rumbled south across the prairie, they relaxed in the smoking car, talking with conductor Joe Reed. The first stop was Pond Creek Station (Jefferson), about twenty-two miles into Oklahoma Territory. The engine took on water, and a couple of passengers came and went. The train pulled out after 9:30 p.m., crossed the Salt Fork River and rolled on through the government townsite of Pond Creek.[14]

Just as the train began gathering speed south of Pond Creek, the brakes were set and it came to a jolting stop, throwing the passengers forward in their seats. Momentarily, it moved forward again for a few yards, then halted altogether.[15]

As it did, two or three shots rang out, and there was shouting from the front of the train. Conductor Reed jumped up and exclaimed, "What the Sam Hill is the matter?"

"It looks like a holdup," replied Bill, "Have you got a gun on you Joe?"[16]

Reed made his way to the platform and sent the porter forward to investigate. Suddenly there was a rapid volley of shots and more yelling. Indeed, it was a hold-up, the first on the Rock Island in Oklahoma Territory. [17]

Two bandits had slipped aboard the train when it stopped for water at Pond Creek Station. After the train crossed the river and passed through Pond Creek, the two men climbed across the tender and into the locomotive cab, threatening the engineer with drawn guns. When the engineer saw the robbers, he "ducked apprehensively," and one of the startled gunman fired, sending a lead slug ricocheting around the cab. The bandits ordered the train crew to stop south of town where a bonfire had been built on the tracks. The crew complied but applied the brakes too quickly, bringing the train to a jolting stop. They then restarted and chugged forward until reaching the first road crossing south of Pond Creek, where four or five other bandits awaited their arrival.[18] In the style of the Dalton and Doolin gangs, they began firing to keep the passengers in the cars.[19] The location chosen for the robbery, however, was "singularly unfitted for an enterprise of the kind." The prairie extended level and unbroken for several miles offering no cover to screen the outlaws from pursuit.[20]

The bandits ordered the engineer and fireman out of the cab, and they "were compelled to cross the cattle guard."[21] The express agent briefly opened the car door to see what the trouble was, but then quickly closed and locked it. The outlaws began firing at the express car, boldly announcing they would "blow it to smithereens," but U.S. Express Company guard Jake Harmon and express messenger John

Crosswight refused to open its doors and continued to "hole up" in the locked car. Several minutes passed as the robbers made more threats, occasionally firing shots into the car. They finally resorted to placing a lighted stick of dynamite at the base of the car's door on the west side of the train. The ear-splitting explosion sent a hail of wood splinters and baggage swirling about the inside of the car. Harmon and Crosswight were both knocked to the floor, and Crosswight was briefly stunned by the concussion. At that point, guard Harmon escaped through the rear of the baggage car and into the passenger cars. By then at least twenty minutes had passed, but the bandits were focused on the express car. Shaken by the blast and a barrage of bullets, express messenger Crosswight decided to open the door, but the explosion had jammed it. He told the bandits to go to the opposite side of the train calling for them to "Hold on! I'll open the door."[22]

For the time being, the outlaws appeared to have temporarily won their way. "At this stage of the game," reported witnesses, one outlaw, "with a 45 Colt revolver in his hand," entered the express car.[23] The bandits then began working to open the safe, oblivious to the fact their robbery was about to be thwarted.

For one thing, guard Harmon, although terribly "frightened," was free and making his way toward the rear of the train with his Winchester shotgun.[24] Also unknown to the bandits, was that the minute the train first stopped, the brakeman grabbed a lantern, jumped from the rear car and ran to Pond Creek, where he was met by several citizens of the town, who were congregated at a local theatre. He yelled, "They're dynamiting the express car!" As they looked down the tracks, citizens could see the train's flashing lights and hear the faint sound of gunfire. Arming themselves with whatever weapons they could find, several townspeople began running south along the tracks toward the scene. By then,

Sheriff R. H. Hagar had hastily formed a posse and was also on his way.[25]

Another unforeseen problem for the outlaws that night, was the intervention of Bill Fossett, who recalled:

> The train robbers took the engineer and fireman back to the place where they were going to force the express messenger to open the door on the west side of the train. They had the porter, engineer and fireman as protection and as it was dark you didn't dare shoot for fear of killing one of the train crew. I went out on the platform and could see the shadows of the men but could not distinguish one man from the other, as the only lights were those shining through the windows of the express car two cars away.
>
> I came back and walked through the train and I have never been able to figure out why I happened to pick a man sitting next to the aisle in the chair car. I asked him if he had a gun? He answered, "No, Why?" I said, "You look to me like a man who would have a gun and don't you leave this seat while this is going on."
>
> The train robbers continued to pound on the door of the express car on the west side, but the messenger would not open the door. The express company had a guard who came through the end door and into the smoker [car] apparently frightened to death. He was so badly scared that he crawled under one of the seats. The messenger was in the express car alone and the outlaws laid a stick of dynamite on the coin plate [sic: koin plate; a metal plate at the base of the door that engages a door locking pin.] and touched it off, making a terrible explosion and shattering the door so that the messenger could not open it. The messenger told the outlaws that if they would come around to the east side of the car he would open the door for them. Some went around the engine and some crawled underneath the train, the messenger opened the door and they lifted a man inside.[26]

William D. Fossett, circa 1895.

By this time, guard Jake Harmon had made his way toward the rear of the train:

> I went out the rear door of the car and stepped off the east side of the smoking car. I tried to work my gun but a cartridge had caught in it. I went through the chair car and finally got my gun to work. I stepped off the car and saw the engineer and fireman climbing into the door of the express car. The robbers were cursing and ordering them to get in or they would kill them. There were three men standing east of the door of the express car. One of them held a revolver in his hand pointed into the car. I took aim and fired. The smoke was so dense I could not see the men after the first shot. They returned the fire.[27]

Harmon and Fossett acted almost simultaneously, without one another's knowledge. As Harmon was getting in to position at the rear of the train, Bill remained in the coach car and recounted:

> One man went out in what is called a barrow pit [where fill dirt and rock are scraped along side the right-of-way] and commenced shooting back and through the passenger coaches. I had changed my position then to the east side. I knew [that] the fellow who was shooting back through the train ... was none of the train crew. So I took a shot at him and he fell and the other robbers piled out of the express car and ran for their horses.... The outlaws took a few shots back but all those shots went wild and nobody was hurt.[28]

While the fleeing outlaws took parting shots at the train, it was reported that Harmon and Fossett "poured hot shot into the four remaining robbers and drove them off."[29]

Moments later, the shooting stopped, and the thick smoke cleared. Jake Harmon then walked toward the engine and found a dead outlaw about twenty-five feet from the express car. He "was lying on his back with his elbow resting on the ground and a [Colt] revolver clutched in his right hand pointing straight up in the air."[30]

Harmon wrested the revolver from the man's death grip and walked back toward the passenger cars. By this time, Bill had left the passenger cars, cautiously making his way along the road that crossed tracks. He "found two horses saddled and brought them down to the train...."[31] The fact that there were two horses indicated that, "...more than this one robber must have been put out of the fight."[32]

As dozens of townspeople and passengers milled around the train, Bill ran into a man that he knew:

> ...among them [the crowd] was an old friend, Joe McEllen, who had been sheriff of Kingman County, Kansas while I had been city marshal of Kingman. He said, "I have two boys who will take the horses back to town." About this time this fellow whom I had told to keep his seat came forward and offered his services. I said, "I thought I told you to stay where you were; now get back there."[33]

About this time, Sheriff Hagar came in from the darkness with a prisoner he had captured riding along a nearby road. The action was over. The unexpected resistance and gunfire from Fossett and guard Harmon had routed the bandits. Harmon was said to be "rattled a little, but Will Fossett stood at his elbow and helped Jake pull himself together." Harmon later boasted that he would have "got more than one, but the cartridges [for his shotgun] would not work right."[34]

The outlaw's body was placed in the express car and the train was backed up to Pond Creek where it was unloaded.[35] After a delay of an hour and a half, the Rock Island's Express No. 1 then pulled out toward Enid.[36]

The .45-caliber, 1878 Colt Frontier Model double-action revolver taken from bandit Bob Hughes. A bullet hole in the belt is visible slightly left and above the hammer spur.

Bill and Jake Harmon stayed the night in Pond Creek to testify at a coroner's inquest the next day. In his capacity as a railroad detective, Bill was also there to investigate the attempted robbery, figuring he could track the outlaws who escaped. He also wanted to keep an eye on the man in the chair car who had identified himself as F. F. Young. He too, remained in Pond Creek, instead of continuing his journey by train.[37]

Deputy U.S. Marshal Chris Madsen arrived in town the next day, characterizing the robbery as "the bungling work of amateurs." The fact that the horses taken at the scene were "good horseflesh," led some people to speculate the robbery was the work of an organized gang like the Daltons, but Madsen and other lawmen laughed at the idea, saying the fiasco did "not resemble their [the Dalton's] handicraft," not to mention the fact that Bob and Grat Dalton had been killed, and brother Emmett wounded and captured during the bank robbery attempt in Coffeyville, Kansas, two years earlier. Since that time, Bill Dalton had teamed up with Bill Doolin and other ex-Dalton gang members, forming a new outlaw enterprise variously known as the Dalton gang, the Doolin gang, and the Doolin-Dalton gang. Nonetheless, the Pond Creek holdup did not match that gang's smooth style.[38]

The prisoner captured by Sheriff Hagar the night of the robbery attempt, refused to talk, gave several different names, and claimed he was a bum trying to get a free train ride. Lawmen were not persuaded because he was a "walking arsenal" when arrested. He finally identified himself as Will Wade, saying he lived on a quarter section adjoining the slain robber and Coleman Dalton (Henry Coleman Dalton), west of Enid.[39] Early on, the dead outlaw had been identified as J. W. Pitts, but by April 12, he was thought to be "a desperado by the name of Bill Rhodes."[40]

Authorities asked Coleman Dalton to go to Pond Creek to "observe" the dead outlaw and prisoner Will Wade. He denied knowing either man and refuted newspaper accounts of a possible Dalton involvement. He added that, "[my] brother Bill is not at present in the United States nor probably ever will be again." He claimed he recently escorted Bill's wife out of the country to join her husband in "a foreign land."[41]

The holdup not only fell short of Doolin-Dalton gang standards, the slain robber himself did not fit their image. *The Pond Creek Tribune* wrote:

> There was nothing on his person to identify him. He had two purses, one with $2.10 in it, the other was empty. On the inside pocket of his coat was an unsigned letter containing threats against certain persons whose names are withheld for obvious reasons.
>
> The dead man stood in life about five feet five inches and weighed about 120 pounds; he had a slightly receding forehead and a small irresolute chin which was partially overcome by firm, decisive lips; his eyes were blue and a light brown mustache curled away from a short upper lip that unconsciously exposed two rows of even, white teeth. He wore a cheap coat of brown material and his checked pants were stuffed into a pair of boots that encased his legs almost to his knees. He wore a soft hat. There was nothing about his appearance to indicate that he had been a "bad" man; certain it is he was not a "terror." It is claimed that he was a gambler years ago in Kansas, but now his hands are sun-browned and his face wore the callous of long-continued sun exposure.[42]

At the coroner's inquest, F. F. Young, referred to by newspapers as "a noted character,"[43] gave a strange account of the robbery. Fossett said, "He seemed ... very anxious to testify and his testimony was altogether different from what had really happened. I called him down on it," said Bill, "and he finally acknowledged he did not know much about it as he was in the chair car all the time."[44]

On April 11, the day following the inquest, two of the suspected train robbers were apprehended in Hennessey after trying to trade their jaded horses. The local marshal and a posse surrounded and arrested the pair in their camp near town. They were identified as John T. O'Conners and Frank Lacey, both of whom had often been seen in the local area. They were placed in the charge of Fossett and fellow railroad detective Allen, for return to Pond Creek.[45]

Local authorities eventually settled on the slain outlaw's identity as Bill Rhodes, alias J. W. Pitts, allegedly a member of the old Jesse James gang who had arrived in the territory from Clay County, Missouri.[46] Rhodes apparently was the name he used in most local circles. In their attempt to make positive identification, deputies took the horses and saddle outfits of the slain and captured robbers to nearby towns. Several men in North Enid said, "That's Rhodes' horse...," when the outfits were displayed there on Wednesday.[47] Apparently, some people also knew the man as "Fuller Rhodes," but all agreed on having seen him numerous times around "L" (Grant) and Garfield counties. By Thursday April 12, the dead man's body and belongings remained unclaimed, and he was buried in a pauper's grave by local lawmen and the undertaker.[48]

Questions as to whether it was Bill, Jake Harmon, both of them, or another person who fired the fatal shots, were raised by subsequent accounts of the incident. In his *Indian-Pioneer History* interview of 1937, Bill states, "...I took a shot at him and he fell...." In his 1929 *Kingfisher Times* newspaper account, however, Bill claims not to have had a gun that night and speculates that during the melee, "... he keeled over, pistol in hand. Someone had brought him down by a shot from the train."[49] Another account was offered by Grant County

Attorney C. C. Daniels, a Pond Creek resident who rushed from town to the robbery scene that night:

> On arriving at the train I found a man standing at the last car with a sawed-off shotgun in his hand...The man with the sawed-off shotgun identified himself as a railroad detective and said he was on the train as a guard because the railroad expected trouble from the citizens of Pond Creek.[50]

Initially, the identity of the dead outlaw was also in question. In both of his later recollections, Bill refers to the slain bandit as "Bob Hughes," but newspapers of the period never mention Hughes as a real name or an alias, perhaps because the name "Hughes" resulted from identification years after the robbery. Further, Deputy U.S. Marshal Chris Madsen, who investigated the robbery, recounted the events in his 1936 book, *Four Score Years a Fighter*. Madsen also refers to the slain robber as Bob Hughes and states, "Fossett does not tell you that he killed Hughes [aka Rhodes & Pitts], but others who were there at the time say he was the only one with a gun and the grit to use it." E. D. Nix, U.S. Marshal for the territory at the time of the 1894 robbery, also identifies the slain bandit as Hughes in his 1929 book, *Oklahombres*.[51]

Following the coroner's inquest on April 11, Bill returned to the robbery scene at the crossing south of Pond Creek. He found an old grain sack with two new patches on it, each one of a different material. The sack had a leather drawstring around the opening. The outlaws apparently intended to carry their loot in it but dropped it during their getaway. Bill also examined the horses captured after the robbery, noting that their hind shoes had been pulled off, but not long before, because dirt had not yet filled up the nail holes.[52]

The Pond Creek law office of county attorney C. C. Daniels.

While he gathered evidence and asked questions, Bill sometimes discussed his findings with County Attorney C. C. Daniels, who noted that the detective was "keen-minded," shrewd and secretive:

> ...the railroad detective who shot the train robber came to my home a number of time for converences [sic], trying to run down clues we gathered from time to time. He was intelligent, capable, cautious, and gave expression only to the words necessary to convey his meaning. He would never discuss any facts connected with the case where it was possible for anyone else to hear anything that was said. He always insisted that we go out on the prairie, where we could see in every direction, making sure that no one else could get close enough to us to hear anything we said, without being seen.[53]

Bill took his evidence to Topeka and explained his findings in a meeting with Rock Island General Solicitor M. A. Lowe and U.S. Express Company Superintendent Dan Rawson. He told them he could find the material used to patch the sack, as well as the horseshoes removed from the horses. His simply planned to follow F. F. Young, the man on the train who had acted suspiciously that night and who later gave false testimony at the inquest.[54]

After returning to Pond Creek, Bill kept tabs on Young, who was staying at a ranch house owned by Billy Malaley. He was sure Young was tied in with the outlaws and would lead him to them. He wasn't disappointed. The day following Bill's return from Topeka, someone brought Young a horse, and he rode south from Pond Creek toward North Enid. Bill followed at a distance:[55]

> ...just so as to catch sight of him now and then on a far rise of the prairie. He rode south to within three miles of

North Enid and then turned west toward a part of the country, which had a pretty bad name. But he did not go far. After traveling about three miles I saw him ride into a big ravine and approach a dugout that was set in the west side of it.[56]

After watching the dugout awhile, Bill rode back to Pond Creek, convinced that if he searched it, he'd find the conclusive evidence and, maybe, the other outlaws. He made another trip to Topeka to discuss matters with the railroad. On the return train ride, his wife, Laura, boarded at Caldwell where she had been visiting family. He outlined his plans to her and left the train at Pond Creek Station, while she continued to their home in Kingfisher.

Bill wanted to surprise the suspects by searching the dugout at night, but needed someone to back him up. Laura Fossett apparently had the same thought, and after arriving in Kingfisher, she told Bill's son, Lew, about his father's plans. Lew hopped the next northbound freight and headed for Pond Creek that same night.[57]

I told Lew to make himself at home in the hotel as I was going out into the country and probably would not be back until late that night.

"I heard about it," Lew said, "I'm going with you."

I told him he was not going.

"You'll take some stranger out with you" Lew said, "and you'll get killed." Lew said if that happened it would make an outlaw of him, as he would follow the fellows who killed me until he got them.

There was something to think about in what my son said. I had seen too many young fellows hit the outlaw trail not to know that.... In those days it was a slim line that separated some law officers from those who operated on the wrong side of the law. One year they were deputy sheriffs or deputy marshals and the next year the sheriffs and marshals were after them. It was all from being exposed to the rough life in a new country.[58]

It was after midnight when Bill and Lew[59] rode across the prairie toward the ravine where Young had earlier been tracked:

>We approached the ravine where the dugout was without any trouble, tied our horses in a clump of brush and crawled up to the back end of the dugout. There was a little window just above the surface of the ground. We began shooting through it with Winchesters and two women and two or three young men ran out and went into the brush. We did not bother them further, but posting my son as a guard outside I entered the dugout with my dark lantern in one hand and a gun in the other.
>
>There was no one inside and one of the first things I found hanging by a nail on the wall, was a little boy's pant, with two pieces cut out of it, one of them from the waist lining. The goods was [sic] the same as the sack [at the robbery scene] had been patched with. I also found two pairs of horseshoes and making a good search I found a letter in a man's coat. The letter had been written only a few days earlier from Pawnee, Oklahoma.[60]

The letter was addressed to Nate Sylva who, according to claim papers Bill had found, owned the dugout he was searching. The letter, in effect, stated that the gang would meet in El Reno on Saturday, May 12, to sell their stolen horses and mules, and "fix to rob the Rock Island on May 15, the day it carried a government payroll for soldiers at Ft. Sill. The letter was signed by Felix Young, the man Bill had been suspicious of all along.[61]

Bill and Lew returned to Pond Creek with their evidence. As he expected, the horseshoes and nail holes fit exactly, and the cloth perfectly matched the patches on the grain sack. It was Friday, May 11, when Bill showed the evidence to Rock Island officials, the day prior to the proposed meeting by Sylva and Young in El Reno. Before leaving Topeka, Bill wired Wichita policeman Bedford Wood, his former deputy while he was marshal in Kingman. Wood boarded the train at Wichita and the two men headed toward El Reno early Saturday morning.[62]

When the train pulled into the station at North Enid, Oklahoma's three most famous deputy U.S. marshals also got on baord:

> At North Enid, Bill Tilghman, Chris Madsen, Heck Thomas, and three or four other deputy United States marshals got on the train. They told me they had found out "who" had held up the train at Round Pond [Pond Creek]. It was the Daltons [probably meaning Bill Dalton and the Doolin gang]. They had a woman with them, a woman who was an associate of the outlaws, who had told them all about it. I told them that if they would get off with me at El Reno I would show them that they were being misled.[63]

With federal arrest warrants in hand, Bill and Bedford Wood began searching the streets of El Reno by midday Saturday. They first spotted Sylva and arrested him without incident, recovering eighteen horses and mules that were hitched on a side street:

> When I arrested Sylva, Felix Young ran west across the street and into the alley where he had his horse tied. I chased him in between some buildings and killed his horse in the alley. He then ran down the street that runs east and west by the Kerfoot Hotel. I shot him in the leg before he got to a little creek in west of the Rock Island tracks. He stopped then and held up his arms, but still had the six-shooter in one hand. I told him to throw his six-shooter toward me as far as he could, which he did and I took him

back to jail. ...I turned Young and Sylva over to Madsen and some deputies who took them to Pond Creek.

Madsen claimed he had shot Young's horse, but at that time Madsen was several blocks away and there was a row of buildings between him and the alley where the horse was killed. A person could not have seen a row of soldiers had they been where Madsen was. I killed Young's horse.[64]

The capture of Sylva and Young in El Reno placed all the known train robbers behind bars, at least for a short time. Frank Lacey and John O'Conners, who were captured in Hennessey the day after the robbery, had already been jailed in Wichita "to avoid lynching."[65] There are no records that show the disposition of charges against the two men.[66]

Young and Sylva were eventually jailed at Pond Creek, where Will Wade had been incarcerated since the night of the attempted holdup.[67] Wade, who claimed to be a tramp taking a free train ride when the holdup occurred, was later identified as "Big Jim" Bourland by U.S. Marshal E. D. Nix when Nix wrote his memoirs in 1929. Nix erroneously reported the three men escaped jail at Enid.[68] Bill said he later learned that Bob Hughes and Jim Bourland were the two outlaws who commandeered the train that night after secretly boarding the tender at Pond Creek Station.[69]

A Pond Creek grand jury indicted Nate Sylva for train robbery, but Felix Young was released for "lack of evidence." Before leaving the jury room, however, Young was arrested again on a federal warrant in connection with the stolen horses and mules in his possession the day he was captured in El Reno.[70]

On the night of June 3, 1894, Sylva, Young, Will Wade (Jim Bourland) and at least two other prisoners broke out of the Pond Creek jail by dislodging some loose rocks and digging through an outside wall. After stealing horses, and then a team and buggy, they were last seen "heading for the Creek or Seminole country."[71]

Bill recounted that Young was killed some time later in Wyoming, and that Sylva eventually went to the penitentiary in Missouri for horse theft.[72] Jim Bourland reportedly served time in Texas for subsequent crimes and then "went straight," returning to Oklahoma where he became a respected lawman and a "nemesis to outlaws."[73]

In a strange turn of events, Jim Bourland would make headlines again a few years later; involved in the deadly conclusion of a life and death struggle with the key player of an investigation set in motion by Bill Fossett.

8

RUNNING DICK YEAGER TO GROUND

One year, almost to the day, following the attempted Rock Island holdup at Pond Creek, bandits attacked the same night express train, this time near Dover.

Late on the night of April 3, 1895, two men scampered aboard the tender and crawled toward the smoke-belching locomotive as it paused during the brief stop at the depot. They covered the crew with Winchesters and ordered engineer Gallagher to pull out south as scheduled, but to stop again about a mile from Dover where the tracks ran through a cut a short distance north of the Cimarron River. The nervous train crew complied but overshot the location and had to back up to a spot where three other bandits waited.[1]

When the train finally stopped, a volley of shots came from the embankment above the tracks, as the outlaws made sure passengers stayed in the cars. Conductor James Mack walked forward to investigate and was met by a pair of cocked revolvers, then escorted back to the express car. When express messenger J. A. Jones refused the conductor's pleas and the gang's demand to open the door, they began blasting away at the car with their Winchesters. Wounded by several random shots, Jones finally opened the door, and the outlaws went to work on the safe. Attempts to drill holes and explode dynamite in them barely peeled the paint from the "through safe" that had been locked in Kansas City and could be opened only by express agents at the final destination of Ft. Worth.

Frustrated by their efforts, two of the bandits, identified as Bill Doolin gang members "Tulsa Jack" Blake and "Red Buck" Waightman, entered the coach cars and forced the train's porter to walk ahead of them with a grain sack while they robbed the passengers. Former U.S. Marshal William Grimes tossed in some small change after hiding his elegant gold watch under the stove. Bill Fossett's son, Lew, was also a passenger that night. When the bandits demanded his money he calmly replied, "You're playing a dead card there."

After shaking down over 200 passengers, the bandits rode off into the night with a grand take of about $250. The train then pulled away toward Kingfisher where authorities were notified of the holdup. Former marshal Grimes provided officers with details of the robbery, but he mistakenly identified one of the bandits as Dick Yeager, an alias for Zip Wyatt. [2]

The Rock Island quickly passed word of the robbery to Deputy U.S. Marshal Chris Madsen in El Reno, where he and a posse boarded a special train that hurried north to Dover. Lawmen were on the outlaw's trail by sun up, following their tracks northwest along the sandy banks of the Cimarron River.

They then split into two groups, hoping to overtake the bandits and cut off their escape route.

Deputy U.S. Marshals Isaac Prater and William Banks headed a posse of six men that pushed along a trail the outlaws didn't bother to hide. At mid-afternoon, they found the bandits camped in a grove of blackjack trees along the north side of the Cimarron. The deputies quickly raised their rifles and called for the gang's surrender, but the surprised outlaws scrambled for cover and answered with gunfire. A furious battle erupted, "which lasted three quarters of an hour, and in which fully 200 shots were exchanged." The robbers, "each having a 45-90 Winchester and two revolvers," out gunned the lawmen, but during their getaway, one was fatally shot and two others wounded, as they withdrew down a hollow that could not be covered by the deputies.[3]

Based on the initial misidentification of former marshal Grimes, the dead outlaw was thought to be Dick Yeager (Zip Wyatt), but a week later, the slain man was positively identified as "Tulsa Jack" Blake.[4] His death marked the beginning of the end for the Bill Doolin gang. Within three years all gang members except one, who served penitentiary time, would meet violent deaths in shootouts with lawmen.[5]

The eventual demise of the Doolin gang concluded an era of glamorized outlawry that began when Oklahoma Territory, and much of the West, was young. In those earlier days, men who worked outside the law were often popularized, winning public support in areas plagued by social conflict. Many of Oklahoma's early settlers distrusted deputy marshals because a few had used their offices to unfairly obtain the best tracts of property during the land rush. Some homesteaders considered themselves poor, defenseless victims of the government, wealthy banks and railroads. For them, outlawry was a justifiable method for the oppressed to fight back.[6]

The *Ardmore State Herald* made this view explicit:

> Their [the outlaw's] life is made up of daring. Their courage is always with them and their rifles as well. They are kind to the beknighted traveler, and it is not a fiction that when robbing a train they refuse to take from women.
>
> It is said that Bill Doolin, at present the reigning highway man is friendly to the people in one neighborhood, bestowing all sorts of presents upon the children. It is his boast that he never killed a man.
>
> This is fully a romantic figure as Robin Hood ever cut.[7]

A similarly glorified reputation belonged to Dick Yeager before he became a vicious killer. His real name was Nathaniel Ellsworth Wyatt, better known by his nickname "Zip." The moniker reportedly was given to him because of his ability to stay a few jumps ahead of authorities after a horse-stealing incident in his youth. During his teens, Zip worked as a cowboy in the Cherokee Outlet, where he became acquainted with Bill Doolin, "Little" Dick West, "Bitter Creek" Newcomb and others. In 1889 he made the "run," settling near the Cimarron River northeast of Guthrie, in an area known as "Cowboy Flats." He located his aging parents, a sister and two brothers on the same claim. Growing up, Zip received little guidance from his drunken father and preferred riding and shooting to schooling and working. His older brother, Nim, an expert gambler known as "Six-Shooter" Jack, died in a Texas saloon brawl in 1891. By then, Zip was well on his way to developing his own reputation as a bad man.

Although authorities were not aware of it until some years later, Zip and a cohort killed the night telegraph operator in a failed robbery attempt of the Santa Fe station at Wharton (later renamed Perry) in November 1889. For the next two years his escapades mostly involved getting drunk and shooting up towns, but on June 3, 1891, two citizens of Langston were wounded in a running gunfight with Zip after he went on a shooting rampage. He fled to Kansas, and on July 4, 1891, Zip stole some riding equipment from a livery stable in Greensburg. Kiowa County deputy Andrew Balfour tracked him to Pryor's Grove, where a holiday celebration was in progress. Balfour spotted Zip and called out: "Hold up young fellow, I have a warrant for you." Zip wheeled around, pulled a pistol and said, "And I have this for you," as he shot Balfour in the stomach. The officer returned fire, slightly wounding his assailant with two shots of his own before dying.

Wyatt fled to his home state of Indiana, where he was eventually captured, but on New Year's Eve 1891, he escaped from the federal jail at Guthrie. He wound up in the Cheyenne-Arapaho country, organized his own gang and began using the alias Dick Yeager.[8]

The key members of the Dick Yeager gang were Isaac "Ike" Black and his wife Belle, and Jennie Freeman, a farmer's wife who ran off with Yeager when he was in hiding after his jailbreak at Guthrie.[9] Black, originally from Kansas, reportedly had been an El Reno policeman in 1892, but ended up in a shooting with lawmen over the illegal cutting of timber in the Glass Mountains, part of a wider region known as the Gyp Hills.[10] From their hideout in the rugged mountains of western Oklahoma, this gang became, "a terror to all farmers and country storekeepers in that section through which they ranged."[11]

Their hit and run break-ins of country stores and postal stations in the area escalated on March 28, 1894. Two men broke in and robbed the home of Edward Townsend, the operator of a post office and store at Todd in Blaine County. The well-known and highly respected Mr. Townsend was shot to death resisting the robbers. The description of the assailants fit Dick Yeager and Ike Black.[12] His murder set the whole countryside to arms. As Marquis James, who grew up in Enid, later wrote: "Kill one settler and you rouse up a swarm of settlers."[13]

Thus, Yeager and Black gained an even more notorious reputation. Like the Doolin gang, they operated in the same territory between the Gyp Hills and the Rock Island Line to the east. Not surprisingly, the pair was suspected of being in on the Rock Island train robbery near Dover in April 1895, but according to James, this was later refuted:

> It was thought then (and for that matter a long time) that Dick and Ike had been at the Cimarron [bridge south of Dover] with Bill Doolin [Doolin's gang] . . . Yet the most dependable evidence denies Yeager and Black had any part in the Rock Island holdup. Their presence in the Gyp Hills with Doolin was a coincidence.
>
> Ike Black was an outlaw of so little account as to be hardly worth the trouble of arresting except for mileage. Dick Yeager stood in a different light.[14]

At the time, however, there was no distinction between the hunt for Yeager and Black and the Dover train robbers; it was just one big search for outlaws, acclaimed "the greatest manhunt Oklahoma ever had."[15] Several posses took up the venture, and on June 4, 1895, Yeager and Black were cornered in a cave near the Woods-Blaine county line. After a daylong gunfight, the outlaws escaped on foot, leaving behind Belle Black and Jennie Freeman, who were captured.[16]

From his home in Kingfisher, Bill Fossett had kept up with the chase for Yeager and Black. Although he considered Yeager "a second-rate outlaw at best," because he had never robbed a bank or railroad, he felt sure Yeager would eventually get around to it.[17] Bill discussed the matter with Deputy U.S. Marshals Bill Banks and Isaac Prater, who had shot it out with the Dover train robbers. The three men apparently had a good intelligence-gathering network and devised a trap for Yeager and Black. According to Bill:

> Banks and Prater got notice that Yeager and Black and their gang would attempt to rob the store at Columbia [northeastern Kingfisher County] on the 23rd of July. I met Mr. Banks on Uncle John's Creek on Sunday the 21st of July, northeast of town, and had a talk with him. Banks went directly to Columbia on horseback to meet a party who was keeping him posted. Mr. Prater and another gentleman went around with a team to Columbia and had sent shotguns ahead loaded with buckshot. Banks borrowed a key to the schoolhouse, which stands in a good position from the post office, to lay in wait for the outlaws when the attack was made.[18]

They waited, but the trap was spoiled by gunplay on the afternoon of July 23. On a road near Sheridan, north of Columbia, three local deputies confronted a man on horseback riding along side two men in a wagon. Believing it was Yeager and his gang, they called for the men's surrender, but the order went unheeded, setting off a brief gunfight. The lone rider was killed, and the men in the wagon wounded. It turned out to be a tragic case of mistaken identity, as both groups of men took the other to be outlaws.[19] The shooting, said Bill, alarmed Yeager and Black who fled the area "without making any attack on the store."[20]

By this time, more than 200 manhunters combed the Gyp Hills region, where the outlaws seemed always to surface. This number included several county posses, groups of armed settlers and members of the Anti-Horse Thief Association, settlers who had organized to defend against the thievery of Yeager, Black and other desperados who plagued the area.[21]

W. D. "BILL" FOSSETT

Nathaniel Ellsworth Wyatt, known as "Zip" Wyatt and Dick Yeager, worked as a cowboy before turning to banditry.

The Glass Mountains

On July 25, the outlaws resurfaced in Blaine County, robbing a store at Oxley. They headed south toward Watonga, but then doubled back toward the hills and made camp near Salt Creek. A posse soon overtook and surrounded them, but the uncanny pair shot their way free again in a "volley of bullets" that left a Blaine County deputy wounded. Black was also wounded, hit in the head with buckshot. The gunfire scared the outlaws' horses off, but Yeager and Black escaped on foot.[22]

After capturing a horse and cart from a farmer near Okeene, they fled into the Glass Mountains. On July 29, another posse cornered them in a canyon. A twenty-five minute gunfight ensued, but Yeager and Black broke through the posse's line. One deputy claimed "to have knocked Yeager down twice and Black once with shots from a Winchester," bearing out the belief the outlaws wore some kind of steel chest plates. Amid the confusion of the fight, the desperate pair stole two of the lawmen's horses and were on the loose again.[23]

Following the shooting fiasco near Sheridan and the gun battle near Okeene, Bill and Deputy Banks became more determined than ever "to start on the hunt and show no quarter." Bill checked with his railroad bosses:

> I then telegraphed to the railroad officials asking permission to go into the Glass Mountains with Banks and try and capture them as we had heard from a reliable source that they intended to make a raid on the Rock Island passenger train and also hold up some of the Kingfisher banks....[24]

Railroad officials in Chicago gave Bill permission to take up the chase. Several men in Kingfisher had previously expressed enthusiasm about joining him but backed out when it came time to form the posse. That left just Bill and Deputy

Marshal Banks until Bill's son, Lew, "insisted on joining the expedition." Although reluctant to do so, Bill consented, and the three men set out for the Glass Mountains on Monday night, July 29.[25]

They reached the mountains by noon the following day. With Yeager and Black both wounded, tired and hungry after weeks of constant pursuit, Bill planned to drive them from their Glass Mountain hideouts and back to the prairie where, by then, over a thousand men had "spread themselves to shoot the quarry down." Lew Fossett almost surely took to the task with mixed feelings because he and Ike Black had attended school together in Caldwell, Kansas. Bill was also well acquainted with Black's parents.[26]

On Tuesday, July 30, Bill and his men picked up the trail, following it southwest through Greever Canyon:

> We then followed the outlaws, zigzagging in every direction, to a point north of the Canadian River near the Amos Chapman ranch. There the outlaws found that Banks and a crowd were after them and told the ranchman they would plant themselves on a sand hill and kill their pursuers as they came. The ranchman was instructed to give out that information. The outlaws then doubled on their course going north through the hills and came to a house about three miles ahead of their pursuers, robbed the occupants, taking a new suit of black clothes, three revolvers, a pair of shoes and some shirts.[27]

Knowing that Yeager and Black needed food and supplies, Bill and his posse laid in wait at a nearby country store. When the two men failed to show, the pursuers picked up their trail leading back to Greever Canyon. Under a bright moon, they tracked the pair after dark, finding a campsite where the outlaws had built a fire and made coffee. Bill estimated that by waiting at the store, his posse was about two hours behind Yeager and Black.[28]

Through the night, they stayed with the outlaws' tracks as they weaved back and forth through the rocks and brush and finally, onto the flatlands. Bill was sure they were on the right trail:

> ...one of the outlaw's horses having a broken hoof which was easily detected from any other track ... We followed Yeager and Black that night as long as their tracks were to be seen by moonlight. Yeager was riding behind Black, slapping Black's horse along.[29]

On Thursday, August 1, the outlaws' tracks took "a straight course toward the foothills northeast of Cantonment." Although Anti-Horse Thief Association members and settlers throughout the region had "thoroughly organized," they refused to follow any trail into the hills for fear of ambush. They told Bill that if "his party would drive the outlaws out of the canyons, they would assist." Having learned earlier that Yeager and Black had hidden fresh horses in a pasture not far from Cantonment, Bill believed they were then headed for that location. He was right:

> When they came out of the hills they struck the bottomlands close to a little grove northeast of Cantonment six miles, called Cottonwood Grove. There a man saw two men on horseback, one driving the other man's horse along in front of him with a whip. The farmer had a field glass and saw that it was Yeager and Black. He started out to get a posse of farmers. Yeager and Black stopped at a little house back in a cornfield.[30]

Yeager and Black stopped at the well for water and then went inside Maggie Nolan's home, where she got them something to eat. In the meantime, the farmer alerted the posse, and about fifteen to eighteen men converged on the house while others took up firing positions in the cornfield. When Yeager and Black emerged, Alva Deputy Sheriff Marion Hildreth called, "Throw up your hands!"

The two men were caught by surprise and out in the open but never hesitated. They responded with "Colts and Winchesters," firing at their pursuers, who returned with a barrage of rifle fire. Black was hit in the head and died instantly. Yeager took a bullet in the right breast but managed to stagger away on foot through the cornfield, the posse sending a hail of bullets after him.[31] Fearing Yeager's ability to pick them off if they plunged into the tall corn, where sight was restricted to just a few feet at a time, the lawmen did not immediately give chase.[32]

When they finally regrouped, it was dusk. They found Yeager's tracks leaving the cornfield and leading easterly over a sand hill to a doctor's house about a mile away. There the posse discovered that Yeager's wounds had been dressed before he took the doctor's horse and rode away. By then it was dark, and the posse opted to stay the night at the doctor's house rather than chase their wounded, but dangerous, prey through the night.[33]

The next morning, Friday August 2, Bill and his men trailed the horse from the doctor's house for six or seven miles to the east, where they met the horse heading back home without a rider. They continued on the original eastward track to near Homestead, in Blaine County. At that point, they discovered Yeager had commandeered a one-horse cart and a fourteen-year-old boy to drive him on east and then north, toward the Cimarron River. By then it was Friday night, and Yeager "sent the horse and boy back and started on foot again."[34]

The following day, the posse found where Yeager had pressed another young boy and a one-horse cart into service, crossed the Cimarron and turned back east.[35] It was evident "Yeager had been wounded so badly that he could not ride on horseback."[36]

The chase was now in southwestern Garfield County, and about "forty men were in pursuit." The posse finally stopped at Turkey Creek to rest their jaded horses.[37] Bill said that could they have obtained fresh mounts, the pursuit would have ended sooner:

> No one would let us have any fresh horses or we could have got around in front of him and headed him off. The posse after him didn't try to get in front, but trailed along behind and of course could not shoot at him for fear of hitting this innocent boy.[38]

About two o'clock in the afternoon, Yeager and his boy hostage crossed the Rock Island tracks at Waukomis, "hotly pursued by the posse." [39]

Bill, Lew, and Deputy Banks temporarily broke off the chase and headed for Hennessey to get fresh horses:

> From there I wired Mr. Hitt, general manager, [of the railroad] the results of the chase. After getting something to eat we, we took fresh horses and started on the trail again, overtaking the posse a few miles northeast of Hennessey. It was a bright moonlight night . . . They claimed they had him surrounded in about three acres of cane [sic: corn], which was seven or eight feet high. After watching them awhile I told the boys, Banks and Lew, that that fellow wasn't in there, even if they had seen him about eleven o'clock [p.m.] as they claimed because there was too much chance to escape.[40]

The corn patch where Yeager supposedly still hid was near Skeleton Creek. He had earlier turned the boy with the cart back home from that point. By that time, a posse from Enid, headed by Deputy A. J. "Ad" Poak, joined the search.[41]

Bill was certain that Yeager had slipped away from the corn patch, recalling that the outlaw "had a sweetheart" who lived "about twelve miles southeast of there." With Lew and Deputy Banks, he rode down the creek to a point "about due east of Hennessey," where they rested until dawn Sunday morning. At daybreak, they began inquiring at farmhouses, learning that a man was seen walking along the creek bottom late the night before. At one farm they found where Yeager forced a man to help him steal his neighbor's horse.[42]

Once he was mounted, Yeager had told the farmer, "Don't give me away too soon. I think I've given them the dodge but if you see the sons of bitches, tell them that while they are getting me, I'll get them."[43]

By the time Bill gathered this information, it was about ten o'clock Sunday morning. The posse from Enid, some men from Sheridan, and members of the Anti-Horse Thief group had arrived in the area. They soon found a new trail that lead southeast from Sheridan, thence into Logan County, where they spotted the stolen horse heading back home. Nearby were footprints leading into a cornfield southwest of Marshall.[44] Enid deputy Ad Poak and Hennessey deputy Tom Smith entered the field on foot, while the rest of the posse surrounded it. As noiselessly as possible, the two men slowly stepped through the tall corn. Finally, they saw a sandy, open patch of ground ahead of them. Stretched across the middle of it, lying face down, was the motionless form of Dick Yeager. His clothing was tattered and clotted with blood, and he wore one boot and one shoe. To his right lay his Winchester and pistol.

Poak whispered to Smith, "Let's give the poor devil a chance."

The deputies leveled their Winchesters and Poak called out, "Put you hands up Dick, we've got you."

Yeager raised his head and looked around toward the voices behind him. Then, without a word, he grabbed for his pistol. Both officers fired at the same time, hitting Yeager in the stomach and hip. Yeager rolled over still holding the pistol.

"Drop that gun," yelled Smith.

Yeager dropped the gun and stiffly rose one hand.

"Both hands!"

"I can't," replied Yeager, "my arm's broke."

As the officers walked up and grabbed his weapons, Yeager asked who they were. When they told him they were deputy sheriffs, he replied:

"Thank God for that. At least the marshals didn't get me."[45]

Using a wagon from a nearby farm, the posse took the wounded fugitive to a little church in Sheridan where Sunday services were just letting out. By then, every man who participated in the final search arrived, and immediately an argument erupted over jurisdiction and rewards. Deputy U.S. Marshal Bill Banks argued for custody based on federal warrants for jail escape and post office robbery. Enid Sheriff Elzie Thralls assumed command of the group, saying his deputies were due the reward because they "never let up on the trail." The men from Sheridan didn't take kindly to the attitude of the Enid men, causing special deputy Billy Fox to assert, "If anybody tries to take this man to Guthrie my guns are liable to go off."

Even Yeager, who lay listening to the dispute, got in on it, whispering to Tom Smith, "If you'll give me my six-shooter for about two seconds, I'll stop the argument." The men finally decided the reward should be divided between the Garfield County officers and the farmers from Kingfisher County and that Yeager should be jailed in Enid.[46]

On Sunday afternoon August 4, they transported Yeager by wagon to Hennessey and placed him on the eight o'clock night train to Enid.[47] The controversial arrangement for jurisdiction prompted the *Kingfisher Free Press* to write:

> Just why he should have been taken there when his recent crimes have been committed in this county, Logan and Blaine, is not known. It may be that the Enid Posse expect to claim the reward which is reported to have been offered for his capture; a reward which should be distributed among the farmers of Kingfisher and Blaine County to whom the credit of Yeager's capture is unquestionably due.[48]

Examining physicians gave Yeager "only one chance in ten to recover." He languished on a cot in the Enid jail and, for a time, seemed to improve. He enjoyed the attention of hundreds of visitors, some coming many miles to see the notorious outlaw, who was the subject of a punishing one hundred twenty-five-day manhunt. He was cordial to most people and boasted of his many adventures, but was less polite when facing accusers of his most dastardly crimes.[49]

When Kiowa County, Kansas, Sheriff James Bonsall arrived to see the man who had murdered his deputy four years earlier, Yeager turned his head and wouldn't speak. He did the same to the widow and four children of Edward Townsend, the man he murdered at the post office and store at Todd. They, however, saw enough to identify Yeager as the killer.[50]

"With three, .44 caliber Winchester balls in his body"[51] Yeager's condition continued to worsen through late August. Each issue of the *Enid Daily Wave* reported on his failing condition, noting his remorselessness for victims, and his contempt for various deputies. On August 24, the paper reported:

> ...A smile always plays over his face when [Deputy U.S. Marshal] Madsen or Fossett is spoken of and at one time he said that if there had never been worse men on his track than Madsen and Fossett, he would not have been captured.[52]

Early Saturday morning, September 7, 1895, Zip Wyatt, alias Dick Yeager, died from his many wounds. His last visitor was a kindly old Tennessean named Dr. H. B. McKenzie, who asked if he wanted to see anyone or say something on his "last day on earth." Defiantly, Yeager replied, "Nobody to see, Doc, and nothing to say."

Barely half a dozen people gathered at the jail's wooden gate the Sunday morning Dick Yeager's pine coffin was loaded aboard a wagon and taken to the paupers' field south of town.[53]

Although Bill never said as much, he seemed intent on assuring Dick Yeager would not attain hero status among the many Oklahomans who followed the outlaw's career. Some years after the Yeager pursuit, he told historian Marquis James that Yeager was "a second stringer—just another cowboy who took a wrong fork in the road."[54] It is apparent that Bill wanted to make sure Yeager stayed a "second stringer" when he took up the chase by explaining, "While Yeager and Black never bothered the Rock Island Railroad, I felt it would be only a short time before they did...."[55]

The Rock Island recognized Bill for his part in the pursuit and capture of Dick Yeager with a promotion to Chief Special Agent of all its lines west of the Missouri River.[56] In Enid, however, stories of the capture generated contention.

The *Enid Daily Wave* asserted that Bill tried "to take upon his shoulders the credit for the capture of Zip Wyatt."[57] The censure apparently came because he had given newspapers an account of the chase. The *Kingfisher Free Press* returned fire saying Bill was "reluctant" to discuss the chase and wanted "farmers who had been in hot pursuit of the outlaws for weeks" to receive the credit, adding:

> No man in this country doubts his courage, and it is beyond all controversy that, in the pursuit of Yeager and Black, deputy marshal [William] Banks, Fossett and his son "Lew" went into the jungles and canyons of the Gloss [sic] Mountains without other company no matter what the reasons were.[58]

The newspaper then chided the "gallant" law officers from Enid who "ran in after Zip Wyatt was run down, exhausted and asleep."[59]

The *Wave's* criticism may have resulted from the enmity created by the recent "Railroad War," in which the town bitterly fought the Rock Island, Bill's employer. In the end, the newspapers made a bigger issue of it than did Bill, who was not known to have commented on the squabble.

9

CHIEF DEPUTY FOSSETT

With the turn of 1897, the operation of the territorial marshal's office at Guthrie was under increasing scrutiny from Justice Department auditors and inspectors. Trouble had been brewing for two years after inspectors found sizeable discrepancies in the handling of office expenses during the administration of Marshal Evett D. Nix. The *Enid Daily Wave* described the initial problem in October 1895:

> The United States Attorney General has discovered that the expenses of the Oklahoma and Indian Territory federal courts consume nearly two-thirds of the government appropriation for territorial court expenses and is about to start an investigation. If our two territories consume so

much money, how does Utah, New Mexico, and Arizona get along with so little? Something rotten somewhere.[1]

The investigation centered on fees paid for unnecessary arrests, charges for mileage never traveled, and other "official extravagances."[2] The summary of a lengthy report to the U.S. Attorney General revealed that Marshal E. D. Nix had received kickbacks on federal contracts, created fictitious pay vouchers, padded expenses to the tune of $850,000 and committed perjury during the government's investigation. The ensuing scandal resulted in Nix's resignation in January 1896. Nix, who once directed an army of one hundred-fifty deputy marshals, was generously bade farewell as a man who "served the people well" by putting "bandits in their graves."[3]

With Nix gone, President Grover Cleveland appointed Democrat Patrick Nagle of Kingfisher to the post. Nagle promised to reduce the force of deputies to the "barest number possible for effective operation."[4] His term was marked by a public uproar over the escape of Bill Doolin and thirteen other prisoners from the federal jail in July 1896. The notorious Doolin had been captured by Deputy U.S. Marshal Bill Tilghman only five months earlier.[5] Although criticism of Nagle softened somewhat after Deputy Marshal Heck Thomas and a posse tracked down and killed Doolin seven weeks later,[6] his office also faced charges of unscrupulous bookkeeping.[7] Nagle bowed out six months after Republican President William McKinley took office in 1897.[8] By then, congress was considering a new system of fixed salaries for marshals and certain territorial court officers, in a move "to kill the fee system."[9]

The marshal's post was in limbo for five months while party factions squabbled over a list of potential appointees. McKinley finally dropped all names and went after a "comparatively new man."[10] He selected Enid rancher and lifelong Republican Canada H. "Harry" Thompson as the new Marshal of Oklahoma Territory. Thompson's experience in law enforcement consisted of a term as a sheriff in Kansas and work as a special agent for the Rock Island Railroad.[11] He took control of the office on November 8, 1897, naming Bill Fossett the chief deputy in charge of field operations. New commissions as deputies were issued to Heck Thomas and Bill Tilghman, among others. The appointment of Fossett, a "fearless and faithful officer," was said to guarantee "efficiency" in the marshal's office.[12]

The day after Bill and other deputies were sworn in, the *Oklahoma State Capital* reported that "Miss Fossett, daughter of Chief Deputy Fossett, has been made stenographer to Marshal Thompson."[13] Nineteen-year-old Mary Frances "Mamie" Fossett had divided the last few years of her life between her father and stepmother's home in Kingfisher and school in Wichita. She also had made frequent trips to Pueblo, Colorado, for visits with her grandmother and other members of the Footman family, likely including her divorced mother, Elizabeth Footman Fossett.[14]

Mamie was not the first female to work in the marshal's office, but her appointment apparently produced considerable publicity and speculation about "female deputies." Two other women were employed as clerks during Marshal William Grimes' term in the early 1890s, and at least one of them, Miss S. M. Burche, still worked there when Canada Thompson became marshal.[15] When Mamie joined the staff, the possibility that the women's duties extended beyond that of "clerk" and "stenographer" was raised by a story in the *Guthrie Daily Leader*. It noted that Misses Burche and Fossett "are the first women to do active work as United States Deputy Marshals." Accompanying the brief article was a poem written by Freeman E. Miller, a professor of English at

Oklahoma A & M University (later, Oklahoma State University). Among its lines were:

> And to their sweet endeavors, we gladly must submit,
> For when a maiden wants a man there's no escaping it!
> They've spoiled our old vocation — they've placed it under ban —
> These winsome, maiden marshals that go after any man.[16]

The story and poem may have given rise to another article found in the vertical files on U.S. Marshals in the Oklahoma Historical Society library. Dated 1898, it was evidently written by an out-of-Oklahoma newspaper under the headline, "Female Officers of the Law."

> It is not infrequent these days for an officer of the law to name a woman as a deputy. But she is nearly always what is called an office deputy. She performs mere clerical duties and never takes to the field. But Oklahoma has set the pace. United States Marshal C. H. Thompson, of Guthrie, has appointed two women as deputies for fieldwork. That a woman should choose the vocation of professional thief taker in the most civilized portion of the land would be strange enough. It is infinitely more so when she chooses field duty on the worst territory in the union.... So it would seem that these girls posses metal of exceptional kind to willingly undertake such duties.
> The young women are Miss S. M. Burche and Miss Mamie Fossett. They are of that adventurous class of females who invaded the newly opened territory in search of homesteads. They are young, fairly good-looking, well

educated, fearless, and independent. Their duties are by no means confined to keeping Marshal Thompson's books.[17]

Details of any actual fieldwork performed by the two women have not been found, so it may have been that Mamie's joining the marshal's staff simply created conjecture about the next logical step. In any case, the speculation over the duties for female marshals was short-lived in the face of the very real and pressing business of rounding up outlaws.

Following the death of Bill Doolin in August 1896, gang members "Dynamite" Dick Clifton and "Little" Dick West pulled off a few small robberies but mostly laid low until the following year. Clifton received his nickname for hollowing out lead bullets and placing a small amount of dynamite in them for added effect on impact. "Little" Dick West was a diminutive, tough little ex-Texas cowhand, whose habit of eating and sleeping outdoors had made him a valuable lookout for the Doolin gang.[18]

This vicious duo joined up with Al and Frank Jennings and Pat and Morris O'Malley to form what became the Jennings gang. The Jennings outfit was so inept that Clifton and West, who had ridden with the "best of the worst" in the likes of Bill Doolin, eventually departed in disgust.

Al Jennings, once a prosecuting attorney in Canadian County, and his brother Frank became outlaws after another brother was killed in a gunfight. The O'Malley brothers, meanwhile, had served as deputy marshals under E. D. Nix. As this little group delved deeper into banditry, West and Clifton joined them, but not for long. In August 1897 the gang tried robbing a Santa Fe train south of Edmond. Using two dynamite shots, they severely damaged the express car but barely scratched the Wells Fargo safe. They left the scene with "little, if any, valuables." Two weeks later, they attempted to stop a train on the Missouri, Kansas & Texas Railroad at Bond

Switch (now Onapa), southwest of Muskogee. They stacked heavy timbers on the rails and set them aflame, but the engineer on the approaching train opened the throttle, blasted them off the tracks, and roared on as the bungling bandits stood slack-jawed. In October, the gang tried its luck on a Rock Island train, stopping it on a sidetrack a few miles south of Minco (the siding is the site of today's Pocasset). Again, dynamite failed to crack the safe, leaving the outlaws with only a couple of hundred dollars in personal valuables after shaking down the passengers.

Following other misadventures with Jennings and his cohorts, Clifton and West left the gang to go out on their own. On November 7, the day before Thompson and Fossett took charge of the U.S. Marshal's office at Guthrie, word came from Indian Territory that "Dynamite" Dick Clifton had died in a fiery shootout with lawmen near Checotah. On December 6, Deputy U.S. Marshal Bud Ledbetter arrested the Jennings brothers and Pat O'Malley in the same locale. "Little" Dick West then became Oklahoma's most wanted criminal.[19]

For three months following the death of "Dynamite" Dick and the capture of Al and Frank Jennings, West dodged officers by holding up in hideouts and visiting friendly settlers in Kingfisher and Logan Counties.[20] Using an assumed name, West finally felt safe enough to take work from Ed Fitzgerald and Harmon Arnett, who owned adjoining farms along Cottonwood Creek, a few miles southwest of Guthrie.

In early April 1898, Logan County Sheriff Frank Rinehart heard a rumor that led him to believe Dick West was in the area. He passed the information to Deputy Marshal Heck Thomas who consulted with Chief Deputy Fossett. On Thursday night, April 7, Bill organized a posse consisting of Sheriff Rinehart; Deputy Marshals Thomas and Bill Tilghman; and possemen Ben Miller and Albert Thomas, Heck's son.[21]

The officers rode to the Fitzgerald farm in the pre-dawn hours of April 8. Finding "no traces of their man," they then "cut across the fields to the Arnett farm, about a mile distant." On the way they saw "a man scouting along the timber to their left." Tilghman and Heck Thomas cut across the creek toward the man, who apparently spotted the officers, "changed his course" and disappeared again.

In the meantime, Bill, Rinehart and the possemen rode on to the Arnett house. Leaving the possemen with the wagon and horses, they approached the front of the house on foot and walked around toward the barn. When they came within sight of it, they saw a man standing near a shed connected with the barn. A moment later he stepped out of view and began running "toward the timber." Bill and Rinehart ran forward, calling for him to halt:

> He replied by turning and firing three shots at the officers with a revolver. One shot went dangerously near Rinehart and one by Fossett. The officers then began firing. Sheriff Rinehart fired two shots with a double-barreled shotgun, and Deputy Fossett fired three shots with a Winchester. At the first shots West turned and fired again and as he did so started to run again, loading his revolver as he ran. The second shot from the Winchester struck him in the left side and passed clear through him, coming out of his right shoulder. He fell forward and was dead when the officers reached his side.[22]

West's body was taken to Guthrie and placed in charge of the undertaker. A coroner's jury found that he "came to his death at the hands of Officer Fossett while resisting arrest."[23]

Fifty-nine years after "Little" Dick West died in the shootout along Cottonwood Creek, posseman Albert Thomas offered a slightly different reason for the outlaw's demise. Thomas said Sheriff Rinehart was using his 10-gauge shotgun loaded with buckshot that day. He claims that when Bill Tilghman and his father arrived at the spot after West had fallen, they examined "the wound in his body" and determined "that it was made by buckshot."[24] At the time of shooting, however, the coroner's jury stated that a shot fired from Bill Fossett's Winchester killed West, and no one presented evidence to the contrary.[25]

In March, Mamie Fossett apparently left her job as stenographer in the marshal's office. It was reported that "Mrs. Fossett and Miss Mamie" had left on a trip to Kansas City and Chicago.[26] The trip may have included preparations for her forthcoming wedding. The Fossetts had lived in Guthrie since Bill was appointed chief deputy. They resided on First Street, about half a block north of downtown but still owned their house and property in Kingfisher.[27] It was in Kingfisher, prior to their move to Guthrie, where Mamie apparently renewed her acquaintance with a young man from Kingman, Kansas.

Richard Hugo Miller and Mamie both grew up in Kingman during the 1880s. Although Miller was two years older, they attended school together. Richard was the son of Kingman businessman and city councilman Peter Miller, the owner of several jewelry stores in Kansas. In October 1897, Peter Miller expanded his chain store operation to include Kingfisher, where he placed his son Richard in charge.[28] Richard and Mamie were married by "probate Judge Stevens at the rooms of Mrs. W. D. Fossett"[29] in Kingfisher on May 21, 1898, the *Guthrie Daily Leader* noting:

> Miss Fossett has resided in this city with her parents and up to last week had been visiting in Chicago since March. She is an amiable and accomplished young lady, and for awhile had been engaged in stenographic work in

the marshal's office. Mr. Miller is a popular business young man of Kingfisher.[30]

One of Mamie's wedding presents included the gift of a white horse from her father. It had belonged to "Little" Dick West and was "acquired" by Bill after the outlaw's death. West reportedly rode it during the Rock Island train robbery near Minco in 1897, and Bill said West was running "to his white horse, standing at the edge of some nearby timber" when he was fatally shot.[31]

Putting an end to "Little" Dick West was not the only task that faced the marshal's staff in early 1898. In January a perplexing case of torture and murder by mob vengeance occurred in Pottawatomie County, and Bill was charged with solving it.

This sordid affair was set in motion by the murder of Mary Leard on the evening of December 30, 1897. The Leard family farmed property just inside the Seminole Nation, on land leased from a Seminole Indian. Eight-year-old Frank Leard said that a big Indian, a stranger with a scar on his cheek, rode into the yard about supper time and asked his mother for the loan of a saddle. Mrs. Leard refused, saying that her husband was not home and, "I don't know you." The stranger left but returned about dark. He chased Mary Leard from the house and, after a brief struggle, struck her in the head with his rifle. Mrs. Leard fell dead in the yard, and the Indian rode away after demanding money from young Frank, who told him, "Papa has got the money and gone with it."[32]

When Julius Leard returned home the next day, he and some neighbors immediately set out to find the killer. Word of the murder spread to white settlers in the Seminole Nation, as well as to those in nearby Pottawatomie County, Oklahoma Territory, a couple of miles west of the Leard farm. Close friends and relatives of the Leard's became involved. One, a man named Sam Pryor, assumed the job of finding the killer. He directed several bands of whites, who scoured the countryside and arrested, without authority, any Indian they saw. Over the next few days, scores of young Seminoles were rounded up and taken to the Leard home, where a gathering mob threatened revenge. Some were questioned for information, while others became suspects and were threatened and beaten. Leard vowed retaliation, saying that if he didn't find the real murderer, he would have to kill two or three Indian boys. Frank Leard looked at each suspect brought in, but could not identify any of them as his mother's killer.[33]

With each failure at identification, the mob, varying in number from twenty to fifty men, became more agitated. Events at the Leard house attracted those from the "whiskeytowns," and even northern Pottawatomie County, people with no concern in the affair, but who were caught up in the blood lust of it. They gathered around a fire in Leard's yard and became more violent each night. Some suspects were pulled from the ground with ropes around their necks. After passing out, they were let down then kicked and beaten.[34] The mob finally settled on a method for retribution. They would burn someone, even though Frank Leard could identify no suspect. To legitimize their actions, mob leaders sought to involve as many outsiders as possible. They called in friends and relatives from several miles away, then finally settled on two Seminole victims, Lincoln McGeisey and Palmer Sampson. Julius Leard himself, read fake confessions to the crowd, and he falsely claimed his wife was raped after she died. By this time, an Indian Territory deputy marshal had half-heartedly investigated the matter but left, apparently too fearful of the mob to intervene.[35]

In the early morning hours of January 8, scores of men marched McGeisey and Sampson west from the Leard farm, across into Oklahoma Territory to the edge of some timber, south of the village of Maud. There a crowd of nearly 300, including a few women and children, watched as the two Indians were chained to a tree and burned alive. Mob leader Samuel V. Pryor then threatened vengeance against anyone in the crowd who divulged information about the burning.[36]

A few days later, newspapers broke the story of "two charred remains, of once living beings." Territorial Governor Cassius M. Barnes, the U. S. Congress, and Justice and Interior Department officials called for an investigation. Fear of an Indian uprising was debunked when Seminole Nation leaders promised and maintained complete order. Even so, no one offered information about the burning, because mob leaders had closed the ranks of instigators, on-lookers and frightened citizens by threats and a code of silence.

Oklahoma Attorney General Caleb Brooks directed U.S. Marshal Thompson to send deputies to Pottawatomie County. Thompson gave Bill Fossett, his chief deputy, the daunting task of leading a small field unit that faced overwhelming odds. At the time, the trimmed-down marshal's office consisted of twelve deputies for the entire territory, and only six could be spared for this operation. Law authorities knew that local residents were unified, uncooperative, and would likely resist by violence. Equally perplexing was that arrested suspects would face Pottawatomie County grand juries and trials, where local sympathizers would never convict the burners for murder. The United States, on the other hand, could prosecute only for conspiracy, not murder. Although a lesser charge, prosecution for conspiracy became the chosen tactic.

Thompson planned for his deputies to move in quickly before public sentiment could rise. They were to use a cover story to get people talking, gather evidence, and make as many conspiracy arrests as possible. Aided by seven, specially deputized possemen, considered "proven" local men, Bill and other deputy marshals, including Heck Thomas and Bill Tilghman, fanned out across Pottawatomie County and the Seminole Nation.[37]

Using a team and wagon, Bill went first to Shawnee, and then on to the site of the burning, where he arrived about sundown one evening. He planned to stay at a nearby house, but found only "small children," whose parents were away at the time. After unhitching his team, the children's parents showed up. They were visibly upset by his uninvited stay at their home.

To soothe their apprehension, Bill launched into his "cover story" of being a Colorado cattleman on business in the area and willing to pay any reasonable fee to stay the night. The couple became curious, and began asking the particulars of his business. Bill told them he wanted to lease pastureland, but wasn't sure if he should "bring a bunch of cattle and men in under the present conditions." He then showed them a Denver newspaper story of the burning, "which seemed to satisfy them."

Assured by his explanation, the couple became more talkative, telling him the proposed ranching activity was not safe because they expected an Indian outbreak at "any minute." The seemingly innocent conversing continued, sustained by Bill's curiosity. The talk finally got around to the burning, and the couple mentioned several names, "including the one who touched the match to the fuel around the boys." The next morning Bill returned to Guthrie, where he obtained warrants for six of the mob members based on names he was given by the couple.[38]

By the end of the first week in February, Bill and fellow deputies gathered enough evidence for the U. S. Court at Guthrie to issue more than seventy warrants.[39] He and fellow deputies then returned to the region by way of Wewoka, "so as to come in from the east and not create any suspicion." After spending the night in the Seminole Nation, they crossed into Oklahoma Territory near Maud, where they split up, going in different directions to serve the warrants. One of the suspects Bill arrested was the clerk of a store near the burning site:

> I sized him up as a man who would make a good witness for the government if I could weaken him enough so he would come through and tell the truth. When we got to Shawnee I put all the prisoners except this clerk in the [train's] smoking car. I took him into the chair car and started in to try to get some information.... I said, "You are the biggest fool I ever knew. You have a nice wife and family and here you are on the way to the penitentiary or maybe to be hanged." I talked to him along that line until he began to cry. I said, "You might as well tell the truth and if you do I'll try and protect you as much as possible." He said, "I'll tell the truth and another man in this party will tell the truth too." When we got to Guthrie instead of putting those two in jail with the rest I took them to my house and kept them there until we fixed bond.[40]

Presumably, the time-honored police technique of "leaning" on suspects produced even more names and evidence. Eventually, the seventy suspects arrested for conspiracy in the initial roundup all pleaded not guilty. They were released on bond to appear at the next term of court.

In the preparation for preliminary hearings, authorities summoned several Seminoles to Tecumseh and Shawnee, as potential witnesses. These included several young men that the mob had held as suspects prior to the burning. Some of them borrowed advances against their witness fees from Bill and Assistant U. S. Attorney Thomas McMechan. The generosity backfired with near disastrous results when a few of them used the cash to go out on the town, only to be decoyed to the back room of a saloon in Shawnee and beaten.[41]

As the investigation progressed, prosecutors learned that both McGeisey and Sampson were innocent, and that the story of rape after death was fabricated, but when it came to indicting the burners, threats from mob leaders kept witnesses silent.[42]

Away from the mob's home region, however, there was growing evidence of a changing public mood. The *Guthrie Daily Capital*, among many newspapers that once believed the burners' story and supported their actions, declared the investigation was revealing horrible facts:

> Truth almost staggers the mind when it is confronted with the indignities and cruelties practiced by this senseless mob of human beings and the acts of those men will be handed down as one of the darkest plots in the history of the Southwest.[43]

The broadening probe and unyielding criminal cover-up eventually led to the appointment of a special prosecutor to deal exclusively with the burning case. Former Territorial U.S. Attorney Horace Speed got the job, and Marshal Thompson assigned Bill to protect and assist Speed during a new evidence gathering trip through the Seminole Nation and Pottawatomie County that summer.[44] Speed and Fossett planned to go after the most violent offenders in the mob, habitual criminals with prior records, who were more apt to be identified by local citizens. With a team and wagon full of supplies, including firearms that the deputies fully expected were necessary for their own defense, the band of lawmen set out for Pottawatomie County.[45]

The most dangerous moments of the trip occurred the second night out, when a group of "nightriders" approached their camp. Bill and Speed were asleep in the wagon when they heard horses in the distance. Grabbing his Winchester, Bill hopped down and moved away from the fire, to the edge of the camp. When the riders were about a hundred feet away, he stepped from the shadows, levered his rifle, and announced, "Come closer and we'll shoot!"

The surprised riders pulled up, all eyes on the big man who stood facing them, rifle at the ready. Beyond Bill they could see the glowing campfire and a wagon, but not prosecutor Speed, who was hunkered down behind the sideboards, his own Winchester pointed at them. The men sat their horses and "talked a few minutes among themselves." They then turned and rode off the way they came.[46]

When the two-week expedition ended, enough information had been gathered for a grand jury in Muskogee to bring scores of new indictments for kidnapping and arson. It also laid the groundwork for more arrests in Pottawatomie County.

The investigation and trials continued through the spring of 1900. Prosecutors finally obtained six convictions, which included three of the mob ring leaders and the Indian Territory deputy who failed "to speak or act" in the name of the law. Although the prime suspect in the death of Mrs. Leard was apprehended for questioning, authorities lacked evidence to hold him, and the big Indian "with a scar on one cheek" disappeared.[47]

The so-called Seminole Burning case represented the first successful prosecution of lynchers in the Southwest. Bill and fellow deputy marshals accounted for most of the initial arrests, but in the end, concluded prosecutor Speed, mob members "escaped very cheaply for an inhuman piece of work."[48]

In January 1899, Marshal Thompson assigned Bill and Deputy Marshal Tilghman to western Oklahoma, to "ferret out" a band of postal thieves. Hundreds of rural homesteaders, in a wide region west of El Reno, were losing articles purchased from mail-order houses, often their only source for goods because they lived so far from large towns and rail lines.

Believing that postal workers were behind the scheme, the lawmen put together several dummy packages to pinpoint the source of theft. They soon learned the pilfering centered near Bridgeport.

On February 3, Fossett, Tilghman and postal inspectors raided a postal worker's home at Bridgeport and recovered a large amount of property comprised of almost "every article that could be sent through the mail." The following week, they made similar raids in and near Weatherford, recovering a wagonload filled with stolen merchandise valued at $2,000.

In his report to the U.S. Attorney General in Washington, District Attorney S. L. Overstreet praised Fossett and Tilghman as deserving the "highest commendation for their very efficient services rendered not only in this case, but in all matters entrusted to them."[49]

Sometime in 1899, about a year following the marriage of Mamie Fossett and Richard Miller, a fire destroyed Miller's jewelry store in Kingfisher. The building and its contents, were a total loss and completely uninsured. Richard and Mamie .then moved to Chickasha, Indian Territory, where Miller resumed his profession as a jeweler at a shop in the Palace drug store.[50] On March 12, 1901, Mamie gave birth to a daughter at the couples home. The *Chickasha Daily Express* announced that "Jeweler Miller and his wife are receiving congratulations of friends," but then added, in error, that the child was a "ten pound boy baby."[51] Irene Madaline Miller was Bill Fossett's first and only grandchild. U.S. District Court records for the month show Bill spent eleven days in El Reno, where he transported federal prisoners for trial. Chickasha was only a short hop away by Rock Island train, so it's likely he spent some time with Mamie, Richard and his new grandchild.[52]

Three months prior to his grandchild's birth, Bill and Laura Fossett divorced. In a petition filed at Kingfisher on November 28, 1900, Bill's second wife, of fifteen years, sued him for "mental suffering and cruelty," charging he had been "away from home for long periods of time," and acted as if "he did not owe her any consideration." Bill did not contest the matter, and the divorce was granted "for costs of this suit." Trouble between the couple apparently had occurred five years earlier, but was followed by reconciliation. A Kingfisher newspaper item of November 1895 noted, "Laura L. Fossett vs. Wm. D. Fossett, divorce, dismissed."[53]

In May 1901, the federal jail at Guthrie was renovated to include the addition of more steel bars and improvements to the "bull pen," where Bill Doolin, among others, had launched escapes. The wooden upper walls of the mass holding area were removed and replaced by bars, and a locked steel cage, where a twenty-four-hour lookout could be stationed atop it, was added between the bull pen and office area. This was to make it "impossible for the prisoners to make a rush, overpower a guard and gain their liberty."[54]

In the late spring, Bill engineered the appointment of a new deputy, creating a furor among Oklahoma's hard-lined political partisans. It was expected that members of the party in power choose one of their own for a federal job, so when Bill, as chief deputy marshal in the presiding Republican administration, selected Democrat Joe Grimes, there was great consternation among Republicans. Bill, however, did not budge. Grimes, from Kingfisher, was highly qualified as a trusted, experienced officer and former payroll and freight guard. He was also Bill's close friend, and one of the most versatile characters of his time.

Grimes, who raised cattle and farmed, eventually became best known as owner of the three largest steers in the world. He displayed "Tom," "Dick" and "Harry," each weighing over three thousand pounds, at state fairs across the country. Joe later performed in Pawnee Bill's Wild West shows.[55]

Another deputy marshal's appointment went to Bill's twenty-eight-year-old son, Lew. By that time, Lew was married and operating a bar in Guthrie's Royal Hotel on Harrison Avenue. If his qualifications were considered tenuous, no one said as much. He was a skilled horseman and tracker, and a veteran of several manhunts with his father.[56]

Lew was no slouch when it came to exhibiting grit either. A couple of years earlier he had been the "door-keeper" at a prize-fighting exhibition in Kingfisher. When the main event came up, fight promoters announced that receipts were "inadequate to justify the sluggers" go at each other "full tilt." The audience went wild and "wanted to fight for the return of money." Lew drew a pistol and kept the unruly crowd from pilfering the moneyboxes until order was restored. The *Kingfisher Free Press* reported:

> No one interfered with the man who had the nerve to pull a gun on a lot of men who made demand for money or its equivalent.[57]

Joe Grimes with prize bulls, Tom, Dick and Harry.

Mamie Fossett, on the white horse of deceased outlaw "Little" Dick West, talking with women in front of Kingfisher's Post Office, circa 1898.

10

THE LAW, LAWTON AND THE LAND LOTTERY

In June of 1901, Deputy U.S. Marshals Lew Fossett and Joe Grimes were part of a small contingent of federal officers who accompanied Bill to Lawton[1] for the opening of the Kiowa-Comanche Lands. This opening was by "land lottery," rather than a race for claims. The Department of Interior offered over three and one-half million acres for settlement after giving homestead allotments to individual tribal members and setting aside another half million acres for Indian pasture. On July 9, homesteaders started registering for the lottery, at either El Reno or Lawton, in anticipation of the drawing to begin several days later.[2]

Bill and Joe Grimes made the trip to Lawton early, part of the way as guards for a shipment of money to Ft. Sill. They sent a buggy and team ahead of them from Kingfisher and then rode the train to Marlow, where they picked up several thousand dollars of government money that was hidden in grain sacks filled with oats. The precaution was necessary because the influx of land seekers to the area had attracted highwaymen and cutthroats from across the territory, all roving the countryside in search of easy victims.

> We went down on the train and landed in Marlow about 9 p.m., then left Marlow about 12 midnight. It was a beautiful moonlit night and we made a safe trip [to Ft. Sill], but by the moonlight, every tree and stump looked like old satin.
> We stayed almost a week in the Ft. Sill guardhouse before going on to Lawton.[3]

Arriving at the Lawton townsite, Fossett and Grimes put up the first tent on what was to become the public square. In the days that followed, there was never a dull moment in their peacekeeping assignment. Designers of the land lottery, who ·hoped to avoid the disputes and conflicts of prior openings, did not figure that nearly 170,000 persons would register for only 13,000 available quarter-section parcels.

Lottery registration closed on July 26, and the actual drawing for homesteads began three days later in El Reno. Registration cards were alternately drawn from two boxes, one for the El Reno district, the other for the Lawton district. Beginning August 6, lottery winners selected their quarter-section parcel from a large map, choosing homesteads in the order their name was drawn.[4]

The sale of Lawton townsite lots in a cash auction to the highest bidder was also set to begin August 6. As the day approached, men of wealth, willing to pay large sums for a town lot, mingled with thousands of homestead lottery losers looking for a second chance, all jamming into the bustling little tent town. Lawton was "wide-open" with "every kind of gambling device known to the frontier." Bill and his men, who by then included deputies Heck Thomas and Bill Tilghman, were hard pressed to keep order. Many settlers complained about the gambling, but the "irony" observed the *Chickasha Daily Express*, is that the "Oklahoma law prohibiting the sales of cigarettes or cigarette paper is enforced, but there is no law that can touch the gambler."[5]

On Sunday morning, August 4, trouble started at a gambling den on Goo Goo Avenue, a street whose main attraction was a tent show, where a woman singer could be heard for blocks as she belted out the popular song, "Just because she made dem Goo Goo eyes." An old soldier was reportedly robbed of several dollars in a shell game, and a furious mob raided the tent, grabbed the gambler and threatened to hang him. Bill and his deputies arrived on horseback and rescued the man, making the mob even angrier.

The explosive crowd followed the deputies and their "prisoner" to the courthouse square, where the man was placed inside the tent that served as the lawmen's headquarters. The deputies then formed a protective circle around the tent, and Bill strode toward the throng in an effort to back people away. He finally drew a line in the dirt with his boot, warning, "Anyone who crosses that line will be shot."

By this time, the crowd was growing, and as Bill returned to the tent, a tall, barrel-chested man motioned for everyone to follow him as he began walking in Bill's direction. For a moment the pack started moving, then faltered and finally stopped. Their leader looked back and boasted, "I'm from Texas, follow me men and we'll clean them up!"

No one moved except Bill, who mounted and rode forward, reining in directly in front of the Texan. Bill looked him in the eye and almost whispered, "Do you want to see men killed here for a few dollars?"

"What does a life amount to?" said the Texan, snapping his fingers. "It doesn't amount to that!"

The showdown's next move belonged to the Texan who finally turned to the assembly and said, "Let's go back and clean out those gamblers." For the next thirty minutes the crowd directed its energy into tearing down nearly every gambling tent on Goo Goo Avenue, effectively putting a temporary end to such activities in the new town.[6]

The confrontation was one of several arising from the fact that upwards of 40,000 persons were bunched in and around the hot, dusty little townsite, where only seven deputy marshals and a few dozen soldiers faced the task of keeping peace. Deputy Joe Grimes observed there was so much money carried on the streets of Lawton in those first days that nearly every person became a tempting target for thieves, resulting in "murders and robberies night and day."[7] According to the *Lawton Daily Democrat*:

> Conditions are becoming intolerable and Marshal Fossett with his six deputies are as powerless as an infant to handle the 15,000 to 20,000 people in and near this place. Fifty assistants would have been little enough considering the fact that we are all trespassers alike and the outlaws soon understand this condition.[8]

On the roads entering Lawton, dozens of hijacking cases were reported, most committed by an emerging new generation of Oklahoma badmen that included nineteen-year-old Bert Casey, a name Bill would reckon with in the months to come.[9]

Beginning August 6, the government auctioneer barked out the bids for town lots "hour after hour, and day after day," as he stood on a dry goods box next to an old building moved in from Ft. Sill to serve as the land office. With each sale, a soldier escorted the high bidder to the land office for payment. If necessary, a buyer could go to one of the two makeshift banks to withdraw the needed cash, but he had only thirty minutes to get back to the land office and make payment. If he failed to make the deadline, the lot was resold. The long lines and frenzied activity of the scene, at this and prior land openings, gave rise to the expression, "a land-office business."[10]

One of Lawton's first banks, started by two Hennessey men, held the hoards of cash from the auction. The bank consisted of a vault inside a tent, and Bill's little law force became its defenders. Sitting in makeshift chairs, with rifles on their laps, they guarded the "bank" around-the-clock, two men by day and two by night.[11]

Even after the lot sale ended, Lawton maintained the dubious reputation as one of the wildest towns ever born by a land opening. At one point, there were eighty-six saloons, one for every 100 inhabitants. As a former Kansan, which was also the home to famous temperance crusader Carrie Nation, it must have given Bill a good laugh to know that one Lawton saloon displayed the sign, "All nations welcome here, except CARRIE."[12]

Bill was back in Guthrie for only a short time after the Lawton opening before traveling again. In early September, he was in Washington, D.C. to escort a murder suspect back to Oklahoma. According to the *Oklahoma State Capital,* Clay Axhelm was in a government asylum "under treatment for insanity" and was now "cured" enough to stand trial.

The trip apparently combined business with pleasure, the newspaper noting that Bill's young niece accompanied him. The *State Capital* further remarked:

> Miss Fossett pluckily agreed to keep watch over Axhelm, who is charged with murder in Oklahoma, half the time during the long journey, and she had [sic] Uncle Will share that duty till the man is landed back in Guthrie.[13]

The young "niece" may have been fifteen-year-old Nellie May Fossett of Caldwell, Kansas, the youngest child of Bill's brother John.[14]

Evidently, Bill did not consider traveling a chore; in fact, he seemed to relish it. In the spring of 1900 he had gone to El Paso, Texas, to pick up James Walcher, wanted for murdering a prominent Kingfisher County man. Walcher was captured in Mexico, and in a rather straightforward extradition process, Mexican authorities pushed him across the Rio Grande Bridge and into the arms of the El Paso County Sheriff, who jailed him until Bill arrived.[15]

Bill's apparent wanderlust developed early and never waned over the years. As a young man he once made a 2,000-mile horseback trip from Oshkosh, Wisconsin, to the Pacific coast.[16] Even after his early trail driving days, his craving to see new country led to several game hunting and stock buying trips around the country, and while living in Kingfisher, Bill and the mayor had traveled to Milwaukee to investigate the possibility of building a water works plant. His former employment and long association with the Rock Island Railroad undoubtedly facilitated some of this moving about, which was to continue in the year's ahead.[17]

Bill Fossett and Joe Grimes, circa 1902.

W. D. "BILL" FOSSETT

William D. "Bill" Fossett, 1902.

11

NEW ORDER AT GUTHRIE AND GETTING BERT CASEY

A series of events during the final months of 1901 soon led to changes in the U.S. Marshal's office at Guthrie. When President William McKinley began his second term early in 1901, Canada H. Thompson was reappointed marshal of Oklahoma Territory, leaving virtually the entire marshal's staff intact. In September, McKinley was cut down by an assassin's bullet and was succeeded by Vice President Theodore Roosevelt. A month later, the decisive, no-nonsense Roosevelt removed Territorial Governor William Jenkins for a financial scandal, appointing Thompson Ferguson as governor. In the spring of 1902, Canada Thompson resigned the marshal's post, and Roosevelt promoted Bill Fossett from chief deputy to full U.S. marshal.[1]

Bill's nomination was affirmed by the U.S. Senate on March 31, 1902, and he was officially sworn in April 7.[2] Politically, Bill and "Teddy" apparently saw eye-to-eye, Roosevelt later remarking that he had "a good deal of trouble

W. D. "BILL" FOSSETT

with his marshal appointments in Oklahoma ... but I made no mistake when I appointed Mr. Fossett."[3]

Initially, the appointment garnered both praise and reproach. Bill's close friend, Horace Speed, the U.S. Attorney for Oklahoma, personally carried Canada Thompson's resignation to Washington, and Bill made the trip with him. Their appearance in Washington brought swift action by Roosevelt and the U.S. Senate, prompting the *Daily Oklahoman* to claim that the matter was "done in a hurry so that nobody would have time to file charges and affidavits."[4]

The speed of selection, on the other hand, avoided the usual, protracted confirmation fight which, not surprisingly, the *Kingfisher Free Press* considered desirable:

> It has been an established "custom" for a "fight" to be organized against every man whose name has been suggested for an appointment to an office. This custom has become tiresome and disgusting to the Administration and also to all self-respecting citizens of Oklahoma and the celerity and secrecy established in this instance will be generally endorsed.[5]

Secretary of Interior Ethan Hitchcock also supported Bill's appointment, saying he "made a good record in the maintenance of order" when the Kiowa-Comanche country was opened.[6] In contrast, the *Chandler Tribune* claimed the opening at Lawton was anything but orderly:

> Well, if the "order" maintained at the opening by Fossett and his gang is pronounced GOOD in Washington, it is to be wondered what they deem bad order.
>
> It is a notorious fact that among all the openings which Oklahoma has ever had, the last was the vilest and characterized by greater lawlessness.[7]

The *Tribune* ranted even more viciously in its diatribe about Republican Party appointments and Bill's personal character:

> If any of the men who have endorsed him have ever received Bill Fossett at their homes and encouraged their wives and daughters to maintain terms of social intimacy with him or with the females with whom he is said to openly associate, then they are not fit to fill the official positions they hold.[8]

The insinuation was left standing without support or further elaboration. As a public officer holder, Bill was wide open to personal attack and could do nothing but ignore the newspaper. In any case, Oklahomans highly valued their marshal's crime fighting ability, and for that, he received high marks:

> ...He has done good work riding Oklahoma of its outlaws, being in several expeditions where there were desperate men to deal with.[9]

If Fossett ever had a clear mandate to deal with "desperate men," it was to wipe out the Bert Casey gang, a task he had started before taking charge of the marshal's office.

Bert Casey grew up in the Washita River bottoms southwest of Arapaho, where he most surely was influenced by the outlawry of his uncles, Jim and Vic Casey.[10] Young Casey graduated from horse stealing to highway robbery, and on the evening of August 4, 1901, nineteen-year-old Bert and at least two other men waylaid a party of travelers who were on their way to the Kiowa-Comanche Land Opening at Lawton.

Dr. Zeno Beemblossom and his eleven-year-old son Jay rode the train from Oklahoma City to Rush Springs, where they were met by two friends who provided a wagon for the final leg of their journey to Lawton. Twelve miles west of Rush Springs, they decided to camp for the evening. As they prepared camp, three riders, later identified as Bert Casey, George Moran and either Mort Perkins or Levi Reed, emerged from the brush and demanded they "throw up their hands." Instead of complying, Dr. Beemblossom "reached for his revolver," and one of the highwaymen fired. The bullet "cut the left sleeve" of Dr. Beemblossom's shirt and struck "Jay in the right side, passing through his kidneys." The bandits fleeced the party of their belongings and rode away. Jay Beemblossom was hurried back to Rush Springs where he died later that night. Casey, already wanted for the March 10 murder of a man he shot and robbed along the banks of the Canadian River in the Chickasaw Nation, had gained the full attention of lawmen in both Indian and Oklahoma Territory.[11]

Less than a month after Jay Beemblossom was killed, the Casey gang stole some mules and a buggy from a farm in southern Washita County. Lawmen eventually tracked the outlaws to the Hughes ranch east of Cordell, where brothers Ben and Jim Hughes were known to provide a haven for men dodging the law. The posse arrested Casey, but as they rode away with their prisoner toward Cloud Chief, they met a hail of bullets from an ambush set by five men. Amid the gunfire and the bucking of startled horses, Casey was hit in the shoulder but managed to escape, as the posse took cover to fight off their attackers. In the months that followed, the bandit outfit held up several country stores and trading posts in Washita County, where witnesses positively identified two of the robbers as Bert Casey and cohort Ben Cravens.

On New Years Day 1902, Bill Fossett, then chief deputy U.S. marshal, and Washita County Sheriff John Miller led another raid on the Hughes ranch hoping to capture Casey, but they came up empty handed.[12] Simultaneous to Bill's raid at the Hughes ranch, Washita County deputies rounded up Casey gang members Levi Reed and Jim Simms, south of Cordell. Reed had escaped the federal jail the previous summer and was turned over to Bill and his posse, who hauled him back to Guthrie.[13] Jim Simms, who was taken to jail at Watonga, Blaine County, where he previously served time for horse theft, broke out of jail on January 5, and fled to rejoin the Casey outfit.[14]

No one was more interested in the capture of Levi Reed than Dr. Zeno Beemblsoom. Following his son's murder, he gave up his medical practice and devoted his life to tracking down the killers. On the morning of January 3, 1902, he read newspaper accounts of Reed's recent capture and immediately took the train to Guthrie. Arriving at the federal jail, Beemblossom asked if he could take a look at Reed and, perhaps, identify his son's killer.

Bill was well acquainted with the doctor, their paths crossing many times during the preceding five months as both sought the Casey gang. After a brief discussion, Bill and jailer J. L. McCracken directed Beemblossom to be seated near a stove in the corridor while a guard brought Reed from his cell. The guard told Reed he was being taken to the bathroom and upon leaving his cell, the *Oklahoma State Capital* reported that, "when his gaze fell on the man sitting near the stove, the prisoner gave a quick start, his face blanched and his lips turned blue."

The men's eyes met, and Beemblossom jumped to his feet blurting out, "You---!" as he grabbed for his revolver. Bill and McCracken expected as much, and they "were on him in an instant," forcing Beemblossom into the jail office, while Reed was returned to his cell. When his rage passed, Beemblossom became "so weak that he had to be assisted to the street by officers." According to newspaper reports,

Beemblossom identified Reed as the man who killed his son"[15]

Twelve days later, on January 15, 1902, the Casey gang struck again. After hiding out in the Chickasaw Nation, Casey and his cronies rode west into the newly opened region of Caddo County, where they robbed several groups of homesteaders as they plodded along country roads in their wagons. The holdups were reported to Caddo County Sheriff Frank Smith, who got on the gang's trail.

Smith and two deputies finally caught up with the outlaws at an old Indian hut west of Anadarko on January 15. The officers swung from their horses and crept toward the hut hoping for surprise, but Casey's gang opened up with rifles. Sheriff Smith was immediately felled by a bullet to the chest, and deputy George Beck was hit in the arm. From the open ground in front of the hut, Beck struggled to return a few shots, but the outlaws' overwhelming firepower finished him. A third officer retreated to Anadarko for help, and when Casey emerged from the hut, he came up to Smith, "kicked the dying officer in the face and stood on his hands while robbing him."[16] The Casey gang then fled the bloody scene to become the most wanted bad men in the Twin Territories of Indian and Oklahoma Country.

The day following the shooting, Bill took horses and a pack of prized bloodhounds from Kingfisher and with fellow lawmen, boarded a Rock Island train heading south toward Caddo County, but they were unable to pick up Casey's trail.[17]

Rewards for the Casey gang reached nine thousand dollars during the spring and early summer of 1902. By then, no less than thirteen men who, at one time or another, had been members of the Casey gang were behind bars, but Casey, along with Ben Cravens, Jim Simms and an unknown number of others were still at large. A continuing rash of holdups and Casey "sightings" made it clear the young outlaw had not given up his hit and run robbery sprees. On June 30, Roger Mills County Sheriff Jack Bullard and deputy John Cogburn were checking out a suspicious number of livestock and saddles at a campsite along Dead Indian Creek, when shooting broke out. Area homesteaders, who heard the firing, arrived to find the two lawmen dead. Sheriff Bullard had been hit numerous times, and Cogburn had a single, mortal wound to his back. The murders were ascribed to the Casey outfit.[18]

In the summer of 1902, lawmen came under increasing pressure to capture, or otherwise do away with, the brutal Bert Casey. To accomplish this task, two nearly identical but independent plans were hatched. Bill Fossett, who by that time was U.S. Marshal, instituted one of them. He would release two, carefully chosen federal prisoners, former Casey gang members, who would rejoin Casey and attempt to capture him.

A comparable scheme was devised by a group of county lawmen headed by Caddo County Sheriff Jim Thompson, a cousin of ex-U.S. Marshal Canada H. Thompson. Jim Thompson had succeeded Sheriff Frank Smith, who was slain by Casey earlier in the year. The sheriffs' plan was to use a "spotter," or undercover officer, to locate Casey, setting him up for capture. Neither Bill nor the sheriffs were aware of each other's plan.[19]

Sometime in late August, Bill and Deputy U.S. Marshal J. L. McCracken, the federal jailer, decided that Fred "Wes" Hudson, who had once run with Casey and was being held for post office robbery, would be the likely candidate for their scheme. Hudson accepted the proposal to get Bert Casey "dead or alive," on condition that charges against him be dropped, that he be deputized as a deputy U.S. marshal, and that he receive all rewards for Casey's capture. Hudson also wanted another man to go with him and selected whiskey peddler F. M. "Ed" Lockett as his accomplice.

Bill consented to the deal and after further discussion, it was anticipated that the ruse could be accomplished in about a month. Thus, with only a promise that they would return with Casey, Bill deputized and armed Hudson and Lockett, then sent them on their way.[20]

The two men soon fell in with the Casey outfit, and in the days that followed, the gang continued its usual run of criminal activity in Washita and Caddo Counties and the western fringes of Indian Territory.

A month following the start of Hudson and Lockett's mission, the county sheriffs' group settled on their one man "spy" in Luther "Lute" Houston, who was reportedly recruited for the job by Indian Territory Deputy Marshal Chris Madsen. Houston was the former brother-in-law of Jim Hughes of the infamous Hughes ranch, where Casey and other outlaws often sought refuge. Hughes had been married to Lute's sister, Mattie, and although they were divorced, Jim and Lute apparently still got along. The coincidental intricacy of relationships by those involved in the plan, Bill later noted, included the fact that the Hughes brothers were related to Bob Hughes, the outlaw killed in the attempted train robbery at Pond Creek in 1894. Another intriguing association was that Jim Bourland, also one of the Pond Creek train robbers who had since served time and gone "straight," was, by then, a deputy to Caddo County Sheriff Jim Thompson, an organizer of the plan to send a "spy" to watch for Casey.[21]

While lawmen anxiously awaited word from their respective undercover agents, Lute Houston kept an eye out for the gang to show at the Hughes ranch, and Hudson and Lockett dutifully rode the outlaw trail with Casey.

As September and most of October slipped by, Bill probably had second thoughts about releasing federal inmates on such a dubious mission. Even so, all was going as planned until sometime in mid-October, when a Hughes informant discovered that Lute Houston was about to send a telegram to Deputy Marshal Chris Madsen.[22]

Jim Hughes promptly and cruelly took care of the problem. Hudson later testified that he heard Jim Hughes and Bert Casey discuss the fact that Houston was a spy. He further related that he reluctantly watched one dark night as Casey and Jim Hughes took Houston "down the bank of a creek and hung him."[23]

When Deputy Marshal Houston's body was finally discovered on October 29, it remained unidentified for several days. Madsen, who recruited Houston, along with the sheriffs who deployed him, did not know until several days later that they had lost their "spy." Bill, meanwhile, was still unaware of Houston's activities.[24]

By this time, several of Casey's men had been captured in Caddo County, which whittled down the gang's size, leaving only Casey and Jim Simms, along with Hudson and Lockett. The marshal's two operatives later told authorities they kept out of sight, traveling around the countryside in a spring wagon with "only one of them being in sight, the others being secretly covered in the bottom of the wagon" so as to not arouse suspicion.[25]

With things getting hot in Caddo and Washita County, the gang made its way toward Woods County, where Casey decided to rob a bank. The target was in the town of Cleo, and once near the area, Casey sent Hudson and Lockett to look it over. The two men rode into town, walked around awhile, got a shave and returned to camp.

Hudson then apparently decided on a showdown with Casey before the bank robbery. That night, Hudson called Lockett aside and explained his plan:

> We can't afford to go into this holdup, as someone is going to get killed. So in the morning when we are

warming up our guns, you sit down in front of Simms and I'll sit down in front of Casey. You keep your eye on me and when I nod, I'm going to make Casey throw up his hands or I'm going to kill him, and I want you to take care of Simms.[26]

They proposed to take the action following breakfast. Hudson and Lockett planned to finish eating first, then begin "warming their guns over the fire." Said Fossett:

It was a habit of outlaws, as well as a good many other people, to examine their guns the first thing of a morning—to warm them up, they used to say.[27]

According to plan, Hudson and Lockett ate first, sat at the fire, got out their guns and "began to twirl them around and limber up," while Casey and Simms sat eating with their guns holstered. Suddenly, Hudson looked at Lockett and nodded.

"Put up your hands, Bert!" demanded Hudson.

Casey, normally no man's fool, did a foolish thing. He reached for his revolver. Without hesitation, Hudson fired and Casey rolled over, squeezing off a shot that went wild. Lockett, meanwhile, the "weak sister" of the two, lost his nerve, and after shooting Casey, Hudson turned and fired at Simms as the outlaw fumbled with the gun's hammer that had failed to fall. Hudson then turned back toward Casey, who was still alive and struggling to bring his weapon back up. He quickly thumbed two more shots into Casey, and it was over.

A farmer, out early and looking for cattle, witnessed the brief gunfight. Hudson and Lockett asked him to go to Cleo and bring local officers to the scene. Within a short time, the "entire neighborhood had assembled at the place," and word of Bert Casey's death "spread like wild fire."[28]

Bill received the news in a telegram delivered to his office in Guthrie about noon, November 3, 1902. He and jailer McCracken set out by wagon for Cleo to pick up the outlaws' bodies. They returned four days later, Fred Hudson and Ed Lockett accompanying them with Casey's body. Simms' remains had been turned over to authorities in Watonga.

Bill was ecstatic and obviously relieved, not only at getting Bert Casey, but with the success of the uncertain plan that accomplished it:

> The greatest nerve ever displayed and certainly the most that I have ever heard of was that of the four men, in hand to hand fight over the campfire, between the two deputy marshals, Lockett and Hudson, and the two outlaws.[29]

If, by then, Bill was aware of the brutal death of Lute Houston, whose body was discovered only five days earlier, he did not mention it.

In accordance with the agreement, all previous charges against Hudson and Lockett were dropped, but as Bill predicted, there were "hard feelings" toward the two men from persons on both sides of the law. The two former "undercover deputies" collected only a small portion of the reward money on Casey. Bill then advised them that it was in everyone's best interest for them "to get out of the country."[30]

Hudson and Lockett headed for Arkansas, where they found plenty of trouble unrelated to the Casey affair. Their short stint as deputy U.S. marshals was not nearly enough to suppress their deeply ingrained outlaw habits.

In 1904, Ed Lockett was shot and killed by the night marshal in Harrison, Arkansas.[31] Meanwhile, Hudson, widely known from earlier times in Arkansas as "Little Wes," killed a deputy marshal during a gunfight in Jasper.[32] That was followed by another slaying when "Wes" shot a bartender in Forsythe, Missouri. Hudson was acquitted in both shootings, but by late December 1905, Oklahoma authorities wanted him for the ongoing Lute Houston death investigation.

A principle investigator of Houston's death was Caddo County Deputy Sheriff Jim Bourland, who had built murder cases against Hudson and the Hughes brothers. On his way to Arkansas to arrest Hudson, Bourland spotted his man at the Perry, Oklahoma, train depot. With the help of a local officer, he arrested Hudson and delivered him to jail in Anadarko. Following a trial in early May 1906, Hudson was acquitted of Houston's death, but was bound over as a prospective witness against the Hughes brothers at Hobart, Kiowa County.[33]

On the evening of May 21, the Hughes brothers were also acquitted, and two nights later, the final chapter in the Fossett – Casey – Hudson – Bourland saga was played out in an Anadarko saloon.

Hudson was in town to celebrate, but Bourland arrested him for carrying a firearm. The pistol was retained by a Justice of the Peace pending Hudson's appearance the following morning.[34]

Bourland, known as "Big Jim" for his size, held positions as both a deputy sheriff and a deputy U.S. marshal. Years later, Bill said that he sensed there might be trouble between the two men. Even though Bill had recommended that Sheriff Jim Thompson hire Bourland as a deputy, and:

> ...although Borland [sic: Bourland] had assured Sheriff Thompson that he bore me no ill will as a result of my part in the Round Pond [Pond Creek] holdup, I am satisfied that it was on my account that he was persecuting this Hudson boy....[35]

In the early hours of May 23, Bourland learned that Hudson, who appeared to be armed, was drinking in the Robinson Saloon. "Big Jim," still "hopping mad" about Hudson's acquittal, pushed through the bat wing doors in search of his adversary.

The two men spotted each other at the same time and, without speaking, each went for his gun. As saloon patrons scattered for cover, "Little Wes" triggered the first shot from his light-caliber .32 revolver, the tiny slug hitting "Big Jim" in the midsection. At the same instant, Bourland had his "new .45-caliber automatic handgun" in play, squeezing off four, quick shots. Two shots missed, the other two hit Hudson in each leg.

Both men were down, mortally wounded but still alive when taken to a local hospital. Doctors removed several inches of Bourland's damaged intestine but could not save him. He died a short time later. Hudson, at first, refused to let doctors remove his shattered right leg.

At one point Hudson inquired, "What did I do to Jim?"

"You killed him," someone said.

Hudson died several hours later, doctors reporting he expressed satisfaction at having outlived Bourland.[36]

At the turn of 1903, Bill approached his first year anniversary on the job in the top marshal's position, an occasion met with great satisfaction by the recent elimination of the Casey gang.

Fossett's daughter and son-in-law, Mamie and Richard Miller, moved from Chickasha to Guthrie about this time, and when Chief Deputy Marshal C. B. Hunt resigned on February 1, a staff position opened up. Hunt, who moved to Perry to "engage in business," was replaced as chief deputy by Office Deputy Don Willits, and Willits was replaced by Richard Miller.[37] Miller apparently had no prior experience as a lawman, but it likely was not required in an administrative position. It was also common practice in the nineteenth Century hey-day of the "spoils system," to hire friends and family for certain jobs.

During Bill's term as marshal, an average of only twelve to sixteen field deputies served Oklahoma Territory from the headquarters' office at Guthrie. This was a far cry from the earlier days of Marshal E. D. Nix, when 150 deputies were on the job, each of whom could have two of their own possemen. The smaller staff apparently resulted in the overlapping of some duties. Several office reports and newspaper items show "Deputy Marshal R. H. Miller" transporting prisoners back and forth between territorial jails.[38]

Deputy marshals still worked under a pay system of fees and expenses during this period but it had been finely tuned to include maximums and daily allowances. Bill could remember the time when unscrupulous deputies, some working both sides of the law, used the old system to obtain higher fees by abusing poor homesteaders:

> One of the most frequent, most lucrative and most dastardly abuses practiced by them was made possible by a federal law that forbade the cutting of green timber on government land. In those days, the southwestern portion of Oklahoma was covered with dense areas of mesquite. Small cedars filled the deep canyons. For the benefit of those who have not seen mesquite, I might liken it to a discarded, deserted peach orchard, scrubby and useless. Most of the wood is underground. It makes good firewood, but that is about all. Some of the cedars were large enough for the manufacture of fence posts.
>
> The poor settlers, reduced to extremity by the severity of unplowed wilderness, would cut and haul a load of posts a hundred miles, perhaps to earn the wherewithal to

buy a few meager grocery supplies and thus feed their starving families.

It became a favorite means of graft among those "brave" deputy marshals of that undesirable type I have described to swoop down upon some miserable homesteader, hauling a load of ill-shaped fence posts or firewood to market, arrest him, take him before a United States commissioner and have him bound over to the next term of court.

The nearest commissioner was in Wichita, from 300 to 400 miles distant; while the federal court, presided over by the famous hanging jurist-Judge Parker, was at Fort Smith, Arkansas. Each mile that homesteader traveled to commissioner or court, often driving his own skinny team and paying his own subsistence, added to the deputy's fee.

The commissioner would charge his fees to the government; the deputy would charge his arrest fee, his mileage fee, transportation for himself and prisoners, subsistence, and sometimes the routine fees for guards to keep the "outlaw farmer" from escaping. There have been well-authenticated instances when a deputy had run his account to $700 or $800 in a few days' time by gathering 40 to 50 homesteaders, and with very little expense.[39]

Even after 1900, federal law prohibited the cutting of mesquite in Oklahoma. This law was so repugnant to Bill that he reached an understanding with the Department of Justice. He explained "that mesquite was detrimental to the land and thus won leniency in the attitude of the department." As marshal, he never allowed the arrest of homesteaders for such an injudicious regulation, a fact he was always proud of.[40]

Bill approached administrative affairs just as sensibly. If for no other reason, the sloppy, and sometimes fraudulent, management of expenditures by prior marshals gave him cause to handle official matters with exacting authority. Under his tenure, there were no disbursements without receipts and proper documentation, whether from witnesses, jurors, or his own deputies. He also made sure deputies kept travel claims to a minimum. In one letter, he told a Ponca City field deputy:

> Enclosed herewith, signed grand jury subpoena No. 7012 for service for the Pawnee Court which convenes on the 24th day of November, 1902. If you find that any of these witnesses are nearer some other deputy and can be more expeditiously served by him, please return it to this office with a memorandum showing where the witness can be found.[41]

The attention to detail paid off when a federal auditor's report found the marshal's office at Guthrie "one of the three best conditioned in the United States."

> Such a report speaks volumes for Oklahoma and Mr. Fossett as well. The fact should be taken into consideration too, that this was the first examination of the Oklahoma office in two years, yet in all this time the books were correct in detail, and all conditions were found good by the inspector.[42]

The Federal jail at Guthrie.

12

MANHUNT FOR THE MURDEROUS MARTINS

Bill and his field deputies spent the spring of 1903 in pursuit of three men whose crime spree had escalated from extortion, to robbery and finally, murder. The Martin brothers, Will and Sam, along with sidekick Clarence Simmons, grew up near the Logan County community of Mulhall. By 1902, the marauding three-man gang was wanted for several store and post office robberies in western Oklahoma and parts of Kansas and Colorado.[1]

No one knew it at the time, but in early 1903 the gang returned to its home territory in Oklahoma to begin a new wave of criminal activity. In the early morning hours of March 3, they entered the Rock Island train depot at Hennessey after the late-running southbound train departed. The bandits strong-armed several passengers, bound and gagged the night station operator and went to work on the safe with "an ax and other tools."[2]

Their work was interrupted when a young man named Gus Cravett walked into the depot:

> He had borrowed a lantern at the station and was taking it back, not knowing the robbers were in the city. They ordered him to halt, but he thought the order came from the railway men and that they were just joshing him....[3]

Cravett kept walking, and when within "a foot and a half of the track," one of the robbers, stationed as a lookout, fired his .30-40 caliber Winchester rifle. Cravett collapsed with a scream, dying "almost instantly."[4] The gunshot "awakened several nearby residents" and brought the town's night watchman running with his pistol in hand. After taking a few shots at local citizens and the watchman, the trio mounted horses and fled west in the direction of Lacey.

The following day, Bill, along with deputies J. L. McCracken and George Foster, joined the pursuit already taken up by Deputy U.S. Marshal Bill Holt and local officers. On the ground near the Hennessey depot, Bill found some "long copper shells" from a high-powered rifle.

Over the next two days, the hot chase doubled back to Crescent and Mulhall, the outlaws stealing several horses, mules and buggies along the way. Bill and his men finally "overtook the robbers," and "near Sheridan, a running fight took place." Lawmen closed in, capturing the bandits' horses and a cache of ammunition. Bill noticed the rifle cartridges were .30-40 caliber "Krag." They matched the ones he had found at the depot, apparently fired from a Model 1895 Winchester like the rifle seen carried by one of the bandits. Officers tried to seal off the area that night, but the Martin gang took out on foot, escaping through a ravine that led north.

Just before dawn the next morning, the outlaws came to a house, where they forced a farmer to supply them with a buggy, a team and food, including some freshly "cooked spare ribs." When Bill and his posse picked up the trail ·at sun up, they had an easy job of tracking:

> The officers again got the trail by means of the spare rib bones which the men threw from the buggy, also on account of a wobbly buggy wheel. Later they came upon the buggy broken down and followed the trail after that by means of the track left by one of the men who was wearing a runover heel boot. The chase was kept up all that day, but the officer's teams were worn out and they could not gain on the outlaws.[5]

By March 7, the bandits were on the move west into Woods County. A local posse ran up on them at Isabella, and "for twenty minutes the two parties engaged in a battle of bullets." The Martin outfit escaped again that night, and after stealing more horses, they eventually outdistanced the posse as they meandered toward the Glass Mountains. By that time, some victims of the gang's horse thievery near Mulhall had recognized the bandits as some "home talent boys named Simmons and Martin."[6]

An exasperated Fossett reported:

> They have stolen fifty horses since the Hennessey robbery; fully thirty teams have been tired out by officers— ten teams by myself and my deputies.[7]

Three months later, the Martin gang resurfaced in the Osage reservation. On Sunday, June 14, they waylaid travelers along the Pawhuska-Bartlesville Road, holding their victims captive in a secluded spot beside the road, while waiting for new prey to come along. In a period of five hours, the Martins robbed over one hundred travelers, relieving them of valuables and livestock, before releasing their captives and riding away.[8]

The gang rode west during the next two weeks, robbing a store in Woods County on July 2. Four days later, someone sighted them near Geary, in Blaine County. On the morning of July 8, the body of Geary City Marshal John Cross was discovered near a smoldering campfire not far from town. He apparently had been shot from his horse while checking the campsite. The marshal's badge and watch were missing.[9]

The *Guthrie Daily Leader* exaggerated the event as a "running gunfight," adding:

> A strong posse of the Sheriff and deputies and United States marshals are in pursuit, with the outlaws attempting to reach the Wichita Mountains. They are believed to be the same men who looted the town of Hennessey several months ago.[10]

Bill left Guthrie to join the latest manhunt, but lawmen lost the outlaws' trail nearly a week of searching. No sooner had he returned to Guthrie than word came that a posse was closing in on the gang again near a spot on "Little Beaver Creek," in Comanche County. The report stated they are "believed to be the same men who killed Marshal Cross at Geary last week."[11]

With reward money mounting, more than 200 citizens and officers combed Comanche County in a renewed search, but the Martins eluded lawmen once more, this time by carefully making their way back toward Osage country and what would be their final shootout.

On August 8, Deputy U.S. Marshals Wiley Haines, Warren Bennett and Constable Henry Majors rode out of

Pawhuska to check reports of some armed men, who had made camp a few miles southeast of town. The lawmen found the outlaws' camp hidden behind a knoll, surrounded by deep ravines near Bird Creek. They dismounted, spread out, and silently worked their way toward the camp, but there was no surprising the wary Martin brothers and Clarence Simmons. When one of the outlaws' horses snorted, the bandits grabbed their rifles and began shooting.

The officers, caught almost entirely without cover, charged the camp, firing as they moved forward. Two shots from Wiley Haines killed Will Martin. Sam was also hit and mortally wounded but still alive when subdued by Bennett after a brief struggle. Only Clarence Simmons made it to his horse and escaped. Deputy Haines had also received a severe bullet wound in the fight and along with Martin, was carted off to a doctor in Pawhuska. Deputy Haines refused a general anesthetic, and as the doctor pulled bullet fragments from his right shoulder, his left hand pointed a pistol at Sam Martin, who lay wounded, but still alive, on a table nearby.

Haines eventually recovered from his wounds, but Sam Martin died the night following the shootout. Before passing, he confessed to many crimes, including the slaying of Gus Cravett at Hennessey. Sam also boasted of robbing "more people than any gang in history." Among the gang's plunder collected at the shooting scene was a silver watch and badge belonging to Geary City Marshal John Cross.[12]

The bodies of Sam and Will Martin were transported to Guthrie, where Marshal Fossett telegraphed the dead men's father about the disposition of the remains. The belated reply was to "dispose of them according to the law." That prompted the *Oklahoma State Capital* to comment, "They have already been disposed of according to the law ... they will now be disposed of according to custom." The Martins were buried in the potter's field of Guthrie's Summit View Cemetery.[13]

W. D. "BILL" FOSSETT

A week following the shootout near Pawhuska, Warren Bennett notified the U.S. Marshal's office that Haines was recovering well. Bill responded by letter:

> I am proud and the territory should be and no doubt is proud of such officers, and to know that I have not been disappointed, believing that if my deputies got an even show with any band of outlaws they would come out victorious.
>
> I regret very much Wiley Haines being wounded, but thank God, it is no worse . . . Do me a kindness and have everything done for him that can be, and if you can't get proper attention and medical aid where he is, have him brought to Guthrie to my house and taken good care of at my expense.[14]

During Bill's term as U.S. marshal, Guthrie had grown to become quite a sophisticated town for turn-of-the-century standards. By 1903, the "Queen City of Oklahoma Territory" had several streets paved with bricks, along with electricity and running water. Construction of a streetcar system also began that year, and the growing business district included fine restaurants, hotels, an opera house and a library.[15]

Bill's entire immediate family lived in Guthrie during this period. Lew Fossett and his wife Anna operated the bar in the Royal Hotel on Harrison Avenue, while Lew served as a deputy. Son-in-law Richard Miller worked as an office deputy at headquarters on the corner of Harrison and Division Street, he and his family living only a short walk away. Richard and Mamie Miller both occasionally helped Lew and Anna at the hotel bar. During this time, Laura Fossett, who divorced Bill in 1900, continued to live on his homestead farm in Kingfisher.[16]

Even with all his business and personal ties in Guthrie, Bill always considered Kingfisher his home, never losing interest in the town, or passing up an opportunity to visit it. His contributions there date from the town's earliest days, when he graded a public road across his property that connected to Main Street. At the road's crossing of Kingfisher Creek, he built a wooden bridge, which initially was used for easy access to the notorious Sandy Point dance hall. The bridge was later replaced by a more substantial suspension bridge on which cars and wagons could cross. Near the same spot along the creek, a wooded area was designated as a public park that became known as "Fossett's Grove."[17]

In 1901, Bill had joined with several '89ers and local businessmen in purchasing a new buggy and supplies for the president of Kingfisher College. The same group of men later pledged funds toward completion of a new dormitory and the maintenance of buildings.[18]

The Congregational Churches of Oklahoma established Kingfisher College in 1894, and after holding classes in several temporary locations, the campus was moved to a 120-acre parcel just east of downtown in 1897. For several years, a three-story brick building combined to serve as classroom, chapel, kitchen, dining room and dormitory, all in one. Enrollment soon grew to 150 students, complete with athletic teams and a music department.[19] In 1904, Bill donated one thousand dollars to the school, helping to further build an endowment. "A generous subscription," said its president, "in the aid of its work of education."[20]

Bill's love of horses was reason enough to make frequent visits to Kingfisher. He not only raised them on his farm north of town, but also was an avid fan and owner of racehorses since his days as city marshal in Kingman, Kansas. At the Kingfisher County Fair one year, Bill's horse "Grey Eagle" won two events in one day, taking "first place in the gentlemen's driving contest" and the "free-for-all trot" for three-year-olds.[21]

Only one month after the April 22, 1889, land run, wood-framed buildings began rising from the cluster of tents in downtown Guthrie.

In less than ten years from its founding, Guthrie took shape under the dominating architectural style of brick and stone. Here, West Harrison Avenue is bustling with traffic at cotton market time.

Looking east along Harrison Avenue from Division Street.
The Hotel Royal and the Brooks Opera House are on the left.

This suspension bridge across Kingfisher Creek from the town's main street to Fossett's property replaced the original wooden span he built leading to the Sandy Point Dance Hall. The bridge was removed when the creek was rechanneled in the 1930s.

While he was U.S. marshal, Bill also kept some of his best stock in Guthrie. One newspaper commented that "in his stables here are some of the finest gaited and blooded animals in Oklahoma." He later presented President Roosevelt with one of his thoroughbred mounts, along with an expensive saddle.[22]

Always ready for a run, his highly spirited horses sometimes did so at inopportune times. The *Oklahoma State Capital* once reported that "Marshal Fossett experienced an exciting runaway last evening," when a neck yoke slipped from a tongue, as he drove his black team of horses along Springer Avenue:

> The team was in a dead run and the broken tongue struck first one then the other horse at each jump. Finally the pole dropped to the ground.
> The team ran to Vilas Avenue, then west to the precipice made there by the Choctaw [Railway] in excavating a right-of-way. The buggy was broken loose from the team and the horses jumped the fence at the top of the precipice and cleared the entire embankment after one leap, landing safely and without bruises thirty-feet down. With the exception of the buggy there were no damages.[23]

Bill seemingly took such events in stride, just as he did when, at aged fifty-two, he married for the third time. He eloped with sixteen-year-old Jessie Belle Jacobson, the young daughter of Office Deputy J. M. Jacobson. A Probate Judge in Wichita, Kansas, married them on February 3, 1904. The following day, the *Wichita Eagle* teasingly reported, "U.S. Marshal W. D. Fossett was in the city yesterday on some important business."[24] Following a honeymoon in New York and Atlantic City, Bill and Jessie Belle returned to Guthrie and took up housekeeping on East Vilas Avenue.[25]

13

POLITICS AND A PRAIRIE WOLF

The presidential election of 1904 offered the first opportunity for Theodore Roosevelt to win the office in his own right. The assassination of William McKinley in 1901 had automatically placed, then vice president, "Teddy" Roosevelt in the White House as the nation's youngest chief executive.[1]

A short time later, McKinley appointee Canada H. Thompson resigned the Oklahoma Territorial marshal's post early, and Roosevelt selected Fossett for the job. As holders of the nation's oldest law enforcement job, marshals could function independently within their own federal judiciary district, but their presidential appointments lasted only four years at a time.[2] Although Fossett's term was not concurrent with the presidency, it would expire in 1906, and any possibility for reappointment rested with the outcome of the 1904 election, or at least so it seemed.

Republican appointee or not, it was in complete character for Fossett to support Roosevelt. "Carrying a big stick" and offering a "square deal" may not have been Bill's slogans, but they perfectly fit his creed.

The Republican convention was held in Chicago that June, and Bill attended as a delegate. With the announcement that the popular Roosevelt unanimously won the nomination, delegates responded with a deafening ovation. Bill was among those appointed to serve on the special committee that traveled to Washington, formally notifying Roosevelt of his selection. The trip, with his wife Jessie, was followed by a visit to the president's "Sagamore Hill" residence on Oyster Bay, Long Island.[3]

The gregarious, energetic Roosevelt, once described by his daughter as wanting to be "the bride at every wedding and the corpse at every funeral,"[4] could charm, inspire and motivate people. Bill came away from Oyster Bay clearly impressed, saying "the event was the grandest he has witnessed" with speeches by Roosevelt and House Speaker Joseph Cannon "illuminating beyond comparison."[5]

In November, Roosevelt handily won the election over Democrat Alton B. Parker, and within a month of his March 4, 1905, inauguration, he was off to Oklahoma to hunt prairie wolves (coyotes).

As a vigorous outdoorsman, Roosevelt favored game hunting as much as did Fossett a manhunt, and this hunt became pivotal to Bill's career. The site was in the area known as the "Big Pasture," a 480,000-acre parcel reserved for common use by the Comanches and Kiowas, along the Red River.[6] Denton County, Texas, cattle barons Burk Burnett and W. T. Waggoner, who leased "Big Pasture" range from the Indians, organized the hunt, and the two men made sure one of the hunters was John R. Abernathy, a local rancher that Roosevelt had heard about and wanted to see in action.[7]

Abernathy was known as "Catch-'em-alive-Jack," a title earned for his unusual ability to catch wolves alive. He discovered his talent by accident, when a stray wolf attacked two of his dogs. Jack jumped into the middle of the brawl and thrust a gloved hand into the wolf's mouth, luckily far enough back to avoid the canine teeth. Pinning the wolf with his knees, he grabbed both upper and lower jaws with his free hand and then clamped them shut, as he worked his other hand out the side of its mouth. He then wired the jaws shut and bound the wolf's legs. Abernathy turned the unusual feat into a profitable business. For a time, he earned a living on wolf bounties before becoming a successful rancher and deputy sheriff in southwestern Oklahoma.[8]

President Roosevelt arrived in Frederick in early April, and following a grand reception and speechmaking, the hunters drove about twenty miles into the "Big Pasture," to a base camp along Deep Red Creek. The party included several ex-Rough Riders, some cowhands and ranchers, Captain Bill McDonald of the Texas Rangers, Comanche Chief Quanah Parker and, of course, Jack Abernathy.[9]

Governor Thompson B. Ferguson, Fossett and several others from Guthrie, journeyed to Frederick for the welcoming festivities. Bill later paid a visit to the chief executive's hunting camp, but had to overcome a temporary identification problem first. Under the headline, "Bill Showed 'Em," the *Guthrie Daily Leader* reported:

> Hon. William D. Fossett, United States Marshal from Oklahoma, yesterday attempted to enter the "Big Pasture" where President Roosevelt is hunting. The soldiers, not believing his identity, took him into custody. He was taken before the regimental officers later and made himself

known and was permitted to proceed to the camp of the president.[10]

The hunt, or "coursing" as Roosevelt termed it, required several teams of greyhounds to essentially run the prairie wolves to exhaustion so they could be killed or captured alive by the hunters, following on horseback. It sounded simple enough except for the natural hazards as described by Roosevelt:

> The coursing was done on the flats and the great rolling prairies which stretched north from our camp toward the Wichita Mountains and south toward the Red River. There was a certain element of risk in the gallops, because the whole country was one huge prairie-dog town, the prairie-dogs being so numerous that new towns and the abandoned towns were continuous with one another in every direction. Practically every run we had was through these prairie-dog towns . . . the wonderfully quick cow-ponies, brought up in this country and spending all their time among the prairie-dog towns, were able, even while running at headlong speed, to avoid the holes with a cleverness that was simply marvellous [sic].... As always in prairie-dog towns, there were burrowing owls and rattlesnakes. We had to be on our guard that the dogs did not attack the latter.... We usually killed the rattlers with either our quirts or ropes. One which I thus killed was over five feet long.[11]

The president witnessed Abernathy live up to his name. During a chase of several miles, Jack and his dogs caught up with one fatigued wolf and began "heading it," as if cutting a cow from a herd. Roosevelt galloped up in time to see the dogs and wolf scuffling, as "Catch-'em-alive-Jack" leaped from his horse and "sprang on top of the wolf." With "greater rapidity than the wolf's snap," Jack jammed his hand in the wolf's mouth crosswise and then clamped its jaws down.

An amazed and admiring Roosevelt later wrote:

> I was not twenty yards distant at the time, and as I leaped off the horse, he was sitting placidly on the live wolf, his hand between its jaws, the greyhound standing beside him, and his horse standing by as placid as he was.... It was as remarkable a feat of the kind as I have ever seen.[12]

The hunting party seemed equally impressed with the down-to-earth president. One newspaper headlined a story with, "Teddy likes 'chuck' too, eats beef and beans like rest of cowboys."[13]

In late April, Abernathy spent a few days in Guthrie as Bill's guest. It may not have been his intention, but the "wolf catcher" apparently made new friends and, possibly, gained backing for the next marshal's appointment. During the visit he willingly recounted events of the recent hunt and declared the president "one of the finest horseman he ever saw."[14]

Bill, meanwhile, returned to the routine matters of transporting prisoners about the territory. On one trip, he had charge of an entire train carload of prisoners bound for district court in Pawnee. The marshal and eight deputies marched forty-two shackled and chained prisoners down the streets of Guthrie to the Santa Fe depot. According to the *Oklahoma State Capital*:

> It was the largest body of unconvicted prisoners ever moved from one place in the territory.
>
> A special car had to be chartered and it was almost like an excursion. The government paid full fair for each man, however, it is probably that few of them will need a

return ticket. They were arrested in Pawnee County or the Osage Nation.[15]

In June 1905, Lew Fossett resigned as deputy marshal to "devote more attention to his horses which Mr. Fossett will take around a [racing] circuit this summer." Lew not only raced some of his father's stock while growing up but, more recently, raised his own horses at his "country home."[16]

By the late summer, Bill began to sense that his reappointment as U.S. marshal was in doubt. While attending the Garfield County Fair in Enid, as "starter for the races," newspaper reporters besieged him with questions about job prospects when his term expired. He responded that the marshalship was not as important as finding who his friends were:

> The thing I am most interested in is the attitude of my friends. Since coming to Enid I have learned that one man, who in the past I had considered my friend, but whom I had been informed was working against me, was yet steadfast in his friendship. There are other instances of the same nature. These discoveries of true friendship are worth a great deal more to me than the marshalship of Oklahoma. I had rather discover my friends and learn of a certainty of false friends and enemies, than to have the salary attached to my office.[17]

He didn't have to wait long to see where the chips fell. Two months later, newspapers were writing headlines about "Fossett's Fight."

In a classic, factional clash over control of Oklahoma's political power base, Bill received the endorsement of virtually every Republican in the territory except one. Judge John H. Burford, himself a candidate for reappointment as chief justice, refused to back the marshal. The November 23,

1905, *Daily Oklahoman* reported the stumbling block was Bill's friendship with U.S. District Attorney Horace Speed:

> Judge Burford charged Fossett with being disloyal to him and stated that Fossett's closest friend (Horace Speed) was his (Burford's) bitterest enemy.[18]

Even though Speed was a Republican, too, Burford feared reprisal from the powerful Republican faction, headed by Bird S. McGuire, Territorial Representative to the U.S. House of Representatives. McGuire endorsed Burford, as did Republican National Committeeman Cash Cade, who also filed papers for appointment as U.S. Marshal. The *Oklahoman* reported that Burford "feared to indorse [sic] Fossett knowing that Cade is a candidate for Fossett's job." The paper further said:

> Even Burford's friends fear he has made a mistake in turning down Fossett's request for indorsement [sic]. Fossett's wide popularity throughout the territory, his clean administration of affairs, and his standing with the department of justice are too great to be tampered with....[19]

While there were no Republican endorsements for Jack Abernathy to become marshal, he did receive qualified party support for "a position of the president's choosing." Even with that backing, however, no one thought his selection as territorial marshal was possible.

On November 22, 1905, Bill departed Guthrie for Washington on a mission to "see the president and present the matter flat footed to him and ask reappointment solely on my record." The meeting brought no immediate commitment from Roosevelt. Although Bill clearly wanted reappointment, he had always avoided factional fights and did so on this occasion. The *Daily Oklahoman* reported him saying, "that if playing politics means stabbing your friends in the back . . . he prefers to return to private life."[20]

With it looking more like Abernathy was gaining the inside track to the marshal's appointment, party leaders finally decided to act. Frank Frantz, a former Roosevelt Rough Rider and the last Oklahoma Territorial governor, serving from 1906 to 1907, wrote to U.S. Attorney General William H. Moody. Frantz said he wanted a man in the marshal's office who not only had integrity and bravery, but also political knowledge and experience. Abernathy, he said, lacked the latter.

Territorial Representative Bird S. McGuire, who became a U.S. Congressman at statehood, was even more blunt:

> He [Abernathy] is what would be regarded as perhaps a dollar and a quarter or a dollar and a half man as a day laborer.... But the fact that he is a man who on his own resources would be incapable of earning more than this amount of money would suggest, it seems to me, a place of lesser importance than the U.S. marshal's office....[21]

The objections failed to sway Roosevelt, and when, on February 5, Governor Frantz was called to the White House along with Abernathy, the governor backed off his hard line stance against the "wolf catcher" and "warmly recommended him."

The news hit Guthrie with the February 6 edition of the newspapers, "Abernathy is Marshal . . . His name goes to the Senate." The *Oklahoma State Capital* didn't mince words, saying that Roosevelt's admiration for the "courage and skill" of Jack Abernathy's wolf catching outweighed Fossett's "clean record" enough to put Abernathy in the marshal's office.[22]

Bill's term was not up until April, but he took consolation in knowing the speculation was over. He publicly thanked his many supporters and gave best wishes to his successor:

> While I am proud of the record of my office during my four years of incumbency, and fully appreciate the many kind words from officials of the department of justice, and from friends in Oklahoma and elsewhere, I realize that President Roosevelt has a perfect right to name a man of his own choosing for the position, and abide the result with the utmost equanimity, believing this to be the duty of all loyal Republicans.
>
> ... When I leave office on April 1, I shall carry with me the knowledge that I have at all times tried to do my full duty. If I can take with me the continued trust and confidence the people of Oklahoma have heretofore honored me with, I shall be content and satisfied.[23]

Later that year, Congress passed the Oklahoma Enabling Act, providing for the election of 112 delegates from Oklahoma and Indian Territory to write the constitution for the proposed new state.[24] Bill ran as a independent Republican candidate from Guthrie's twenty-fifth district but lost out to machine politics again. The *Guthrie Daily Leader* reported it was "a cold piece of villainy" for Republican candidate Henry Asp to have Fossett's petition "declared defective because signers of the petition failed to give their address in full."[25]

The convention concluded its work in March 1907, and an election followed to ratify the new constitution. On November 16, 1907, a presidential proclamation joined the Twin Territories to make Oklahoma the forty-sixth state.

The effect of statehood placed law enforcement responsibilities with county sheriffs, local police departments and city marshals. Federal marshals began operating under two state jurisdictions, the Eastern District at Muskogee, and the Western District at Guthrie. Each force contained only a handful of deputies, dealing solely with federal laws.[26] With statehood, Jack Abernathy automatically became marshal for the Western District of Oklahoma.

It didn't take long for Abernathy himself to prove that his appointment over Bill Fossett was a big mistake. The U.S. Attorney General returned dozens of his quarterly reports, singling out many discrepancies and asking for his "Immediate Attention." Finally, a federal auditor went to Guthrie. His investigation added charges of adultery, indecent behavior and failure to pay alimony and child support, to the voluminous bookkeeping irregularities already discovered.

In November 1910, the U.S. Attorney General wrote Marshal Abernathy:

> ...I shall be willing to accept your resignation, if you will transmit it promptly: otherwise I shall have to deal in a different manner with the subject.[27]

Two weeks later, the *Guthrie Daily Leader* reported, "Abernathy Gets Huffy and Quits."[28]

14

A LAWMAN ON THE TRAIL AGAIN

After losing his bid to become an Oklahoma Constitutional Convention delegate in the fall of 1906, Bill and wife Jessie moved to Kingfisher. In August 1907, Jessie sued for divorce. The *Daily Oklahoman* reported that "his girl-wife" ended their three and a half year marriage on grounds that he "unnecessarily and without cause absents himself from home for long periods of time leaving her alone and unprotected."[1] It was a familiar, almost predictable, allegation against a highly independent man who relished the freedom to go most anywhere, anytime he well pleased.

Barely two weeks later, Bill received word from Guthrie that Richard Miller, his son-in-law, had died of an apparent heart attack. Mamie's thirty-one-year-old husband was proprietor of Guthrie's White Front Café when he died. Friends had become concerned when Richard failed to open his business on the morning of September 14. They broke into his room at the Osage boarding house and found his body. He had been dead for several hours. Mamie and six-year-old daughter Madaline were visiting relatives in Wichita at the time. Richard Hugo Miller was buried in his hometown of Kingman, Kansas, September 17, 1907.[2]

In early 1908, Bill returned to work as a peace officer, taking the position of city marshal in Waurika, the recently designated county seat of Jefferson County. During the Chisholm Trail days, the hills around Waurika were covered with buffalo grass, and the location became a favorite camping spot for trail herders. The Rock Island Railroad laid out the townsite in 1892, first calling it Monika. A railroad executive later renamed it Waurika, an adaptation of an Indian word meaning pure water.[3]

Between its new county seat status and the expanding Rock Island rail yards, Waurika was thriving in 1908. Its growth brought "hordes of undesirable persons," according to the *Waurika News*, including "tinhorn gamblers and others of their ilk [who] have found good picking here."

The newspaper announced Bill's hiring as city marshal on February 7, 1908, and in so doing, couldn't resist a swipe at Oklahoma's current federal marshal:

> Mr. Fossett was instructed by the Board to clean up the town and run every loafer and grafter out of town.
> …Mr. Fossett, the new marshal, was for a term of four years, the United States Marshal for Oklahoma territory. He filled the office in every sense of the word and would now be holding that position if John Abernathy had not caught a wolf with his hands.[4]

Bill had barely begun his new job when Waurika faced an entirely unexpected crisis. In May and June, record setting rains sent water gushing over the banks of rivers from

Southern Kansas to Northern Texas. In Oklahoma, the Arkansas River at Tulsa, and the Red River along the Texas border, produced epic flooding.

In the upper watersheds of the Red River in Stephens and Jefferson Counties, Beaver and Cow Creeks widened to become one broad, muddy torrent pouring south. Downpours along the Oklahoma-Texas border tributaries caused the Red River to force backwater up the streams. Water ran from two to three feet deep down Waurika's main street, in some areas even deeper.[5]

Fossett, no stranger to floods like the one he experienced in Kingman, Kansas, years before, mounted one of his most powerful horses and "plunged into the water time after time." The quickly rising waters left several people stranded, perched on buildings, barns and in trees. The big marshal, still hale and hearty at aged fifty-six, rode out to each victim, tossed them a looped rope, tied it to his saddle horn, and pulled them through the water to safety. Some people were rescued by "clinging to the horses tail," and others were placed in his saddle, while he paddled along side holding a stirrup as the horse swam and high stepped its way to the nearest shoreline. "There were many times when it was feared he would not return," said Waurika resident M. O. Stetler, "but he brought out many people who were stranded on rooftops and other dangerous places."[6]

Fossett's friend Joe Grimes once remarked that as Bill grew older, he often became homesick for "his hometown of Kingfisher."[7] It may have been the reason he left Waurika after less than a year's stay. By January 1909, Bill journeyed back north to resume a familiar career with the Rock Island Railroad at its Oklahoma Division Headquarters in El Reno. The railroad had first offered him his old job back when he lost the marshal's reappointment in 1906. He passed on it then, but now the idea looked much better to him. A short railroad ride of only twenty-four miles allowed him to visit Kingfisher when he got time away from his El Reno office and his job as "chief of police" for the railroad's Southern District.

The Rock Island's ongoing expansion in creating a divisional headquarters put El Reno on the map. The company built new mechanical shops and repair facilities in the rail yards north of town, as well as new staff offices downtown.[8]

Bill managed a detective force of half a dozen men who traveled in all directions from El Reno. They were described as "veritable terrors to evil-doers," guarding railroad passengers and property all along the district's routes. In the first eleven months of 1909, Bill and his men made 534 arrests "of persons for robbing cars, stealing trunks and grips, and picking pockets." The *El Reno Democrat* reported that twenty-three miscreants received long penitentiary terms, while about 200 served jail sentences.[9]

During a rash of freight thefts that appeared to be the work of railroad employees, Bill rigged alarm clocks and placed them in trunks aboard the freight cars. When the trunk lid was opened, the clock stopped, making it easy to determine the time of pilfering and which employee was on the run at that time. In one instance, he traced freight theft by hiding in a car, enroute from Oklahoma City to Clinton. When the train stopped between stations, crewmembers began throwing off what they wanted, but were caught red-handed when Bill suddenly appeared. He gave them "the scare of their lives" but allowed them to stay on the job, without arrest, out of consideration for their families. Bill said he felt "amply repaid" when his trust was no longer abused.[10]

Some trainmen in Chickasha were not as lucky. A Fossett investigation revealed several employees' houses filled with "loot" taken from baggage cars over a period of several months. Bill "threw the book at them" and all received prison terms.[11] As usual, he gave credit to county and local officers who, "have rendered every assistance in locating and arresting criminals." Said the *El Reno Democrat*, "the Southern Division of the Rock Island is a mighty good place for crooks to shun."[12]

By 1910, Lew and Anna Fossett had moved from Guthrie to Kingfisher. The couple managed the Kingfisher Hotel at the corner of Robberts and Sixth, their names often appearing in local social columns as hosts and participants of card and bridge tournaments. Other Fossetts living in Oklahoma at this time included Bill's nephew, John Fossett ("Frank"), in Enid, and Bill's brother Isaac, and his wife, who resided in Custer County.[13]

Laura Fossett, Bill's second wife, still lived in Kingfisher during this time. As one of the town's earliest settlers she was well known and respected. The Kingfisher newspapers frequently noted her comings and goings, referring to her as "Mrs. Laura Fossett."[14]

In 1912, Lew and Anna Fossett gave up management of the Kingfisher Hotel "to move to California to make their home." Their absence was short-lived. Lew was back in Kingfisher by August 1918, leasing and managing the same hotel. The newspaper story announcing Lew's return also mentioned that "W. D. Fossett" would continue management of the hotel's "Oklahoma Café."[15]

By this time, Bill had retired from the Rock Island. He married twenty-two-year-old Ruby Clifton at Marshall, Texas, in 1917. Law enforcement work beckoned again in 1919, and he was appointed Kingfisher's chief of police. He held the one hundred-dollar per month job for nearly two years, then made an unsuccessful bid to become Kingfisher County Sheriff.[16] A short time later, Ruby, his fourth wife, ran out on him, refusing to return. The couple divorced in December 1921. In a switch from the usual pattern, he sued her for neglect and abandonment.[17]

209

The Kingfisher Hotel at the corner of Sixth and Robberts, circa 1910.

Bill's last days as a lawman came in Oklahoma City during the 1920s. In 1910, the State Capital was relocated there from Guthrie, launching the city's rapid growth. That same year, a twelve-story "skyscraper" known as the "Colcord Building" was constructed downtown. It was built by Charley Colcord, Bill's old friend from his cowboy days who, by then, had become a successful entrepreneur.[18]

Oklahoma City was still growing in 1921, and when its police force was expanded from ninety to nearly 150 officers, Chief of Police Carl Glitsch appointed Bill a special city detective. Later the same year, Alva McDonald, U.S. Marshal for Oklahoma's Western District, hired Bill as a deputy marshal.

"Bill," said McDonald, "admitted he was more than sixty-seven years old . . . but he was still strong, and a darned good shot, and he still made a good officer." In truth, Bill had just turned seventy when he pinned on a deputy U.S. marshal's badge again.[19]

In 1924, Bill rejoined the Oklahoma City Police Department as jailer. He was on duty the night of November 1, when word came that his old friend and fellow lawman, William "Bill" Tilghman, had been shot to death in Cromwell, Oklahoma. Bill asked to be relieved of duty and left the jail.

He later told a reporter that he left work that night so he could "get the man who killed Bill," because it was "cold murder." He apparently drove to Shawnee where Tilghman's killer, a prohibition agent named Wiley Lynn, had already been apprehended and jailed.

The famed Bill Tilghman, about the same age as Fossett, had taken the Cromwell city marshal's job only a few months before. Illegal booze and crooked money flowed freely in the tough little town that sprang to life following the discovery of oil in Seminole County. Tilghman had come out of retirement to help clean it up.[20]

Reasons given for the shooting incident vary. Some accounts claim the two men engaged in a personal feud, others say Lynn had been drinking when Tilghman attempted to arrest him. Lynn claimed self-defense and was acquitted at trial.[21]

The night following Tilghman's death, an *Oklahoma City Times* reporter called on Fossett at his one-room apartment on West Second Street. Bill reminisced about his old friend and their exploits. He recalled they had been together in Dodge City, Kansas, and rode "to Oklahoma together" right before the opening in 1889.[22]

Bill had a strained look on his face as he spoke, but maintained his composure. At one point he momentarily "fumbled with a cameo watch charm," then said:

> Don't let them say he was a gunman, for Bill was a good officer, and he never used a gun when it wasn't necessary. He was murdered in cold blood. I worked with and around him too long not to know.[23]

When the newspaperman left to prepare his story for print in the next day's edition, Bill was by himself to trace the memory of his many years. It must have been an especially lonely night in that small, forlorn apartment in downtown Oklahoma City. It was the eve of Bill Fossett's seventy-third birthday.

15

THE PEACEFUL END TO A ROUGH AND TUMBLE CAREER

In 1925, Bill moved back to Kingfisher to stay. He kept himself busy with his horses and tinkering around his farm, sometimes driving into town to visit friends and have supper. He may have slowed his pace at age seventy-three, but his instincts as a lawman were as sharp as ever.

Walking to his car near the Kingfisher Hotel late one night, Bill was about to make the short drive home when, according to the *Kingfisher Times*, "he saw three Negroes headed west of [sic] the north side of Robberts Avenue." Suspicious of their actions at that late hour, he cut across the street to meet them on the sidewalk. Passing the doorway of "Little Joe's Confectionery," Bill saw someone's shadow inside. He opened the screen door to find a young man crouching down as if to hide.

"The Negro claimed he was sick, but Mr. Fossett," said the *Times*, "recognized this as an old 'gag' and began feeling for a gun on the man, but the Negro beat him to it." At that point, two of the boys on the sidewalk jumped on Bill's "back and began wrestling with him" as he tried to secure the gun.

Two other boys, both wielding "big guns," ran up from behind the store where they were posted as lookouts. Now he was up against six of them, and three pointed guns his way. One of them cautioned, "Turn him loose, we don't want to kill anybody."

At this point the bandits apparently panicked and began to scatter, firing in all directions as they ran. One of the bungling candy store bandits shot a fellow robber in the leg, and another round whizzed by Bill's head, barely missing him.

Standing on the sidewalk, Bill soon heard a car start and drive away down the alley. "'Old Bill' Fossett," said the *Kingfisher Times*, "prevented the robbery of Little Joe's Confectionery doing so at considerable risk to himself."[1]

A few days after his seventy-fifth birthday, Bill married seventy-year-old Mary Ball, his fifth wife. Mary was the widow of M. A. Ball, who had purchased his livery business many years before:

> Mary M. Ball and Bill Fossett, both old residents of Kingfisher, were married in El Reno last Saturday evening by the county judge. They are making their home on the Fossett property just north of town. Both are well and favorably known in this vicinity through long residence here, and *The Times* wishes them much happiness.[2]

The couple had only two years together. Mary M. Ball Fossett passed away in August 1928.[3]

As the years slipped by, Bill and his pioneer contemporaries were fast becoming the patriarch members in the exclusive, and ever diminishing, "club" of Kingfisher

'89ers. Then somewhat bent and battle scarred, with receding white hair combed straight back, he enjoyed sharing his experiences with the Rotary Club and other service groups that sometimes held special '89er programs.

Bill, town druggist C. P. "Doc" Wickmiller, undertaker Arthur Bracken and other old-timers regaled in the reminiscing. At those meetings, attended by many who were far too young to remember, Bill spoke of the buffalo herds that disappeared from the Oklahoma plains within a year of his arrival in 1873. He recalled cowmen and cattle trails, "race day" at Kingfisher, the experiences of staking and holding his claim, and the building of the town he dearly loved.

People "had a pretty tough time back then and many left," Bill told listeners at one meeting, but "the fellow who didn't get a chance to sell his land was eventually the lucky man."[4]

"Doc" Wickmiller, Kingfisher's first pharmacist, who had made the "run" with a "hatful of pills" as his drugstore inventory, agreed:

> I am glad that the hard days are over, that the younger generation does not have that trouble starting. I am glad the tent drugstore is no more, also that I am still in Oklahoma and hope to be with you when this will be one of the grandest states in the union.[5]

The pride, perspective and example of men like these made it small wonder that the Oklahoma Historical Society was first established in Kingfisher in 1893.[6]

The Cherokee Strip Cow Punchers Association had an even more exclusive membership than the '89ers. It was made up of men who rode the Chisholm and other cattle trails prior to opening the Cherokee Outlet for settlement in 1893. Organized in 1920, the old cowmen met each September at

"Cowboy Hill" on the Miller Brothers' famed "101 Ranch" at Bliss (now Marland), Oklahoma. Bill and Lew Fossett numbered among the 650 qualifying, original members, and they both attended the annual meeting in 1928, the last time for each of them.[7]

In 1933, when the Oklahoma State Highway Commission set out to accurately map and mark the Chisholm Trail, Bill wrote a detailed, almost mile-for-mile description of the route from the Red River to Caldwell, Kansas. How the Highway Commission used the information is not known, suffice to say his recollection perfectly matched the way the famous trail is officially mapped.[8]

One of Bill's proudest moments came in 1934 as the surprised guest of honor during the convention of the Sheriffs' and Peace Officers' Association of Oklahoma at Guthrie. In April 1939, the Oklahoma City Chamber of Commerce honored him with a reception and banquet. Elmer Solomon, then postmaster of Kingfisher, said he "never saw an old man more pleased than was Bill Fossett...."[9]

That same month, on April 22, Kingfisher celebrated its Golden Anniversary of the 1889 Land Run. Decked out in a three-piece suit and a light-colored Stetson, it was one of Bill's happiest days. "Uncle Bill," as he was affectionately known, renewed "old friendships with pioneer people whom he had not seen in many years."[10]

Victor Murdock and David Leahy, both newspapermen and Bill's old friends, came down from Wichita for the celebration. Fossett and Leahy had known each other since the early days in Caldwell, where Leahy's first job was as a grocery clerk. Dave said he used to sleep in the store, making his bed in the front window. So wild was Caldwell in the late 70s, said Leahy, that once when he "woke up in the morning and looked out, there were three dead men lying in the street and on the sidewalk."[11]

Bill Fossett, circa 1939.

Murdock and Leahy also visited ex-lawman Chris Madsen, then retired and living in Guthrie. Murdock, editor-in-chief of the *Wichita Eagle*, wrote of his visit with the two aging peace officers:

> Be ye born to die in bed, bullets in their deadly course will bend around you. Lethal lead will never lay you low.
>
> In the whole history of Oklahoma, more hot metal streamed by these two men without touching them than shot along-side any mortals in this region.[12]

The statement rang true for Bill Fossett in less than a year. On March 9, 1940, he died at the home of friends in Kingfisher.

Following a funeral at St. Peter and Paul's Catholic Church, he was buried in the Kingfisher City Cemetery, just west of the city limits. The unmarked grave lies only a few feet from the spot where, fifty-one years earlier, Bill and hundreds of others made the run from Kingfisher Creek to establish the town.[13]

Anything but an affair of state, Bill's funeral and burial services were as uncontrived as he was. Doubtlessly, he would have been pleased. In eighty-eight years, his life had crossed paths with all sorts of people, leaving all sorts of memories to be shared that day. Some old-timers spoke of his abilities, and among the most dazzling was his legendary marksmanship.

Once, while transporting some prisoners through Custer County, he killed a wolf with a 300-yard rifle shot. "The prisoners," it had been reported, "were almost afraid to breathe after witnessing such marksmanship."[14]

Another time, he rode across the prairie toward Pawnee with two "well-known desperadoes," each man on horseback, Bill trailing behind. To make sure they didn't spur their horses and run off, he watched for an opportunity to make an impression. When a "jack rabbit jumped up some distance off and too far for an ordinary shot," Bill said, "Watch me halt that old boy." He raised his rifle, squeezed the trigger, and the rabbit "tumbled forward, dead." His prisoners rode on peaceably to Pawnee and jail.[15]

Bill's last federal boss, Alva McDonald, U.S. Marshal for the Western District of Oklahoma, for whom Bill served as a deputy at age seventy recalled:

> ...He was the best shot with a rifle or pistol in the history of Oklahoma.
>
> Why that man could shoot a bird out of the sky with a rifle and he could snap a barbed wire fence with a pistol, shooting from a speeding automobile.[16]

This was one way people thought of Bill Fossett, but not the only way.

Elmer Solomon was a youngster in the 1890s, when Bill served as a railroad detective and chief deputy U.S. marshal. He remembered that he and other boys would run to meet the towering lawman as he rode back into town "carrying only his satchel and ivory-handled Colt" after a long trip chasing outlaws.

"The youth of the community," Solomon remembered, knew the marshal as "a most fearless sort of man." He seemed "almost unapproachable, but really had a kind heart, liked people and wanted them to like him."[17]

Joe Grimes, Bill's long-time friend, added:

> If Bill Fossett had an enemy it was someone who did not know him. Even the prisoners in the federal jail in Guthrie, many of whom Bill had run down and put behind bars, all respected him and called him Uncle Bill.
>
> To Bill, Kingfisher was always home. Last fall when I was sick he made me a visit. He held my hand and

219

cried like a child. He said, 'Joe, I'm so sorry to see you sick. I'm coming back to see you. I would stay longer but I'm homesick to get back to my old hometown Kingfisher.'

Bill could have reached the top of the ladder financially had he not had such a big heart—he was too liberal for his own good.[18]

As a peace officer serving the law in a tough country for the better part of four decades, Bill's career and life may have best been summed up by the *Oklahoma State Register*, when, in 1906, it was written of him upon leaving the U.S. Marshal's office:

> Fossett is a Western man strong in his friendships, generous to a fault and loyal to his obligations. He had been known on the borders of Kansas and Oklahoma for thirty years, and his oldest friends are his best—they swear by him. You can hear a thousand things about "Bill" Fossett, but you never have to go around to find out where he is in relation to his duty or friendships.[19]

EPILOGUE

In 1907, when Mamie Fossett Miller's husband Richard was buried in Kingman, Kansas, the *Kingman Leader-Courier* reported those attending included his wife and "Mrs. W. D. Fossett." Since Bill Fossett was sued for divorce by his third wife, Jessie, only two weeks before, the "Mrs. Fossett" referenced was probably Laura Kelso Fossett, Bill's second wife. It appears that Laura raised Bill's children, Lewis and Mamie, from the time they were about twelve and seven years of age respectively, but they may have spent a great deal of time with Elizabeth, too. Laura divorced Bill in 1900, but continued living in Kingfisher until about 1913, when she moved to Enid. She died in Oklahoma Western Hospital at Ft. Supply in 1950.[1]

Elizabeth Footman Fossett, Bill's first wife and the mother of Lewis and Mamie, essentially disappeared without a trace after their divorce in 1885. Elizabeth may have moved to Pueblo, Colorado, where her mother and brothers lived, but the absence of any known vital records for her, leaves her whereabouts after 1885 a matter of speculation. There is inconclusive census data indicating she may have lived in the Tulsa, Oklahoma, area during the 1920s.

W. D. "BILL" FOSSETT

After Lewis "Lew" Fossett moved back to Kingfisher from California in 1918, census records made no mention of his wife, Anna, listing him as "living alone." Following a brief period managing the Kingfisher Hotel, Lew worked for the Rock Island Railroad a couple of years, and in the mid-1920s he moved to Tulsa to work as a letter carrier for the U.S. Post Office. He had been retired only a couple of years when, on September 6, 1952, he died of tuberculosis at the Eastern Oklahoma State Sanatorium at Talihina, in Latimer County.[2]

The eventual fate of Mamie Fossett Miller remains a mystery to this day.

Mamie's daughter Madaline, Bill's only grandchild, was six-years-old when her father, Richard Miller, died in 1907. Madaline was taken to Kingman, Kansas, where she was raised by her Aunt Minnie Miller, a no-nonsense Kingman businesswoman, and her grandparents, Peter and Louisa Miller. The Fossett side of the family was never discussed.

At age twenty, Madaline married Fredrick W. "Fritz" Klaver on June 4, 1921. They spent their entire married life together on the Klaver homestead north of Belmont, Kingman County. A short time following their marriage, Mamie paid them a brief visit. She appeared to be ill. She soon left, never to be seen or heard from again by her only child. When Bill Fossett died in 1940, his obituary included a cryptic reference that, "according to reports, Mamie Fossett died many years ago." Following her grandfather's death, Madaline received a letter from Charles Fossett, one of Bill's nephews. He told her that Mamie was also deceased "and had never been quite right" after Richard died.

Like an hourglass, Bill's line of the Fossett family had tapered to the mere, thin stem of his only grandchild, Madaline Miller Klaver, but not for long. The Klavers had four children: Betty, Fredrick, Jr., Eugene, and Alice. Three of these children have families of their own, giving Madaline eleven grandchildren: Sherry Fieser Goemmer, Connie Fieser Albano, Kenton Fieser, Beth Fieser Rohling, Deborah Klaver Durr, Billy G. Klaver, Michael D. Klaver, Suzanne Meilert Fields, Stephanie Meilert Holder, Cary Meilert and Samantha Newcomb. These grandchildren gave Madaline twelve great, grandchildren and two great, great grandchildren. Most members of this close-knit family still live in Kingman County.

Madaline Miller Klaver taught school for thirty-three years before retiring in 1971. She then returned to work as a substitute teacher until she was 79. Always feisty, independent and energetic, she was still playing golf at age seventy-five, when she made a hole-in-one. A few years later she received a speeding ticket for going 82-mph in a 55-mph zone. With a "sheepish grin," eighty-year-old Madaline told the officer that

Madaline Miller Klaver

"since she was eighty, she thought she should be able to drive 80-mph." Madaline lived to be just over 101-years-old, passing from life in Norwich, Kansas, June 6, 2002.[3]

Madaline never knew her parents well, but she did have sketchy, yet fond, memories of her grandfather Bill. She remembers him as "big, and kind, and good to her." She once told a story of crawling on a bed with dirty feet and then sitting on top of the headboard. When Bill entered the room, "he just burst out laughing." Family members report that years later, when Madaline was in her teens, Bill made a couple of

223

visits to Kingman, once presenting her the gift of a white horse.

A month before Madaline's death her granddaughter, Deborah Klaver Durr, who provided extensive family information herein, related:

> It is sad what was lost between them. My grandmother is a very generous, giving person, who would give a stranger anything she had. Much like Bill Fossett was described.
>
> I would have to say now that our family made up for the loss my Grandma bore. Her children and grandchildren are very close. I think Bill Fossett would be proud of the brood he helped father.[4]

Altogether, Bill Fossett and his eight siblings produced twenty-two children and scores of grandchildren.

During the last 100 years, the descendants of the pioneer family begun by immigrants John and Susannah Carrigan Fossett have scattered far and wide. Their many occupations and professions have included cow punching, saddle making, farming, ranching, prospecting, railroading, medicine, manufacturing, funeral directing, homemaking, preaching and teaching. There are engineers, geologists, accountants, mission workers, elected officials, a variety of technicians, and dozens of sales, business and management people.[5]

In 1977, when Anna Leah Fossett Goodrich, Bill Fossett's great-niece, began compiling the family genealogy, she expressed concern that the Fossett name and its descendants might "die out entirely."[6]

She needn't have worried.

Notes, Comments and Variants

Chapter 1
The Westward Movement

[1] Albert Richards, "History of Sumner County," *Historical Atlas of Sumner County*, Philadelphia, 1883, p. 7. In July 1870 an act of Congress called for removal of the "Great and Little Osage Indians" from their former reservation in southern Kansas, to a reservation in the Cherokee Outlet of Indian Territory, opening the way for white settlement to begin (Indian Affairs: Laws and Treaties, Vol. I, Laws, U.S. Government Printing Office, Washington, D.C., 1904).
[2] Ibid.; The Homestead Act, 37th Congressional Session II, 1862, Chapter LXXV.
[3] Edward Everett Dale, *Cow Country*, University of Oklahoma Press, Norman, 1942, pp. 8-9.
[4] A reference originating with Major Stephen Long's Expedition of 1819 to the plains' states between the Missouri River and the western mountains.
[5] Edward Everett Dale, *Cow Country*, op. cit., pp. 1-5, 41.
[6] William G. Cutler, *History of the State of Kansas*, A.T. Andreas, Chicago, 1883, p. 1494; W.D. Fossett, interview, Indian-Pioneer History Project for Oklahoma, Works Progress Administration, Aug. 11, 18, 1937, p. 1.
[7] Albert Richards, "History of Sumner County," loc. cit.
[8] The phrase was first used by Indiana newspaperman John Soule and later popularized by New York Tribune editor Horace Greeley.

[9] Mrs. C.E. Goodrich (Anna Leah Fossett), "The Fossetts in America," genealogy, 1974, pp. 1-3. William Fossett stated his birth year as 1851 during his Pioneer History Project interview of 1937. Some second-hand references cite the year as 1852.

[10] Ibid.

[11] Ibid.; General Pension Index, 1861-1934, Roll 312, Document 18, Deposition C by Isaac H. Fossett, September 26, 1900. Winnebago, Minnesota, no longer uses the word "City" in its name.

[12] Minnesota Historical Society, Timepieces, The Dakota Conflict, 2001; Light & Shadow of a Long Episcopate, the Reminisces and Recollections of the Right Reverend Henry B. Whipple, Bishop of Minnesota, 1902.

[13] Burt V. Manigold & Joseph Rosenberger, "Last of the Gunfighters," *Golden West Magazine*, May 1968, pp. 11-12. Burt V. Manigold was Bill Fossett's great-nephew. A few years before his great-uncle died, Manigold began collecting notes for a planned publication on Fossett's experiences. The only known publication by Manigold was in *Golden West Magazine*. In the article, Manigold erroneously identified the location of the traders post massacre as New York. As there were no Indian uprisings during that era in New York; Along with the fact that records show the Fossetts lived in southern Minnesota in 1862 at the time of the Sioux uprising there; Plus the records for his brothers' enlistments in Minnesota Indian fighting units are clear evidence that the massacre incident occurred somewhere near their home in southern Minnesota.

[14] Minnesota Historical Society, loc. cit.

[15] *The Minnesota Adjutant General's Report of 1866*, Personnel Roster of the Minnesota First Cavalry, 1863, Historical Data Systems, Duxbury, Mass. The surname for John and Isaac Fossett is spelled *Fosset* on Civil War era personnel rosters, but they signed their names *Fossett* with the conventional two "t"s.

[16] Burt V. Manigold & Joseph Rosenberger, "Last of the Gunfighters," loc. cit.; Perry Township, Brown County, Ohio, 1860 Census; Amherst Township, Fillmore County, Ohio, 1870 Census.

[17] W.D. Fossett, Indian-Pioneer History Project for Oklahoma, loc. cit.; Certificate of Marriage No. B-75, Faribault County, Minnesota, March 6, 1872; Death Certificate of Lewis D. Fossett, No. 013321, State of Oklahoma Dept. of Health, filed October 15, 1952. Elizabeth Footman was born in Ohio. Her family later moved to Fillmore County, Minnesota. The death certificate for Lewis D. Fossett lists his mother as *Lizzie* Footman, and in subsequent Kansas census records she is listed as Elizabeth.

[18] Mrs. C.E. Goodrich, "The Fossetts in America," loc. cit. Family genealogy shows eldest son John, with his wife Rachel and six children, moved to Kansas in a wagon pulled by oxen in 1874. Isaac and his wife Jenny, who had no children, moved about the same time. John Fossett died in Caldwell in 1879 (Family Search Files, Church of the Latter Day Saints), Susannah in 1876 (Wellington Monitor Free Press, October 19, 1876).

[19] *Portrait and Biographical Record of Oklahoma*, Chapman Publishing, Chicago, 1901, p. 513.

[20] *Daily Oklahoman*, March 10, 1940.

[21] W.D. Fossett, Indian-Pioneer History Project for Oklahoma, loc. cit.

Chapter 2
Along the Cattle Trails

[1] W.D. Fossett, interview, Indian-Pioneer History Project for Oklahoma, Works Progress Administration, Aug. 11, 18, 1937, p. 1. Fossett said he moved to Caldwell, but property and census records show the family actually moved first to the countryside of Falls Township, adjacent to Caldwell, the nearest town. The Chisholm Trail was named for Jesse Chisholm, a Tennessean of Scottish and Cherokee ancestry. He became a trader among Indian tribes of the plains, also acting as a guide and freighter. He spoke English, Spanish and fourteen Indian languages and was often instrumental in making peace between the different tribes and the whites. As a young man he bought captive Mexican children from the Comanches and raised them as his own children. They became experts in the lore of the plains, speaking several languages, as did their foster-father, and were in demand as guides and interpreters. He drove cattle to Mexico in 1865 and set up trading posts in Indian Territory and Kansas. In so doing, he blazed a trail from Texas to Wichita. Chisholm died in his trading camp in what became Blaine County, Oklahoma, in 1868, never living to see his famous trail become legend in western history. He was buried near Geary, Oklahoma, with a stone marker that said, "No one left his home cold or hungry" (Oklahoma Historical Society Marker, 1976; Gwendoline and Paul Sanders, *The Sumner County Story*, The Mennonite Press, North Newton, Kans., 1967, pp. 11-13).

[2] Falls Township, Sumner County, Kansas, 1875 Census. Falls Township was created in March, 1873 (Gwendoline and Paul Sanders, *The Sumner County Story*, op. cit., p. 105).

[3] One of Isaac Fossett's several purchases was along Bluff Creek about four miles southwest of Caldwell where he was deeded 160 acres from Bedford B. Wood in April 1879 (Sumner County Kansas Register of Deeds, April 29, 1879, Book # 2, p. 226). Bill Fossett, who had previously owned property in Falls Township, received a receipt for final payment on 40 and 44/100 acres adjoining Caldwell to the west in 1880 (U.S. Government Receiver's Office, Certificate No. 12035, Wichita, Kansas, April 14, 1880, to William D. Fossett for lot # 1 quarter of Section No. 3, in Township 35 South, of Range 3 West). Bill Fossett's Government Patent to the land was granted May 10, 1882 (U.S. Patent Record No. 12035, U.S. Land Office, Wichita, Kansas). John Fossett bought three lots on Osage Street in Caldwell in 1879 (Sumner County Kansas Register of Deeds, April 16, 1879, Vol. IX, p. 447).

[4] Mrs. C.E. Goodrich (Anna Leah Fossett), "The Fossetts in America," genealogy, 1974, p. 1.

[5] *Sumner County Press*, June 17, 1875; January 6, June 1, 1876; *Caldwell Post*, July 28, 1881; General Pension Index, 1861-1934, Roll 312, Document 16, Deposition A by Elizabeth Fossett Manigold, July 11, 1900. Francis X. Manigold divorced his wife, Elizabeth Fossett, about 1858, after they had been separated a few years. In a dispute over his Civil War pension in 1900, Elizabeth claimed to be unaware of the divorce, saying she knew only that Francis Manigold died after the war.

[6] Mrs. C.E. Goodrich, "The Fossetts in America," op. cit., pp. 1, 3-7; *Sumner County Press*, July 6, 1876. John, tired of explaining he had no middle initial, appropriated the first letter of the alphabet and signed his name "A.J. Fossett." John and wife Rachel had three more children after moving to Caldwell.

[7] *Kingman Courier,* March 1940; *Kingfisher Free Press*, March 11, 1940. Fossett is often described as a big man by those who knew him including Joe Grimes, a former deputy, and B.V. Manigold, Fossett's nephew (Burt V. Manigold & Joseph Rosenberger, "Last of the Gunfighters," *Golden West Magazine*, May 1968, p. 12). N.E. Hobson, who knew Fossett in Kingman, notes his height at 6'4." Alva McDonald, U.S. Marshal for the Western District of Oklahoma, considered Fossett "the best shot with rifle or pistol in the history of Oklahoma."

[8] *Kingfisher Free Press*, April 17, 1939.

[9] *Portrait and Biographical Record of Oklahoma*, Chapman Publishing, Chicago, 1901, pp. 513-514; Louise S. Barnes, Summary of Indian-Pioneer History Project Interview with W.D. Fossett, November 18, 1937, p. 1; *Golden West Magazine*, May 1968, loc. cit.

[10] W.D. Fossett, Indian-Pioneer History, op. cit., p. 8. Ft. Sill was originally called Camp Wichita when established in 1869 by Major General Philip Sheridan who lead a campaign into Indian Territory to stop hostile raiding. Sheridan later named the camp for his West Point classmate, Brigadier General Joshua Sill, who was killed during the Civil War (Ft. Sill Museum, Ft. Sill, Okla). Fossett mistakenly reported in his *Pioneer Papers* that it was General William Sherman, instead of General Sheridan who named Ft. Sill.

[11] Gary L. Roberts, Introduction to: *Oklahombres*, by E.D. Nix, University of Nebraska Press, Bison Press Edition, 1993.

[12] W.D. Fossett, Indian-Pioneer History, op. cit., p. 9.

[13] Ibid., pp. 9-11.

[14] Frederick S. Barde, *Manuscript Archives*, Oklahoma Historical Society, Oklahoma City, p. 2. Barde, a correspondent for the Kansas City Star calls Fossett's companion "Robinson" in his draft for newspaper publication. The "Laughlin" referred to may have been freighter George "Laflin" (Oliver Nelson, *The Cowman's Southwest; being the reminiscences of Oliver Nelson; freighter, camp cook, cowboy, frontiersman in Kansas, Indian Territory, Texas, and Oklahoma, 1878-1893*, Edited by Angie Debo, Bison Books, University of Nebraska Press, Lincoln and London, 1986, p. 36).

[15] W.D. Fossett, Indian-Pioneer History, op. cit., p.11.

[16] Frederick S. Barde, *Manuscript*, op. cit., p. 3.

[17] Ft. Reno was established in 1874 to assist the agents at the Darlington Indian Agency who controlled the Cheyenne-Arapaho Reservation. In Fossett's *Pioneer-History* version he said he walked to Darlington, which was about 5 miles northwest of where Ft. Reno was later located. He probably found the soldiers near the Cheyenne-Arapaho Indian Agency there.

[18] Frederick S. Barde, loc. cit.

[19] W.D. Fossett, Indian-Pioneer History, op. cit., p. 12.

[20] Frederick S. Barde, *Manuscript*, op. cit., p. 4.

[21] W.D. Fossett, Indian-Pioneer History, op. cit., p. 2.

[22] Wayne Gard, *The Chisholm Trail*, University of Oklahoma Press, Norman, Okla., 1954, pp. 62-73; David Dary, *Cowboy Culture*, University Press of Kansas, Lawrence, Kansas, 1989, pp. 168, 184-188; Odie B. Falk, *Oklahoma: Land of the Fair God*, Windsor Publications, Northridge, Calif., 1986, p. 114. Some writers place the date of the first Chisholm Trail drive as 1866. Cattle were driven to Kansas and Missouri along a more easterly trail in the years prior to the Civil War. In 1866, some drives went

into Kansas on what became commonly known as the Chisholm Trail, but the through route to Abilene and the establishment of stock yards at the rail head there came in 1867.

[23] Mary Ellen Jones, *The Nineteenth Century American Frontier*, Greenwood Press, Westport, Conn., 1998, p. 171.

[24] David Dary, *Cowboy Culture,* op. cit., pp. 108-123.

[25] Ibid., pp. 187-192.

[26] W.D. Fossett, Indian-Pioneer History, loc. cit. The trail that ran to Dodge City was better known as the Western Trail (Edward Everett Dale, *Cow Country*, University of Oklahoma Press, Norman, 1942, p. 42).

[27] The Kansas Pacific Railway Company, *Guide Map of the Great Texas Cattle Trail from the Red River Crossing to the Old Reliable Kansas Pacific Railway,* Kansas City, 1874, pp. 5-9.

[28] David Dary, *Cowboy Culture,* op. cit., pp. 198-200.

[29] W.D. Fossett, Indian-Pioneer History, op. cit., pp. 6-7. Fossett did not mention Bull Foot Station (Hennessey) because this portion of his pioneer paper narrative followed his explanation of Hennessey's death.

[30] The number of men who reportedly died with Hennessey varies from two to three. Richard Lane (Editor of *Midnight & Noonday* by George D. Freeman, University of Oklahoma Press, 1984) says positive identification has been given to only two of the men: Drivers George Fant and Thomas Calaway. In his *Wild, Wooly and Wicked* (Clarkson N. Potter, Inc., New York, 1960), Harry Sinclair Drago identifies a third teamster, Ed Cook, in addition to Fant and Calaway.

[31] Harry Sinclair Drago, *Wild, Wooly and Wicked*, Clarkson N. Potter, Inc., New York, 1960, p. 240. Bull Foot Station, which became Hennessey, was located eight miles south of the Buffalo Springs Station, which later became Bison (*Caldwell Commerical*, May 20, 1880).

[32] Ibid.; *Handbook of Texas*, The Texas State Historical Association, 1999. Fossett said that the last buffalo hunts in Indian Territory occurred in the fall of 1874 and the winter of 1875. By that time buffalo on the plains were scarce and the large herds had moved north (W.D. Fossett, Indian-Pioneer History, op. cit., p. 13).

[33] Harry Sinclair Drago, *Wild, Wooly and Wicked,* op. cit., p. 241.

[34] W.D. Fossett, Indian-Pioneer History, op. cit., pp. 5-6.

[35] Harry Sinclair Drago, *Wild, Wooly and Wicked,* loc. cit.; George D. Freeman, *Midnight & Noonday*, Edited by Richard Lane, University of Oklahoma Press, Norman, Okla., 1984, pp. 155-156.

[36] W.D. Fossett, Indian-Pioneer History, loc. cit., p. 8.

[37] Neil Allen Bristow, "Colcord and Bristow family Genealogy," 2001.

[38] *The Autobiography of Charles Francis Colcord: 1859-1934*, Tulsa, Okla., 1970, p. 58.

[39] Charles F. Colcord, "Reminiscences of Charles F. Colcord," *Chronicles of Oklahoma*, 1934, Vol. XII, pp. 5-18; Mrs. George Rainey, *In Memory: Cherokee Strip Brands*, Enid, Okla., 1949.

[40] *The Autobiography of Charles Francis Colcord,* op. cit., p. 59.

[41] Ibid.

[42] Ibid., p. 60. Fossett, in his *Pioneer History* interview recalls Colcord being about 16 years of age and very hot tempered at the time of the incident. Fossett says he was able to get his finger under the hammer before the firing pin fell, thus, preventing an actual shot, but severely injuring his finger.

[43] Charles F. Colcord, "Reminiscences of Charles F. Colcord," loc. cit. Charles Francis Colcord clearly possessed the entrepreneurial skills of his father. He later was part owner of the Comanche Cattle Pool, the largest in the Cherokee Outlet. He went on to become the first Police Chief of Oklahoma City, a deputy U.S. marshal, and well-known Oklahoma businessman.

[44] Anna Fossett Goodrich, "Frank J. Fossett," *Journal of the Cherokee Strip*, September 1977.

[45] Laban S. Records, *Cherokee Outlet Cowboy,* edited by Ellen Jayne Maris Wheeler, University of Oklahoma Press, Norman and London, 1995, p. 155.

[46] Ibid., pp. 155-156; Mrs. C.E. Goodrich ("The Fossetts in America," op. cit., pp. 1-5). In Laban Records' book, Sam's name is mistakenly spelled "Fawcett." Sam Fossett was a son of John Fossett, William Fossett's oldest brother.

[47] W.D. Fossett, Indian-Pioneer History, op. cit., p. 14.

[48] *Sumner County Press*, July 6, 1876.

[49] Ibid., February 28, 1878; Sumner County, Kansas, 1880 Census.

[50] *Caldwell Post*, December 4, 1879; May 18, 1880. J.W. and T.W. Montague are both listed as having interest in the Montague and Manning Cattle Company. They may have been brothers, or father and son.

[51] W.D. Fossett, Indian-Pioneer History, loc. cit.

[52] George D. Freeman, *Midnight & Noonday*, Edited by Richard Lane, University of Oklahoma Press, Norman, Okla., 1984, pp. 186, 193. Harry Sinclair Drago paints a casual arrangement in terms of the titles, duties and selection of local lawmen. He says the police constable obtained help when he needed, often making the rounds of saloons to enlist the aid of tough men to help him enforce the law. During the incident when cowboys

were "shooting up the town" in July 1879, Drago claims the constable got the help of six men, including George Flatt and John Wilson "who were first-class trouble-makers in their own right and rated high among toughs and desperados. . . ." (Harry Sinclair Drago, *Wild, Wooly and Wicked,* op. cit., p. 251.)

[53] *Caldwell Post,* November 18, 1879.

[54] Ibid., November 27, December 18, 1879.

[55] Ibid., January 8, 1880.

Chapter 3
Law in the Border Queen

[1] George D. Freeman, *Midnight & Noonday*, Edited by Richard Lane, University of Oklahoma Press, Norman,1984, pp. 21, 94.

[2] Ibid., pp. 9-11.

[3] W.D. Fossett, interview, Indian-Pioneer History Project for Oklahoma, Works Progress Administration, Aug. 11, 18, 1937, p. 1. Fossett first lived in nearby Falls Township, east of Caldwell, before moving into town.

[4] Robert R. Dykstra, *The Cattle Towns*, Alfred A. Knopf, New York, 1968, pp. 63-64; William G. Cutler, *History of the State of Kansas*, A.T. Andreas, Chicago, 1883, pp. 1502-1503.

[5] Robert R. Dykstra, *The Cattle Towns*, op. cit., pp. 65-66.

[6] Mrs. C.E. Goodrich (Anna Leah Fossett), "The Fossetts in America," genealogy, 1974, pp. 1-6.

[7] Robert R. Dykstra, *The Cattle Towns*, op. cit., p. 114.

[8] George D. Freeman, *Midnight & Noonday* , op. cit., p. 44.

[9] Robert R. Dykstra, *The Cattle Towns*, op. cit., pp. 68-73; William G. Cutler, *History of the State of Kansas*, op. cit., pp. 1495, 1502-1503, 1509.

[10] Nyle H. Miller and Joseph W. Snell, *The Great Gunfighters of Kansas Cowtowns, 1867-1886,* University of Nebraska Press, Lincoln and London, 1963, pp. 97-98; *Caldwell Post*, August 21, 1879.

[11] *Caldwell Post*, July 10, 1879; Miller & Snell, *The Great Gunfighters of Kansas Cowtowns,* loc. cit. Harry Sinclair Drago (*Wild, Wooly and Wicked*, Clarkson N. Potter, Inc., New York, 1960, p. 251), says that Flatt went on a drinking binge following the shootout.

[12] George D. Freeman, *Midnight & Noonday*, op. cit., p. 40.

[13] Hubert Collins, *Warpath and Cattle Trail*, University Press of Colorado, Niwot, Colo., 1928, pp. 8-9.

[14] Miller & Snell, *The Great Gunfighters of Kansas Cowtowns,* op. cit., pp. 99, 358. Meagher is usually pronounced "Mayor."

[15] *Caldwell Post,* June 24, 1880.

[16] *Caldwell Commercial,* July 1, 8, 1880; Miller & Snell, *The Great Gunfighters of Kansas Cowtowns,* op. cit., pp. 99-103, 359; George D. Freeman, *Midnight & Noonday,* op. cit., p. 200.

[17] Harry Sinclair Drago, *Wild, Wooly and Wicked,* op. cit., pp. 253-254.

[18] *Caldwell Commercial,* July 8, 1880.

[19] George D. Freeman, *Midnight & Noonday,* op. cit., pp. 202-204; Miller & Snell, *The Great Gunfighters of Kansas Cowtowns,* op. cit., pp. 365, 471. Spear is sometimes spelled *Speer* and *Spears.* The term "red light district," often used to describe an area where there are brothels, reportedly originated in cowtowns like Caldwell. Railroad crewmen were known to hang their red signal lantern outside the door of a house so they could quickly be found if needed in an emergency. Another version is that the term originated from a Dodge City "sporting house" called the Red Light because of the blood red glass on the front door through which the light shined at night (David Dary, *Cowboy Culture,* University Press of Kansas, Lawrence, Kansas, 1989, p. 221).

[20] *Caldwell Commercial,* July 28, 1880; Miller & Snell, *The Great Gunfighters of Kansas Cowtowns,* op. cit., p. 360.

[21] *Caldwell Messenger,* May 10, 1971.

[22] Ibid.; George D. Freeman, *Midnight & Noonday,* op. cit., p. 186.

[23] *Caldwell Commercial,* November 3, 1881.

[24] Sam P. Ridings, *The Chisholm Trail,* Co-operative Publishing Company, Guthrie, Okla., 1936, pp. 470-471; Harry Sinclair Drago, *Wild, Wooly and Wicked,* op. cit., p. 257; George D. Freeman, *Midnight & Noonday,* op. cit., p. 251. Corroboration of the Talbot's real name as "Sherman" comes from trial testimony by his brother Rollan Sherman (George D. Freeman, *Midnight & Noonday,* op. cit., 250), and from the *Caldwell Commercial* and *Sumner County Press* of December 22, 1881. George Spear was the older brother of David Spear, accused of killing former constable Frank Hunt. Both men were the sons of C.L. Hunt who was with George Flatt the night he was murdered. Bob Munson's name is sometimes spelled *Munsin* or *Munsen.*

[25] *Sumner County Press,* December 22, 1881.

[26] Gwendoline and Paul Sanders, *The Sumner County Story,* The Mennonite Press, North Newton, Kansas, 1967, p. 151; *Caldwell Post,* December 22, 1881.

[27] *Caldwell Post*, December 22, 1881; *Sumner County Press*, December 22, 1881.

[28] Gwendoline and Paul Sanders, *The Sumner County Story*, loc. cit.; George D. Freeman, *Midnight & Noonday*, op. cit., p. 255.

[29] Gwendoline and Paul Sanders, *The Sumner County Story*, op. cit., p. 152; George D. Freeman, *Midnight & Noonday*, op. cit., p. 253; *Caldwell Post*, December 22, 1881; Sam P. Ridings, *The Chisholm Trail*, op. cit., p. 453. The 1881 newspaper accounts and the 1895 trial version differ slightly. At the trial it was reported that both Martin and Munson were in custody and being escorted when rescued by Talbot and others. Trial testimony also said that Talbot and his cohorts escaped by backing into a crowd where they "dodged behind some bystanders," which may explain why Fossett and Wilson did not fire their "drawn" guns (Wellington Monitor Free Press, April 11, 1895).

[30] *Wichita Times*, December 17, 1881.

[31] *Caldwell Post*, December 22, 1881. Meagher was born in Ireland and served as marshal of Wichita in the years 1871-74 and 1875-77. Prior to that he had been a deputy U.S. marshal. He was thirty-eight years old when he died (George D. Freeman, *Midnight & Noonday*, op. cit., pp. 253, 257).

[32] Sam P. Ridings, *The Chisholm Trail,* op. cit., pp. 475-476. Ridings also recalls that during the afternoon fighting, W.N. Hubbel, an ex-Caldwell mayor and store owner, discovered the outlaws' horses saddled and waiting in front of the Red Light Saloon. With the same deliberation "as if he was shooting chickens' heads off, he killed most, if not all, of these horses" with his Winchester. Contemporary news accounts do not mention the systematic slaughter of getaway horses.

[33] George D. Freeman, *Midnight & Noonday*, op. cit., pp. 255-256; Gwendoline and Paul Sanders, *The Sumner County Story,* loc. cit.

[34] George D. Freeman, *Midnight & Noonday*, op. cit., pp. 258-263. Laban S. Records says he and other cowboys working in the Cherokee Outlet helped Talbot and his gang secure fresh horses after they made their way west of Pond Creek. Records says he let Bob Munson "take a $60 horse" with the understanding the horse would be returned as quickly as he could. "I haven't seen the horse since," said Records, in his 1937 memoirs (Laban S. Records, *Cherokee Outlet Cowboy,* edited by Ellen Jayne Maris Wheeler, University of Oklahoma Press, Norman and London, 1995, p. 178).

[35] Ibid., pp. 265-266. Talbot's cousin was reported to be Sylvester Powell, whom Meagher killed in 1877 while marshal of Wichita. Powell reportedly fired several shots into a privy occupied by Meagher, wounding him in the

leg. Meagher came out shooting, killing Powell. The "half-brother " to George Flatt rumor was essentially denied by Talbot in a letter to the *Kansas City Sunday Times* of January 12, 1882.

[36] *Kansas City Sunday Times*, January 12, 1882. Fossett's recollection of the Talbot raid 56 years later was that the gang was trying to rob the bank and that "the marshal [Wilson] hid out" during the fight (W.D. Fossett, Indian-Pioneer History, op. cit., p. 14). The memory does not square with records of the incident.

[37] *Wellington Monitor Free Press*, April 11, September 18, 19, 1895; George D. Freeman, *Midnight & Noonday*, op. cit., p. 267; Miller & Snell, *The Great Gunfighters of Kansas Cowtowns,* op. cit., p. 368.

[38] George D. Freeman, *Midnight & Noonday*, op. cit., pp. 207-208.

[39] Ibid., pp. 214-228; Kansas State Historical Society, *A Moment in Time*, September, 1995. According to cowboy Laban S. Records who knew Brown (Laban S. Records, *Cherokee Outlet Cowboy,* op. cit., pp. 256-258), the bank holdup was a botched inside job that was supposed to cover up fraudulent bookkeeping by bank vice president George Gephart. Ben Wheeler and Gephart, boyhood friends, had hatched the scheme of a harmless robbery but when bank president Wiley Payne showed up unexpectedly that day, Wheeler and Brown thought it was a double-cross and started shooting.

[40] Wayne Gard, *The Chisholm Trail,* University of Oklahoma Press, Norman, 1954, pp. 255-259.

Chapter 4
Kingman

[1] *Caldwell Messenger*, May 10, 1971.

[2] *Caldwell Commercial*, June 29, 1882.

[3] *Kingman Mercury*, August 2, 1882.

[4] W.D. Fossett, interview, Indian-Pioneer History Project for Oklahoma, Works Progress Administration, Aug. 11, 18, 1937, p.14; Mrs. George Rainey, *In Memory: Cherokee Strip Brands*, Enid, Okla., 1949. T.W. and J.A. Montague may have been father and son, or brothers.

[5] Letha Mitchel, "Chikaskia Township-Spivey Town," 1989, research collection, Kingman, Kansas, Carnegie Library; Kingman County, Kansas, Register of Deeds Office, *Numerical Index of Lands*, Vol. 8. The Chikaskia Township plat shows that several sections of land south of what became the town of Spivey, were owned by Montague & Manning in the early to

mid-1880s. Register of Deeds' records also show William D. Fossett and brother Isaac Fossett owned several acres of property southwest of Spivey in Chikaskia Township that were sold to J. A. Montague on May 24, 1886.

[6] John P. Edwards, *Historical Atlas of Sumner County*, Philadelphia, 1883, p. 75.

[7] *Kingman Mercury*, December 6, 1883; William G. Cutler, *History of the State of Kansas*, A.T. Andreas, Chicago, 1883, p. 1527. The Laclede House was originally built as part of Kingman's "south town" before it was moved north of the Ninnescah River in 1882 and "greatly enlarged."

[8] William G. Cutler, *History of the State of Kansas*, op. cit., pp. 1525-1527.

[9] Wayne Gard, *The Chisholm Trail,* University of Oklahoma Press, Norman, Okla., 1954, pp. 198-199; William G. Cutler, *History of the State of Kansas*, loc. cit. Harry Sinclair Drago *(Great American Cattle Trails,* Bramhall House, N.Y., 1965, p. 140) places this trail west of Kingman.

[10] William G. Cutler, *History of the State of Kansas*, loc. cit.

[11] Fred Hurd, *A History of Kingman County: 1871-1969*, Mennonite Press, North Newton, Kansas, 1970, p. 62.

[12] William G. Cutler, *History of the State of Kansas*, op. cit., p. 1528. During the Civil War, black troops were commanded by white officers. Such a role was shunned by career military men but afforded enlisted men, considered "officer material," an opportunity for advancement (National Archives and Records Administration, *Black Soldiers in the Civil War*).

[13] Fred Hurd, *A History of Kingman County,* op. cit., p. 63.

[14] Robert R. Dykstra, *The Cattle Towns*, op. cit., pp. 123-124.

[15] Kingman City Council Minutes, July 7, 18, 1884; May 3, July 6, 1886.

[16] Fred Hurd, *A History of Kingman County,* loc. cit.

[17] Ibid.

[18] *Southern Kansas Democrat*, October 20, 1883; *Kingman Courier*, June 6, 1884; *Meade's Manual: An Internal History of the Atchison, Topeka and Santa Fe Railway, 1916 to 1919*. The line to Pratt was built as the "Kingman, Pratt & Western Railroad" in 1887.

[19] *Kingman Courier*, April 18, 1884.

[20] Kingman City Scrapbook, Kingman, Kansas, Carnegie Library, Vol. III.

[21] Kingman County, Kansas, Register of Deeds' records, April 8, 1884. Fossett bought lots #123 & 125 in April, eventually purchasing four more lots in the same area of north Main Street during the following nineteen months.

[22] Kingman County, Kansas, Register of Deeds' records, May 24, 1886. Fossett and his brother Isaac owned a portion of the property adjacent to

Montague and Manning in Chikaskia Township until they sold it in 1886. In April 1884, while operating the Stone Livery Stable in Kingman, Fossett was only two months away from being appointed city marshal.

[23] *Kingman Courier*, May 9, 1884.

[24] Ibid., June 6, 1884.

[25] Ibid.

[26] Ibid. The road was turned over to the operating department for regular schedules on July 1, 1884. In 1886, the Kingman, Pratt & Western Railroad began extension of this line to Pratt, Kansas. It was consolidated as the Wichita and Western Railroad Company on July 24, 1889, and then acquired by the Santa Fe Railway on December 31, 1898 (*Meade's Manual: An Internal History of the Atchison, Topeka and Santa Fe Railway*, loc. cit.).

[27] *Kingman Courier*, June 13, 1884. W. A. Liggett, the first city marshal, was succeeded by E. A. Newman.

[28] Ibid.; Kingman City Council Minutes, June 9, 1884.

[29] *Kingman Courier*, June 20, 1884.

[30] Kingman City Council Minutes, October 6, 1884; November 4, 1885.

[31] Fred Hurd, *A History of Kingman County,* op. cit., p. 64.

[32] *Southern Kansas Democrat*, December 4, 1884.

[33] *Kingman Courier*, January 7, 1887. Wood was one of two deputies serving when Fossett resigned as marshal of Kingman in January 1887.

[34] Sam P. Ridings, *The Chisholm Trail,* Co-operative Publishing Company, Guthrie, Okla., 1936, pp. 424-426; Nyle H. Miller and Joseph W. Snell, *Why the West was Wild*, Kansas Sate Historical Society, Topeka, 1963, p. 647. Wood succeeded Fossett as assistant marshal of Caldwell in 1882. He later served as a Caldwell policeman and city marshal before going to Kingman. He became a plainclothes police officer and deputy sheriff in Wichita, and was named Wichita Chief of Police in 1907 (*Wichita Eagle*, April 11, 1907). Fossett knew Wood from the time both men were early settlers in Falls Township, east of Caldwell (John P. Edwards, *Historical Atlas of Sumner County*, op. cit., p 51), and Fossett's brother, Isaac "Ike" Fossett had land dealings with Wood (Sumner County Kansas Register of Deeds, Book 2, p. 226, April 29, 1879).

[35] Anita Cheatum, "Address to the Kansas State Senate," January 23, 1996; *Kingman Courier*, April 18, 1884.

[36] Anita Cheatum, "Address to the Kansas State Senate," loc. cit.

[37] Ibid. Highway 54 through Kingman is known as the "Cannonball Highway."

[38] *Southern Kansas Democrat*, November 20, 1884; *Kingman Courier*, November 21, 1884.

[39] *Kingman Courier*, January 2, 1885.

[40] Ibid.

[41] Fred Hurd, *A History of Kingman County,* op. cit., p. 72.

[42] *Kingman Courier*, January 2, 1885; *Clark County Clipper*, October 23, 1930.

[43] *Clark County Clipper*, loc. cit.; *Southern Kansas Democrat*, August 14, 1884; Kingman City Council Minutes, March 29, 1886.

[44] Kingman, Kingman County, Kansas, 1885 Census.

[45] Kingman County Kansas, Appearance Docket Book B, Case No. 494, March 1885.

[46] *Southern Kansas Democrat*, April 23, 1885.

[47] *Kingman Courier*, April 24, 1885.

[48] Ibid.

[49] *Southern Kansas Democrat*, April 23, 1885.

[50] *Kingman Courier*, April 24, 1885.

[51] Ibid.

[52] McPherson County, Kansas, Marriage License, May 10, 1885; *Portrait and Biographical Record of Oklahoma*, Chapman Publishing, Chicago, 1901, p. 513.

[53] *Kingman Courier*, June 12, 1885.

[54] Ibid., June 19, 1885.

[55] Ibid.

[56] Kingman City Council Minutes, July 1, 1885.

[57] Ibid., July 6, 1886; Kingman City Directory, 1887, p. 218.

[58] Robert R. Dykstra, *The Cattle Towns*, loc. cit.

[59] *Southern Kansas Democrat*, June 4, 1885.

[60] *Kingman Courier*, July 24, 1885. This new part-time position may have been in anticipation of the imminent sale of the Fossett & Mead Livery Stable a few weeks later (*Kingman Courier*, August 14, 1885).

[61] *Kingman Courier*, July 31, September 11, 1885.

[62] Fred Hurd, *A History of Kingman County,* op. cit., p. 68.

[63] *Hennessey Clipper*, March 21, 1940.

[64] Ibid.

[65] Fred Hurd, *A History of Kingman County,* op. cit., pp. 68-69.

[66] Ibid.; *Hennessey Clipper,* loc. cit.

[67] *Kingman Courier*, January 22, 1886; March 15, 1940.

[68] Ibid., September 18, 1885.

[69] Ibid., September 25, 1885.

[70] A Kansas Portrait, "The Blizzard of 1886," Kansas State Historical Society, 2001; Fred Hurd, *A History of Kingman County,* op. cit., pp. 74-75.

[71] *Kingman Courier*, August 7, 1885; January 8, 29, 1886.

[72] *Kingman Courier*, April 23, 1886.

[73] Ibid.

[74] *Kingman Courier*, June 11, 1886. Sam died on June 7. He was born in Minnesota on June 25, 1861. In 1884, within a couple of years of the accident (described in Chapter 2), he married Harriet Amanda Walton in Harper County, Kansas (Harper County, Kansas, marriage records). The injury apparently took a heavy toll on his health and finally his life. His obituary said he "was an industrious young man full of life and energy," who suffered greatly toward the end and "sought the forgiveness of God with all his heart" before dying. His funeral was June 8, 1886, at the Kingman Methodist Church. He was buried in Kingman's Walnut Hill Cemetery. In "The Fossetts in America," family genealogy, it's reported that Sam's "health was undermined by exposure of life on the range," apparently a term used when death results from accidents such as his.

[75] *Southern Kansas Democrat*, February 12, 1885; *Kingman Courier*, October 9, 1885; *Belle Plaine News,* September 4, 1886.

[76] W. G. Seaver, *Railroad Man's Magazine*, Vol I, No. 1, New York, October, 1906; *Arkansas Republican*, April 10, 1886; A.A. Grant, *Railroad and County Map of Kansas*, 1887. At the time this map was published, probably early in 1887, the line was shown running only from Belle Plaine to Kingman in the south central part of the state. A railroad map of 1888 shows the line complete from Coffeyville, in southeastern Kansas, through and beyond Reno County.

[77] *Kingman Courier*, September 17, 24, October 8, 1886; January 7, 1887. He continued his city marshal position until January 1887.

[78] W. G. Seaver, *Railroad Man's Magazine,* loc. cit.; *Belle Plaine News*, September 4, 1886.

[79] *Belle Plaine News*, April 17, 1886.

[80] W. G. Seaver, *Railroad Man's Magazine,* loc. cit.; *Kingman Courier*, September 10, 1886.

[81] *Kingman Courier*, September 24, October 8, December 31, 1886; *Kingman Morning Courier*, January 1, 1887; *Kingman Courier*, January 7, 1887.

[82] *Kingman Courier*, May 13, September 22, December 1, 1887; *Caldwell Journal,* January 26, 1888.

[83] *Portrait and Biographical Record of Oklahoma*, loc. cit.

[84] *Larned Tiller & Toiler*, June 1996.

[85] Fred Hurd, *A History of Kingman County,* op. cit., pp. 78-80.

[86] W.D. Fossett, Indian-Pioneer History, op. cit., p. 16.

Chapter 5
The Run

[1] Stan Hoig, *The Oklahoma Land Rush of 1889*, Oklahoma Historical Society, Oklahoma City, 1989, pp. 3-16; John Morris, et al, *Historical Atlas of Oklahoma,* University of Oklahoma Press, Norman, 1976, pp. 20, 23, 26, 33-34.

[2] Odie B. Falk, *Oklahoma: Land of the Fair God*, Windsor Publications, Northridge, Calif., 1986, p. 116.

[3] Stan Hoig, *The Oklahoma Land Rush of 1889*, loc. cit.

[4] Ibid., pp. 14-16; John Morris, et al, *Historical Atlas of Oklahoma,* op. cit., pp. 47-49.

[5] Glenn Shirley, *West of Hell's Fringe*, University of Oklahoma Press, Norman, 1978, p. 7.

[6] Ibid., p. 25.

[7] Ibid., p. 7.

[8] *Kingfisher Free Press,* April 17, 1939.

[9] Ibid.; *Kingfisher Times*, April 15, 1926.

[10] B.B. Chapman, "The Legal Sooners of 1889 in Oklahoma," *Chronicles of Oklahoma,* 1957-1958, Vol. XXXV, No. 4, p. 398; The Kingfisher Study Club, *Echoes of Eighty-Nine*, 1939, p. 19.

[11] Standard Atlas of Kingfisher County, George A. Ogle & Co., Chicago, 1906, p. 60; Chicago, Kansas & Nebraska Railway survey map, April 4, 1889; *The New World*, May 18, 1889. Jacob Admire said that no vestige of the stage station remained on April 22, (The Kingfisher Study Club, *Echoes of Eighty-Nine*, op. cit., p. 24) but the railway survey map, made a few days earlier, clearly marked the station's location.

[12] W.D. Fossett, interview, Indian-Pioneer History Project for Oklahoma, Works Progress Administration, Aug. 11, 18, 1937, p. 15.

[13] Stan Hoig, *The Oklahoma Land Rush of 1889*, op. cit., p. 166.

[14] Ibid.; B.B. Chapman, "The Legal Sooners of 1889 in Oklahoma," op. cit., pp. 398-400.

[15] Ibid.; Stan Hoig, *The Oklahoma Land Rush of 1889*, op. cit., p. 165.

[16] The Kingfisher Study Club, *Echoes of Eighty-Nine*, op. cit., p. 21.

---

[17] *Kingfisher Free Press,* April 18, 1949; *Echoes of Eighty-Nine*, op. cit., p. 21.

[18] *Kingfisher Times*, April 15, 1926.

[19] The Kingfisher Study Club, *Echoes of Eighty-Nine*, op. cit., p. 210.

[20] Melvin Fiegel, "The Founding and Early Development of Kingfisher, Oklahoma," Oklahoma State University, 1965, pp. 13-14; B.B. Chapman, "The Legal Sooners of 1889 in Oklahoma," loc. cit.; W.D. Fossett, Indian-Pioneer History, op. cit., p. 16.

[21] Melvin Fiegel, "The Founding and Early Development of Kingfisher, Oklahoma," op. cit., p. 17; The Kingfisher Study Club, *Echoes of Eighty-Nine*, op. cit., p. 22.

[22] *Pioneers of Kingfisher County: 1889-1976,* Kingfisher Bicentennial Committee, 1976, p. 258; Kent Ruth, et al, *Oklahoma: A Guide to The Sooner State,* University of Oklahoma Press, Norman, 1957, p. 440.

[23] *Kingfisher Free Press*, April 17, 1939; John Alley, *City Beginnings in Oklahoma Territory,* University of Oklahoma Press, Norman, 1939, pp. 56-57; The Kingfisher Study Club, *Echoes of Eighty-Nine*, op. cit., p. 69.

[24] *Pioneers of Kingfisher County: 1889-1976*, op. cit., p. 9.

[25] *The New World*, May 18, 1889.

[26] W.D. Fossett, Indian-Pioneer History, loc. cit., p. 16.

[27] *The New World*, loc. cit.

[28] *Pioneers of Kingfisher County: 1889-1976*, op. cit., pp. 7-9, 258.

[29] Kingfisher, Kingfisher County, Okla., Patent Record, Book No. 1, pp. 54-55. The "park" in question was apparently known as "Fossett's Grove" according to subsequent newspaper stories indicating its use for picnics and social gatherings. The U.S. Land Office Patent Record was signed by President Benjamin Harrison August 8, 1892. The Kingfisher County Register of Deeds recording date was July 7, 1893.

[30] *Kingfisher Times*, April 15, 1926; Emory D. Brownlee, "Why is Kingfisher?" An address to the Eighty-Niner Celebration, 1902. Fossett apparently acted as developer by selling individual lots in "Fossett's Addition." (see also following note # 37.)

[31] *Echoes of Eighty-Nine*, op. cit., p. 21.

[32] *Kingfisher Daily World,* March 26, 1891.

[33] B.B. Chapman, "The Legal Sooners of 1889 in Oklahoma," op. cit., pp. 402, 404, 405.

[34] *The New World*, May 18, 1889.

[35] Atlas of Kingfisher County, loc. cit.

[36] *The New World*, April 4, 1891.

[37] Lee Boecher, *Short Grass Country*, privately published, 1968, pp. 47, 179-180; Kingfisher, Kingfisher County, Okla., County Court Clerk Land Records, 1893 to 1931. The Sandy Point dance hall lasted until shortly after statehood. Fossett platted his southeast 40 acres as an "Addition" to the city and acted as a land developer for portions of the property both north and south of Kingfisher Creek, on the West side of Main Street. Over a period of years he sold and re-purchased several lots many times over, but that portion of "Fossett's Addition" north of Kingfisher Creek never came to fruition as a developed addition to Kingfisher. In the early days, Kingfisher Creek crossed Main Street (U.S. Route 81) twice in its tortuous route through Fossett's property. The creek was re-channeled in the 1930s. Today, it crosses Main Street at only the very northern tip of what was once Bill Fossett's northwest quarter section.

[38] W.D. Fossett, Indian-Pioneer History, loc. cit.; William Edward Hayes, *Iron Road to Empire*, Simmons-Boardman, N.Y., 1953, pp. 122, 125-126. On June 10, 1891, all Chicago, Kansas and Nebraska railroad property was formally conveyed to the parent, Rock Island Company (Hayes p. 126).

[39] John Alley, *City Beginnings in Oklahoma Territory*, op. cit., pp. 96-98. Guthrie was designated the temporary capital of the territory and finally won the title until the capital was later moved to Oklahoma City. Greer County was in dispute between Oklahoma and Texas until declared a part of Oklahoma in an 1896 Supreme Court decision.

[40] Roy Gittinger, *The Formation of the State of Oklahoma,1803-1906*, University of Oklahoma Press, Norman, 1939, pp. 194-197.

[41] Lloyd C. Lentz III, Guthrie, *A History of the Capital City*, Thirty Seconds Press, Guthrie, 1999, p. 75.

[42] John Alley, *City Beginnings in Oklahoma Territory*, op. cit., pp. 48-49.

[43] Harold Preece, *The Dalton Gang*, Hastings House, N.Y., 1963, pp. 36-37.

[44] Nancy Samuelson, *The Dalton Gang Story*, Shooting Star Press, Eastford, Conn., 1992, pp. 61-63, 78-82; Glenn Shirley, *West of Hell's Fringe*, op. cit., p. 45; *Coffeyville Journal*, October 7, 1892.

[45] W.D. Fossett, Indian-Pioneer History, op. cit., p. 17.

Chapter 6
Forty Miles Through Hell to Hennessey

[1] B.B. Chapman, "The Legal Sooners of 1889 in Oklahoma," *The Chronicles of Oklahoma*, 1957-1958, Vol. XXXV, No. 4, p. 382.

[2] Odie B. Falk, *Oklahoma: Land of the Fair God*, Windsor Publications, Northridge, Calif., 1986, p. 112.

[3] Rock Island Technical Society, *Rock Island Railroad History,* 1970.

[4] William Edward Hayes, *Iron Road to Empire*, Simmons-Boardman, N.Y., 1953, pp. 121-122, 143.

[5] George Rainey, *The Cherokee Strip*, Enid, Oklahoma, 1925, pp. 1-13. The term "Cherokee Outlet" is often used interchangeably, but mistakenly, with *Cherokee Strip*. In 1854 the southern boundary of Kansas was established at the 37th parallel, thereby taking in a 2.46 miles wide strip of land previously assigned to the Cherokee tribe. This became the so-called "real" Cherokee Strip. Following the Civil War, a treaty with the Cherokees ceded the land in trust to the United States to become a part of Kansas, and later this *strip* was opened to white settlers. The "Cherokee Outlet," meanwhile, took in about 226 miles in length, was about 58 miles wide and, after 1866, was all in Indian Territory. In recent years, use of the term "Cherokee Strip," has come to mean what was technically, the Cherokee Outlet."

[6] Ibid., p. 14.

[7] William Edward Hayes, *Iron Road to Empire,* op. cit., pp. 135, 136.

[8] Ibid., pp. 122-131.

[9] James R. Mead, *Hunting and Trading on the Great Plains*, University of Oklahoma Press, Norman, 1986, pp. 196, 252; Wayne Gard, *The Chisholm Trail,* University of Oklahoma Press, Norman, 1954, p. 73; Sam P. Ridings, *The Chisholm Trail,* Co-operative Publishing Company, Guthrie, 1936, pp. 409; *The Encyclopedia of Oklahoma*, Somerset Publishers, Inc., St. Clair Shores, Michigan, revised 1999, p. 215; George H. Shirk, *Oklahoma Place Names*, University of Oklahoma Press, Norman, 1987, p. 195; *Enid News & Eagle,* March 3, 1993. When James R. Mead and Jesse Chisholm built the first trading post there in 1866, they designated the creek "Round Pond Creek" because its overflow made an almost circular pond south of the creek. This was located directly east of the trading post and what later became Sewell's Stockade and a stage station.

[10] William Edward Hayes, *Iron Road to Empire,* op. cit., pp. 122-131. There are many stories as to how the name *Enid,* was selected. Hayes believes the authentic one is that it was taken from the book, *Idylls of the King,* by some construction engineer who read literature in his spare time. Another version is that it was named for the deaf mute sister of local rancher W.C. "Bill" Quinlin (Laban S. Records, *Cherokee Outlet Cowboy,* edited by Ellen Jayne Maris Wheeler, University of Oklahoma Press, Norman and London, 1995, p. 297).

[11] Ibid., p. 136.

[12] George Rainey, *The Cherokee Strip,* op. cit., p. 22.

[13] William Edward Hayes, *Iron Road to Empire,* loc. cit; Ralph E. Tanton, *Early Legends Along Osage Creek,* Grant County Historical Society, Medford, Okla., 1975, pp. 31-33.

[14] Ibid.; C.C. Daniels, "Oklahoma: Land of the Fair God," unpublished manuscript, 1947, p. 95.

[15] George Rainey, *The Cherokee Strip,* op. cit., pp. 18-22.

[16] William Edward Hayes, *Iron Road to Empire,* op. cit., p. 137; Samuel P. Ridings, *The Chisholm Trail,* Co-Operative Publishing Co., Guthrie, 1936, p. 539.

[17] George Rainey, *The Cherokee Strip,* op. cit., p. 21.

[18] *Guthrie Daily Leader,* September 19, 1893.

[19] William Edward Hayes, *Iron Road to Empire,* loc. cit.

[20] Frederick S. Barde, "A War Against the Railroad," Oklahoma Historical Society, Manuscript and Archives Division, 1897; Samuel P. Ridings, *The Chisholm Trail,* op. cit., p. 547.

[21] *Cherokee Sentinel,* June 7, 1894; Frederick S. Barde, "A War Against the Railroad," loc. cit.; Ralph E. Tanton, *Early Legends Along Osage Creek,* loc. cit.

[22] George Rainey, *The Cherokee Strip,* Co-Operative Publishing Co., Guthrie, 1933, pp. 373-374.

[23] *Pond Creek Echo,* June 23, 1894; *Cherokee Sentinel* June 20, 1894, and April 20, 1895; *Wichita Eagle,* April 11, 1894.

[24] Samuel P. Ridings, *The Chisholm Trail,* loc. cit.; *Pond Creek Echo,* June 23, 1894; George H. Shirk, *Oklahoma Place Names,* loc. cit.

[25] *Cherokee Sentinel,* June 20, 1894. Almost a year later, in April 1895, the confusion apparently persisted. The *Cherokee Sentinel* published another editorial chastising people for the "injustice" in continuing to call the town Round Pond. By then it was more widely known as Pond Creek, as it is today.

[26] William Edward Hayes, *Iron Road to Empire,* op. cit., 137-138.

[27] Ibid., p. 139.

[28] *Enid Daily Wave,* May 5, 1894. The Rock Island eventually located a station where the line crossed E Street, today's Broadway.

[29] F.J. Callahan, interview, Indian-Pioneer History Project for Oklahoma, Works Progress Administration, March 14, 1938, pp. 23-25.

[30] C.C. Daniels, "Oklahoma: Land of the Fair God," op. cit., p. 157.

[31] William Edward Hayes, *Iron Road to Empire,* op. cit., p. 139.

[32] Marquis James, *The Cherokee Strip*, Viking Press, New York, 1945, p. 14.
[33] Ibid., p. 13; Judge J.W. Byrd, interview, Indian-Pioneer History Project for Oklahoma, Works Progress Administration, Vol. 90, p. 311.
[34] Samuel P. Ridings, *The Chisholm Trail,* op. cit., pp. 548-549.
[35] Ibid.; *Cherokee Sentinel*, June 7, 1894; William Edward Hayes, *Iron Road to Empire*, loc. cit.
[36] Frederick S. Barde, "A War Against the Railroad," loc. cit.; William Edward Hayes, *Iron Road to Empire*, op. cit., p. 140.
[37] *Enid Daily Wave*, July 13, 1894.
[38] William Edward Hayes, *Iron Road to Empire*, op. cit., p. 142. The saw used to cut the bridge was hidden in a haystack north of town for several years. It is now displayed at Enid's Cherokee Strip Museum.
[39] Glenn Shirley, *West of Hell's Fringe*, University of Oklahoma Press, Norman, 1978, pp. 226-229.
[40] Ibid., pp. 224-225.
[41] Ibid., pp. 231-232; William Edward Hayes, *Iron Road to Empire*, op. cit., p. 141; Frederick S. Barde, "A War Against the Railroad," loc. cit.
[42] *Enid Morning News*, March 30, 1912.
[43] Jefferson was later moved about one mile north along the Rock Island tracks from the old Pond Creek Station site (Ralph E. Tanton, *Historical Tales of the Cherokee Strip and the Rhubarb Farm*, Pine Hill Press, Freeman, S.D., 1982, p. 177).
[44] George H. Shirk, *Oklahoma Place Names,* op. cit., pp. 126, 195; Samuel P. Ridings, *The Chisholm Trail,* op. cit., pp. 550-553.

Chapter 7
Raid on the Rock Island

[1] David Dary, *Cowboy Culture,* University Press of Kansas, Lawrence, Kansas, 1989, pp. 308, 330. Fencing of the great ranges began as early as 1882 at which time fewer riders were needed, and many line camps were discarded in favor of operating from a headquarters ranch (Laban S. Records, *Cherokee Outlet Cowboy,* edited by Ellen Jayne Maris Wheeler, University of Oklahoma Press, Norman and London, 1995, p. 71).
[2] Edward Everett Dale, *Cow Country,* University of Oklahoma Press, Norman, Okla., 1942, pp. 211, 220-221, 223; Oliver Nelson, *The Cowman's Southwest; being the reminiscences of Oliver Nelson; freighter, camp cook, cowboy, frontiersman in Kansas, Indian Territory, Texas, and*

Oklahoma, 1878-1893, Edited by Angie Debo, Bison Books, University of Nebraska Press, Lincoln and London, 1986, p. 209.

[3] Edward Everett Dale, *Cow Country,* pp. 224-225, 229-230.

[4] Glenn Shirley, *West of Hell's Fringe,* University of Oklahoma Press, Norman, Okla., 1978, p. 37.

[5] Paul I. Wellman, *A Dynasty of Western Outlaws,* Doubleday & Co., Garden City, New York, 1961, p. 14.

[6] Harry Sinclair Drago, *Outlaws on Horseback,* University of Nebraska Press, Bison Book Edition, 1998, p. xxvii; Glenn Shirley, *West of Hell's Fringe,* loc. cit. Research by both Drago and Shirley show that Doolin had been a top hand on Oscar Halsell's HX Bar ranch before joining the Daltons. After the Dalton's debacle at Coffeyville, Kansas, Doolin returned to the HX Bar north of Guthrie and began recruiting other cowhands for his own gang.

[7] *The Daily Oklahoman,* April 23, 1939.

[8] Ibid.

[9] Glenn Shirley, *West of Hell's Fringe,* op. cit., p. 38.

[10] Harry Fox, son the Rock Island Railway Superintendent Harry P. Fox in a letter to Preston Rishaw, March 1958.

[11] *Kingfisher Times,* October 17, 1929.

[12] W.D. Fossett, interview, Indian-Pioneer History Project for Oklahoma, Works Progress Administration, Aug. 11, 18, 1937, p. 27; *Kingfisher Times,* loc. cit. The interviewer in the Pioneer History Project spelled the name "Umphrey," but other references by Fossett, including the *Kingfisher Times* story, spell the name "Humphrey" or "Humphreys."

[13] *Kingfisher Times,* loc. cit.

[14] Ibid.; *Enid Daily Wave,* April 10, 1894. The conductor's name is variously spelled "Reed" and "Reid."

[15] W.D. Fossett, interview, Indian-Pioneer History, op. cit., p. 29.

[16] *Kingfisher Times,* loc. cit. In the 1929 *Kingfisher Times* story, Fossett said he had no gun on him that night, but as the same robbery account unfolds in the Pioneer History Project interview, Fossett does not mention being without a gun, saying, "I took a shot at him…[the robber]."

[17] W.D. Fossett, Indian-Pioneer History, loc. cit.

[18] *Enid Daily Wave,* April 10, 1894; *Cherokee Sentinel,* April 12, 1894; *Kingfisher Times,* loc. cit.

[19] *Pond Creek Tribune,* April 12, 1894.

[20] *Enid Daily Wave,* April 10, 1894.

[21] *Cherokee Sentinel,* April 12, 1894.

[22] *Pond Creek Tribune*, loc. cit.; *Wichita Daily Eagle*, April 11, 1894; *Enid Daily Wave*, April 13, 1894.

[23] *Cherokee Sentinel*, loc. cit.

[24] W.D. Fossett, Indian-Pioneer History, op. cit., p. 30.

[25] *Pond Creek Tribune*, loc. cit.; *Cherokee Sentinel*, loc. cit.; *Pond Creek News*, April 14, 1894.

[26] W.D. Fossett, Indian-Pioneer History, op. cit., pp. 29-30.

[27] *Pond Creek Tribune*, loc. cit.

[28] W.D. Fossett, Indian-Pioneer History, op. cit., pp. 30-31.

[29] *Oklahoma State Capital*, April 11, 1894.

[30] *Pond Creek Tribune*, loc. cit.

[31] W.D. Fossett, Indian-Pioneer History, op. cit., p. 31.

[32] *Kingfisher Times*, loc. cit.

[33] W.D. Fossett, Indian-Pioneer History, loc. cit.

[34] *North Enid Weekly Tribune*, April 12, 1894; *Enid Daily Wave*, April 13, 1894.

[35] W.D. Fossett, Indian-Pioneer History, loc. cit.

[36] *Enid Daily Wave*, April 10, 1894.

[37] W.D. Fossett, Indian-Pioneer History, op. cit., p. 32; *Pond Creek Tribune*, loc. cit.; *Kingfisher Times*, loc. cit.

[38] *Enid Daily Wave,* April 10, 1894; Nancy Samuelson, *Shoot from the Lip*, Shooting Star Press, Eastford, Conn., 1998, p. 49. By the time of the Pond Creek train robbery, the Dalton gang had all but ceased to exist. Bill Doolin had been a member of the Dalton gang at one time, and Bill Dalton joined the new Doolin gang after his brothers were shot down at Coffeyville, Kansas, in 1892. For a time, the new gang was known by several names, with the surnames "Doolin" and "Dalton" interchangeable when it came to laying blame for almost any law offense in the territory.

[39] Ibid.; *Enid Daily Wave*, April 13, 1894.

[40] *North Enid Weekly Tribune*, April 12, 1894.

[41] *Cherokee Sentinel*, April 26, 1894. Henry Coleman Dalton was the second oldest son in the family and had helped his mother and sisters stake a claim near Kingfisher in the 1889 land run. Two months after the Pond Creek holdup, Bill Dalton, wanted for many crimes, was tracked down and killed while attempting to escape from lawmen in Indian Territory.

[42] *Pond Creek Tribune*, loc. cit.

[43] Ibid.

[44] W.D. Fossett, Indian-Pioneer History, loc. cit.; *Kingfisher Times*, loc. cit.

[45] *North Enid Weekly Tribune*, loc. cit.

[46] Ibid.

[47] Ibid.

[48] *Pond Creek Echo*, April 13, 1894.

[49] W.D. Fossett, Indian-Pioneer History, op. cit., p. 30; *Kingfisher Times*, loc. cit.

[50] C.C. Daniels, "Oklahoma: Land of the Fair God," unpublished manuscript, 1947, p. 111.

[51] Another post-incident identification of the slain bandit as Bob Hughes is in Fossett's 1929 *Kingfisher Free Press* account of the robbery. He says, "The dead man was identified as Bob Hughes, a member of the family that produced several outlaws down in the Chickasaw Indian Country. I had known him slightly." The name "Hughes" was never used by newspapers at the time of the robbery, making it logical that his identification came later, possibly by Fossett, Madsen and Nix, through records in the U.S. Marshal's Office. National Archives and Administration records show that on July 8, 1893, a Bob Hughes was indicted for peddling whiskey to the Indians in Atoka County, the Choctaw Nation. This may have been the Bob Hughes to which Fossett referred.

[52] W.D. Fossett, Indian-Pioneer History, op. cit., p. 32; *Kingfisher Times*, loc. cit.

[53] C.C. Daniels, "Oklahoma: Land of the Fair God," op. cit., p. 117.

[54] W.D. Fossett, Indian-Pioneer History, op. cit., p. 33.

[55] *Kingfisher Times*, loc. cit. Fossett said Malaley's ranch was used "as a hotel" by many transient cowboys in the area. This was the same Billy Malaley who had buried Pat Hennessey's body after the Indian raid in July 1874. Malaley had been a deputy U.S. marshal and a cattleman who was active in the Cherokee Strip Livestock Association. During the 1880s, he lived in Caldwell and operated a ranch in the Pole Cat area of the Cherokee Outlet, a stage stop near what later became Renfrow, Okla., (George D. Freeman, *Midnight & Noonday*, Edited by Richard Lane, University of Oklahoma Press, Norman, 1984, p. 155; Laban S. Records, *Cherokee Outlet Cowboy*, edited by Ellen Jayne Maris Wheeler, University of Oklahoma Press, Norman and London, 1995, pp. 259-267).

[56] Ibid.

[57] W.D. Fossett, Indian-Pioneer History, op. cit., p. 35.

[58] *Kingfisher Times*, loc. cit.

[59] W.D. Fossett, Indian-Pioneer History, loc. cit. In both the *Kingfisher Times* and the Indian-Pioneer History interviews, Fossett said Lew was about "fifteen years old." Lew's death certificate shows his birth date as

January 10, 1873, making him over 21 years old at the time of this pursuit in April 1894.

[60] *Kingfisher Times*, loc. cit. In his Indian-Pioneer History interview version, Fossett remembers the letter being sent from "over about Chandler" [Oklahoma].

[61] Ibid.; W.D. Fossett, Indian-Pioneer History, op. cit., p. 37.

[62] Ibid.; W.D. Fossett, Indian-Pioneer History, op. cit., p. 38.

[63] *Kingfisher Times*, loc. cit. Fossett said he was sure none of the Daltons was involved because he knew the family quite well. He rented property to Eva Dalton Whipple, a sister to the outlaw brothers. Said Fossett: "I would have hated to think that any of the Dalton boys would have caused me any trouble, as long as we had known each other."

[64] W.D. Fossett, Indian-Pioneer History, op. cit., pp. 38-39. Although there were contradictory reports at the time and in ensuing years, Fossett is emphatic about who killed Young's horse and captured Young. The *El Reno Democrat* of May 17, 1894, reports it was Chris Madsen and Deputy Isaac Prater who made the capture under similar circumstances described by Fossett. The *Daily Oklahoman* of May 26, 1894, credits "Kid Marshal" W.A. Murphy with the capture. E.D. Nix in his 1929 *Oklahombres*, says Madsen tracked down Young and Sylva and made the arrests. In his 1936 story, "Fourscore Years a Fighter" (*Daily Oklahoman*, January 19, 1936), Madsen credits Fossett with learning the two men were in El Reno, but then said Fossett called on him (Madsen) to help make the arrests. Madsen then claims to have done all the shooting and was aided by Fossett only after Young was down and injured. Fossett, who doggedly investigated the attempted train robbery from the beginning, may have felt slighted by the continual oversights of the Young capture when he had the last say in his 1937 interview.

[65] *Oklahoma State Capital*, April 12, 1894.

[66] Glenn Shirley, *West of Hell's Fringe,* op. cit., p. 210.

[67] *Kingfisher Times*, loc. cit.; *The Cherokee Sentinel*, May 17, 1894.

[68] E.D. Nix, *Oklahombres*, University of Nebraska Press, Lincoln, Nebr., 1993, p. 190. The escape was from Round Pond (Pond Creek), a widely reported incident of June 3, 1894.

[69] *Kingfisher Times*, loc. cit.

[70] *Daily Oklahoman*, May 26, 1894; Glenn Shirley, *West of Hell's Fringe,* op. cit., p. 211.

[71] *Cherokee Sentinel*, June 7, 1894.

[72] *Kingfisher Times*, loc. cit.

[73] E.D. Nix, *Oklahombres,* op. cit., p. 191.

Chapter 8
Running Dick Yeager to Ground

[1] *Hennessey Clipper*, April 4, 1895; *El Reno Eagle*, April 8, 1895.

[2] *Kingfisher Times*, April 4, 1895, *Hennessey Clipper*, loc. cit.; Glenn Shirley, *West of Hell's Fringe*, University of Oklahoma Press, Norman, 1978, pp. 272-273; Bailey Hanes, *Bill Doolin, Outlaw O.T.*, University of Oklahoma Press, Norman, 1968, pp. 141-142. Hanes wrote that "Zip" Wyatt was one of the bandits, an error apparently taken from several newspaper accounts resulting from Grimes' mistaken identity.

[3] *Hennessey Clipper*, April 4, 6, 1895.

[4] Ibid., April 11, 1895.

[5] Jay Robert Nash, *Encyclopedia of Western Lawmen and Outlaws*, Da Capo Press, Inc., New York, 1994.

[6] Richard White, *It's Your Misfortune and None of My Own: History of the American West*, University of Oklahoma Press, Norman, 1991, pp. 336-337.

[7] *Ardmore State Herald*, March 14, 1895.

[8] Glenn Shirley, *Desperado from Cowboy Flat*, Barbed Wire Press, Stillwater, 1997, pp. 20-38; Jay Robert Nash, *Encyclopedia of Western Lawmen and Outlaws*, loc. cit.

[9] Glenn Shirley, *Desperado from Cowboy Flat*, op. cit., pp. 47-48.

[10] Chris Madsen, "Fourscore Years a Fighter," *Daily Oklahoman*, 1935-1936. The information about Black is offered by Chris Madsen in his serialized memoirs. The cutting of cedar from land claims was, at one time, a federal offense in Oklahoma. The Glass Mountains are sometimes incorrectly referred to as the "Gloss" Mountains, an apparent mistake by early cartographers. In 1873, a survey map for the U.S. General Land Office was handwritten with the stem of the letter "a" partially obscured, making it appear as an "o" (Bill Burchardt, editor, *Oklahoma Today*, Volume XXI, No. 1, Winter 1970-71, p. 31).The name Glass Mountains likely came from the fact that gypsum crystals found there, glistened in the sunlight (Oliver Nelson, *The Cowman's Southwest; being the reminiscences of Oliver Nelson; freighter, camp cook, cowboy, frontiersman in Kansas, Indian Territory, Texas, and Oklahoma, 1878-1893*, Edited by Angie Debo, Bison Books, University of Nebraska Press, Lincoln and London, 1986, p. 133).

[11] *Guthrie Daily Leader*, April 14, 1963.

[12] Glenn Shirley, *Desperado from Cowboy Flat*, op. cit., pp. 54-56. Edward Townsend's wife and children provided the description of the robbers, and following Yeager's capture they made positive identification of him as the killer.

[13] Marquis James, *The Cherokee Strip*, Viking Press, New York, 1945, p. 28.

[14] Ibid., p. 27. For a time, federal officers were paid a mileage fee for the transporting of suspects and prisoners.

[15] Ibid., p. 28.

[16] Glenn Shirley, *Desperado from Cowboy Flat*, op. cit., p. 60. At that time, Woods County adjoined Blaine County. In 1907, Major County was created from a portion of southern Woods County.

[17] Marquis James, *They Had Their Hour*, The Bobbs-Merrill Company, Indianapolis, 1926, pp. 286, 295.

[18] *Kingfisher Free Press*, August 8, 1895.

[19] Ibid., July 25, 1895.

[20] Ibid., August 8, 1895.

[21] *Hennessey Clipper*, August 1, 1895; W.D. Fossett, interview, Indian-Pioneer History Project for Oklahoma, Works Progress Administration, Aug. 11, 18, 1937, pp. 18, 23.

[22] Ibid.; *Kingfisher Free Press*, August 1, 1895.

[23] Ibid.; Marquis James, *They Had Their Hour,* op. cit., p. 290.

[24] *Kingfisher Free Press*, August 8, 1895.

[25] Ibid.

[26] Marquis James, *They Had Their Hour,* loc. cit.; *Kingfisher Times*, January 7, 1926. Some references say Black and Lew Fossett attended school together at Coffeyville, Kansas, but there is no evidence to indicate the Fossett's ever lived in Coffeyville. Marquis James, who was acquainted with the Fossetts, says the location was Caldwell, Kansas.

[27] *Kingfisher Free Press*, August 8, 1895. Greever Canyon and Greever Creek were named for Dave Greever, who owned a ranch just west of the Glass Mountains (W.D. Fossett, Indian-Pioneer History, op. cit., p. 19).

[28] W.D. Fossett, Indian-Pioneer History, op. cit., p. 21; *Kingfisher Times*, January 7, 1926.

[29] *Kingfisher Free Press*, August 8, 1895.

[30] Ibid.

[31] Glenn Shirley, *Desperado from Cowboy Flat*, op. cit., pp. 86, 88. In Fossett's *Indian-Pioneer History Interview,* and his *Kingfisher Free Press* story of August 8, 1895, he simply states the posse fired on them, "killing Black and wounding Yeager." Marquis James in, *They Had Their Hour,*

says "the posse fired without warning." Fossett never clearly states whether or not he, Deputy Banks, or son Lew Fossett, fired on the pair.

[32] Marquis James, *They Had Their Hour,* op. cit.; p. 291.

[33] *Kingfisher Free Press,* August 8, 1895; *Kingfisher Times,* January 7, 1926.

[34] *Kingfisher Free Press,* August 8, 1895.

[35] Ibid.

[36] W.D. Fossett, Indian-Pioneer History, op. cit., p. 23.

[37] *Kingfisher Free Press,* August 8, 1895.

[38] *Kingfisher Times,* January 7, 1926.

[39] *Oklahoma Daily Times-Journal,* August 5, 1895.

[40] *Kingfisher Times,* January 7, 1926.

[41] *Kingfisher Free Press,* August 8, 1895; Glenn Shirley, *Desperado from Cowboy Flat,* op. cit., p. 95.

[42] *Kingfisher Times,* January 7, 1926.

[43] *Oklahoma Daily Times-Journal,* August 5, 1895; *Enid Weekly Wave,* August 8, 1895.

[44] *Kingfisher Free Press,* August 8, 1895; Glenn Shirley, *Desperado from Cowboy Flat,* op. cit., p. 97.

[45] Marquis James, *They Had Their Hour,* op. cit.; pp. 292-293; *Enid Daily Wave,* August 8, 1895.

[46] Glenn Shirley, *Desperado from Cowboy Flat,* op. cit., pp. 103-104.

[47] *Hennessey Clipper,* August 8, 1895.

[48] *Kingfisher Free Press,* August 8, 1895.

[49] *Enid Daily Wave,* August 8, 1895; Marquis James, *They Had Their Hour,* op. cit. p. 294.

[50] Glenn Shirley, *Desperado from Cowboy Flat,* op. cit., pp. 106-108.

[51] *Enid Daily Wave,* August 8, 1895.

[52] Ibid., August 24, 1895.

[53] Marquis James, *They Had Their Hour,* op. cit. pp. 297-298.

[54] Ibid., p 296.

[55] W.D. Fossett, Indian-Pioneer History, op. cit., p. 18.

[56] Ibid., p, 26.

[57] The *Enid Daily Wave* as quoted by the *Kingfisher Free Press,* August 15, 1895.

[58] Ibid.

[59] Ibid.

Chapter 9
Chief Deputy Fossett

[1] *Enid Daily Wave*, October 3, 1895.

[2] *Oklahoma Daily Times-Journal*, January 20, 24, 1896.

[3] *Guthrie Daily Leader*, January 25, 1896; Nancy Samuelson, *Shoot from the Lip*, Shooting Star Press, Eastford, Conn., 1998, pp. 69-70.

[4] Glenn Shirley, *Heck Thomas: Frontier Marshal*, Chilton Co., New York, 1962, p. 210.

[5] *Guthrie Daily Leader*, July 8, 1896.

[6] *Oklahoma State Capital*, August 26, 1896.

[7] Ibid., November 11, 1987.

[8] Ibid., June 10, 1897.

[9] *The Cherokee Advocate*, March 27, 1897.

[10] *Oklahoma State Capital*, October 13, 1897.

[11] Glenn Shirley, *West of Hell's Fringe*, University of Oklahoma Press, Norman, 1978, p. 383.

[12] *Oklahoma State Capital*, November 8, 1897; *Kingfisher Free Press*, November 11, 1897.

[13] Ibid., November 9, 1897.

[14] *Kingfisher Times Weekly*, September 8, 1892; *Kingfisher Free Press*, April 14, June 17, 1895; May 13, 1897. Newspapers indicate she was either visiting "friends" or her "relatives" in Pueblo. Although not mentioned specifically, this could have included her mother, Elizabeth. Federal and Colorado State Census Records of 1880 and 1885, show that four brothers of Elizabeth Footman Fossett (Mamie's mother) lived in Pueblo, Colorado, and in 1901, their mother (Mamie's grandmother) died there (T.G. McCarthy Funeral Home and Roselawn Cemetery records, April 3, 1901).

[15] Nancy Samuelson, "Some Notes on Oklahoma's Female Marshals," *Quarterly for the National Association of Outlaw and Lawman History*, July-September 1998, Vol. XXII, No. 3, p. 5.

[16] *Guthrie Daily Leader*, February 17, 1898. Coincidentally, a female U.S. deputy marshal named F. M. Miller, commissioned from the federal court at Paris, Texas, was once "known to be the only female deputy that worked the Indian Territory (*Muskogee Weekly Phoenix*, November 19, 1891)."

[17] Art Burton, "Women of the Shooting Iron," *Oklahombres Journal*, Winter 1996, Vol. VII, No. 2, P. 14.

[18] Glenn Shirley, *West of Hell's Fringe*, op. cit., pp. 139, 186, 383.

[19] Ibid., pp. 186, 384-385, 390-396, 406-407, 411. Al Jennings served prison time and was paroled in 1902. He returned to law practice, made an unsuccessful run for governor in 1913, and then wrote a garbled and highly fictionalized account of his "success" as an outlaw. He then moved to California and convinced moviemakers he was a "big-time, gun-fighting train robber and old West outlaw." His welcome in Hollywood as a consultant for western movies "greatly exceeded" his actual reputation in Oklahoma. "In the world of pretense, a pretender will find a home, and so it was with Jennings (Ken Butler, *Oklahoma Renegades*, Pelican Publishing Company, Gretna, Louisiana, 1997, pp. 162-165)."

[20] *Oklahoma State Capital*, April 8, 1898.

[21] *Guthrie Daily Leader*, April 9, 1898; Glenn Shirley, *West of Hell's Fringe*, op. cit., p. 413.

[22] *Guthrie Daily Leader*, April 9, 1898.

[23] Ibid. West's grave in Guthrie is incorrectly marked "Killed April 13."

[24] Glenn Shirley, *West of Hell's Fringe*, op. cit., p. 414. Shirley says the information was contained in a letter from Albert Thomas, dated October 7, 1957.

[25] *Guthrie Daily Leader*, April 9, 1898.

[26] Ibid., March 11, 1898.

[27] Business and Residence Directory, Guthrie & Logan County, 1898.

[28] *Kingfisher Free Press*, October 28, 1897, *Kingman Leader-Courier*, September 19, 1907; *Kingman Journal*, September 20, 1907; *Clark County Clipper*, October 23, 1930. Richard Miller was born in Parker's Landing, Pennsylvania, October 13, 1875.

[29] *Kingfisher Free Press*, May 26, 1898.

[30] *Guthrie Daily Leader*, May 26, 1898.

[31] *Kingfisher Free Press*, March 18, 1940.

[32] Daniel F. Littlefield, Jr., *Seminole Burning, A Story of Racial Vengeance*, University Press of Mississippi, Jackson, 1996, pp. 33-34.

[33] Ibid., pp. 35-39, 59.

[34] Ibid., pp. 47-48, 54.

[35] Ibid., pp. 62-64, 73-74, 80.

[36] Ibid., pp. 80-83.

[37] Ibid., pp. 87, 92-98.

[38] W.D. Fossett, interview, Indian-Pioneer History Project for Oklahoma, Works Progress Administration, Aug. 30, 1937, pp. 1-5.

[39] Daniel F. Littlefield, Jr., *Seminole Burning*, op. cit., p. 99.

[40] W.D. Fossett, Indian-Pioneer History, op. cit., pp. 5-6.

---

[41] Daniel F. Littlefield, Jr., *Seminole Burning,* op. cit., pp. 99-100.

[42] Ibid., pp. 120, 124.

[43] Ibid., p. 125.

[44] Ibid., pp. 129, 132.

[45] W.D. Fossett, Indian-Pioneer History, op. cit., pp. 6-7.

[46] Ibid.

[47] Daniel F. Littlefield, Jr., *Seminole Burning,* op. cit., pp. 128, 135, 146, 163-164.

[48] Ibid., pp. 168, 170; Nancy Samuelson, *Shoot from the Lip,* op. cit., p. 81.

[49] Glenn Shirley, *Guardian of the Law*, Eakin Press, Austin, 1988, pp. 291-293.

[50] *Kingman Leader-Courier*, September 19, 1907; *Chickasha Daily Express,* July 6, 1901.

[51] *Chickasha Daily Express*, March 14, 1901; Oklahoma State Department of Health, Delayed Certificate of Birth for Irene Madaline Miller, born March 12, 1901. Bill's granddaughter preferred using "Madaline" to "Irene."

[52] U.S. District Court Expense Record form #270, March 31, 1901.

[53] Kingfisher, Kingfisher County, Okla., County Court Case Record No. 2346, November 28, 1900; *Kingfisher Free Press*, November 28, 1895.

[54] *Oklahoma State Capital*, May 2, 1901.

[55] *Kingfisher Free Press*, March 18, 1940; *Pioneers of Kingfisher County: 1889-1976,* Kingfisher Bicentennial Committee, 1976, p. 93.

[56] *Kingfisher Free Press,* June 1, 1893; April 18, 1949; Business and Residence Directory, Guthrie & Logan County, 1902.

[57] *Kingfisher Free Press*, September 1, 1892.

Chapter 10
The Law, Lawton and the Land Lottery

[1] Lawton, south of Ft. Sill, was named for General Henry W. Lawton, a hero of the Spanish-American War who was killed during the Philippine insurrection in 1899. It was a designated townsite for the 1901 opening, and a post office was established there on July 15, 1901. Lawton did not become an actual town until the day of the opening, August 6, 1901 (George H. Shirk, *Oklahoma Place Names*, University of Oklahoma Press, Norman, 1987, p. 138).

[2] History, City of Lawton, Okla.; John Morris, et al, *Historical Atlas of Oklahoma,* University of Oklahoma Press, Norman, 1976, p. 57; Kent Ruth, et al, *Oklahoma: A Guide to the Sooner State,* University of Oklahoma Press, Norman, 1957, p. 34.

[3] *Kingfisher Free Press,* April 18, 1949.

[4] Ibid.; *Chickasha Daily Express,* July 29, 1901; John Morris, et al, *Historical Atlas of Oklahoma,* op. cit., p. 48; *Lawton: A Child of the Prairie,* Museum of the Great Plains, Lawton, 2001, pp. 18-19.

[5] *Chickasha Daily Express,* August 5, 1901; Beth Thomas Meeks with Bonnie Speer, *Heck Thomas, My Papa,* Levite of Apache, Norman, 1988, pp. 37-38; *'Neath August Sun-1901,* Second Edition, Lawton Business and Professional Women's Club, 1955, p. 162.

[6] Beth Thomas Meeks with Bonnie Speer, *Heck Thomas, My Papa,* loc. cit.; *'Neath August Sun-1901,* op. cit., pp. 143-144, 161. Goo Goo Avenue was later cleaned out and renamed Gore Avenue for Oklahoma Senator Thomas Gore (Museum of the Great Plains, Lawton).

[7] *Kingfisher Free Press,* April 18, 1949. Estimates of the number of people in Lawton for town lot sales vary from 25,000 to 40,000.

[8] *Lawton Daily Democrat,* August 6, 1901.

[9] Ibid.; Ken Butler, *Oklahoma Renegades,* Pelican Publishing Company, Gretna, La., 1997, pp. 53-56, 73. Several members of the Casey Clan had been in trouble with the law. Most notable were Jim and Vic, Bert's uncles, who shot and killed Canadian County Deputy Sheriff Sam Farris in May 1894, as Farris attempted to arrest them as murder suspects in an earlier case. Vic died from his wounds in the shootout, and Jim was slain the following year during a jailbreak, in which he fatally shot Oklahoma City Police Chief Milton Jones (Ken Butler, *Oklahoma Renegades,* op. cit., pp. 54-55).

[10] Kent Ruth, et al, *Oklahoma: A Guide to the Sooner State,* op. cit., p. 158.

[11] *Kingfisher Free Press,* April 18, 1949; Glenn Shirley, *Heck Thomas: Frontier Marshal,* Chilton Co., N.Y., 1962, p. 223.

[12] Kent Ruth, et al, *Oklahoma: A Guide to the Sooner State,* op. cit., pp. 158-159.

[13] *Oklahoma State Capital,* September 14, 22, 1901.

[14] Mrs. C.E. Goodrich (Anna Leah Fossett), "The Fossetts in America," genealogy, 1974, p. 7.

[15] *Kingfisher Free Press,* January 18; June 7, 1900.

[16] Frederick S. Barde, *Manuscript Archives,* Oklahoma Historical Society.

[17] *Kingfisher Free Press*, April 18, 1895; *Kingman Courier*, March 12, 1886.

Chapter 11
New Order at Guthrie and Getting Bert Casey

[1] *Oklahoma State Capital*, April 1, 1902.
[2] *Daily Oklahoman*, April 1, 1902; U.S. Department of Justice, U.S. Marshal's Oath of Office, April 7, 1902.
[3] *Kingfisher Free Press*, March 11, 1940.
[4] *Daily Oklahoman*, loc. cit.
[5] *Kingfisher Free Press*, April 3, 1902.
[6] *Kingfisher Times*, April 3, 1902.
[7] *Chandler Tribune*, April 3, 1902.
[8] Ibid.
[9] *Oklahoma State Capital*, loc. cit.
[10] Ken Butler, *Oklahoma Renegades*, Pelican Publishing Company, Gretna, Louisiana, 1997, pp. 53, 56; *Chickasha Daily Express*, August 7, 1901. Reports of Jay Beemblossom's age vary from 11 to 14, depending on the source.
[11] *Lawton Daily Democrat*, August 6, 1901; *Oklahoma State Capital*, January 3, 5, 1902. One of the bandits was originally thought to be Mort Perkins, but Dr. Beemblossom later identified the men as Levi Reed, along with Casey and Moran.
[12] *Norman Transcript*, August 14, 1902; Ken Butler, *Oklahoma Renegades*, op. cit., pp. 60, 114-115.
[13] *Oklahoma State Capital*, January 3, 1902; *Cordell Beacon*, January 3, 1902.
[14] *Watonga Republican*, January 9, 1902.
[15] *Guthrie Daily Leader*, January 3, 1902; *Oklahoma State Capital*, January 3, 5, 1902. Eventually, Mort Perkins and George Moran were convicted of Jay Beemblossom's murder, and both were paroled after serving a few years in prison (Ken Butler, *Oklahoma Renegades*, op. cit., pp. 135-136).
[16] *Kingfisher Free Press*, January 16, 1902; *McAlester News*, February 27, 1902. The kicking and robbing of Sheriff Smith was related in subsequent court testimony by two captured gang members.
[17] *Kingfisher Free Press*, January 16, 1902.

257

[18] *Shawnee Herald*, July 2, 12, 1902; *Anadarko Tribune*, July 4, 1902. Accounts vary in reporting that Bullard was hit from 3 to 19 times. Cogburn's revolver was unfired, indicating he was slain from ambush first, which alerted Bullard, who then apparently shot at the outlaws before he was cut down by their concentrated firepower.

[19] *Kingfisher Free Press*, October 24, 1929.

[20] *Oklahoma State Capital*, November 8, 1902.

[21] Ken Butler, *Oklahoma Renegades*, op. cit., p. 127; *Kingfisher Free Press,* October 24, 1929. (See the earlier chapter on the Pond Creek train robbery.) The man captured at the scene of the attempted train robbery used the alias Will Wade, but U.S. marshals later determined his real name was Jim Bourland.

[22] Homer Croy, *Trigger Marshal, The Story of Chris Madsen*, Duell, Sloan and Pearce, New York, 1958, p. 110.

[23] *Kingfisher Free Press*, October 24, 1929. Hudson later testified that interfering with Houston's hanging would have endangered his own life and the plan to capture Bert Casey (*Hobart News-Republican*, May 17, 1906).

[24] Ken Butler, *Oklahoma Renegades*, op. cit., p. 128; *Kingfisher Free Press*, October 24, 1929.

[25] *Oklahoma State Capital*, November 8, 1902.

[26] *Kingfisher Free Press*, October 24, 1929. At that time, the town was called Cleo and the gang camped near the actual springs nearby. In 1917 the town became Cleo Springs (George H. Shirk, *Oklahoma Place Names*, University of Oklahoma Press, Norman, 1987, p. 53).

[27] Ibid.

[28] Ibid., *The Weekly Oklahoma State Capital*, November 8, 1902. Accounts vary as to whether or not Lockett ever fired a shot. The shooting death of Bert Casey occurred November 3, 1902. The stone on his grave is erroneously marked "November 8," the day of his burial.

[29] *The Weekly Oklahoma State Capital*, November 8, 1902.

[30] *Kingfisher Free Press*, October 24, 1929.

[31] *Kingfisher Reformer*, March 24, 1904.

[32] *Guthrie Daily Leader*, May 11, 1903.

[33] Ken Butler, *Oklahoma Renegades*, op. cit., pp. 155-165.

[34] *Anadarko Daily Democrat*, May 23, 1906.

[35] *Kingfisher Free Press*, October 24, 1929.

[36] *Anadarko Daily Democrat*, May 23, 24, 1906. Bourland's "automatic handgun" undoubtedly was the Colt Model 1905 automatic pistol, carrying

a seven-round magazine. It was the first, true semi-automatic in .45-caliber, and the forerunner of the famous Model 1911.

[37] *Guthrie Daily Leader*, January 29, 1903. The name is spelled "Willis" by the newspaper, but U.S. Marshal's office records show it to be "Willits."

[38] *Guthrie Daily Leader*, February 16, 1903; U.S. District Court Expense Record, Form #22, June 30, 1903.

[39] *Kingfisher Free Press*, March 18, 1940.

[40] Ibid.

[41] Files of correspondence by W.D. Fossett, Western History Collection, Oklahoma University Library, Norman, Okla.

[42] *Guthrie Daily Leader*, June 9, 1904.

Chapter 12
Manhunt for the Murderous Martins

[1] J. D. Haines, *Wiley G. Haines Frontier U.S. Deputy Marshal*, Eakin Press, Austin, 2002, pp. 44-46.

[2] Ibid.; *Oklahoma State Capital*, March 5, 1903. The men were initially identified as Bob and Ray Martin and Ed Simmons (*Guthrie Daily Leader*, March 9, 1903).

[3] *Oklahoma State Capital*, March 5, 1903. The victim was initially identified as "Justice Craig" by Guthrie newspapers, but the *Kingfisher Free Press* of March 12, 1903, identified him as Gus Cravett.

[4] Ibid.; Glenn Shirley, *They Outrobbed Them All*, Barbed Wire Press, Stillwater, 1992, p. 32.

[5] *Guthrie Daily Leader*, March 5, 7, 9, 1903; *Kingfisher Free Press*, March 12, 1903; Glenn Shirley, *They Outrobbed Them All*, op. cit., p. 37.

[6] *Kingfisher Free Press*, March 12, 1903. Prior to statehood in 1907, Isabella was in Woods County.

[7] Glenn Shirley, *They Outrobbed Them All*, op. cit., p. 41.

[8] J. D. Haines, *Wiley G. Haines Frontier U.S. Deputy Marshal*, op. cit., pp. 50-51.

[9] Ibid., pp. 52-53.

[10] *Guthrie Daily Leader*, July 8, 1903.

[11] Ibid., July 17, 1903.

[12] J. D. Haines, *Wiley G. Haines Frontier U.S. Deputy Marshal*, op. cit., pp. 54-55.

[13] Ibid., p. 56.

[14] Ibid., p. 57.

[15] John W. Morris, *Cities of Oklahoma*, Oklahoma Historical Society, Oklahoma City, 1979, p. 29; Lloyd C. Lentz III, *Guthrie, A History of the Capital City,* Thirty Seconds Press, Guthrie, 1999, p. 100. Guthrie's streetcar system was completed in 1905.

[16] Business & Residence Directories, Guthrie and Logan County, 1900-1907; *Standard Atlas of Kingfisher County*, George A. Ogle & Co., Chicago, 1906, p. 60. The divorce decree of 1900 did not specify how or if the Kingfisher property was divided, but land records indicate that Laura L. Fossett still maintained rights to about 110 acres of land as of 1906.

[17] *Kingfisher Free Press*, June 9, 1892; June 22, 1893. "Fossett's Grove" was apparently a public park, one of two small land parcels set aside for public use when Fossett was awarded his Homestead Patent claim from the U.S. Land Office (U.S. Land Office Patent Record, August 8, 1892).

[18] *Kingfisher Free Press*, May 30, 1901; June 13, 1901.

[19] *Pioneers of Kingfisher County: 1889-1976,* Kingfisher Bicentennial Committee, 1976, p. 274.

[20] *Guthrie Daily Leader*, January 2, 1904. Lack of funds for operating expenses finally closed Kingfisher College in 1922 (*Pioneers of Kingfisher County: 1889-1976,* loc. cit).

[21] *Kingfisher Free Press*, October 8, 1902.

[22] *Oklahoma Leader*, February 15, 1906.

[23] *Oklahoma State Capital*, November 12, 1902.

[24] State of Kansas, County of Sedgwick Marriage License, February 3, 1904; *Wichita Eagle*, February 4, 1904. The marriage license stated Bill's age as "50," when in fact, he was 52.

[25] *Guthrie Daily Leader*, February 27, 1904; *Daily Oklahoman,* August 27, 1907. The 1904-05 Guthrie Directory places their home at 318 E. Vilas.

Chapter 13
Politics and a Prairie Wolf

[1] Theodore Roosevelt was the youngest to serve as president, John F. Kennedy was youngest to be elected.

[2] U.S. Dept of Justice, United States Marshals Service.

[3] *Guthrie Daily Leader*, August 5, 1904; *Lawton News-Republican*, February 15, 1906.

[4] Alice Roosevelt.

[5] *Perkins Journal*, August 5, 1904.

[6] The "Big Pasture" was set aside during the 1901 opening and reserved for the Kiowa and Comanche tribes. It was opened for white settlement by sealed bids in 1906. After statehood in 1907, portions of Comanche County, which at the time of the hunt took in all the "Big Pasture," became the new counties of Tillman and Cotton.

[7] Theodore Roosevelt, *Outdoor Pastimes of an American Hunter*, Charles Scribner & Sons, New York, 1905, p. 100. Roosevelt incorrectly spelled Waggoner's name "Wagner."

[8] John Abernathy, *A Son of the Frontier*, Introduction by Kermit Roosevelt, privately published, 1935.

[9] Theodore Roosevelt, *Outdoor Pastimes of an American Hunter*, op. cit., p. 101.

[10] *Oklahoma State Capital*, April 9, 1905; *Guthrie Daily Leader*, April 13, 1905.

[11] Theodore Roosevelt, *Outdoor Pastimes of an American Hunter*, op. cit., pp. 102-103.

[12] Ibid., pp. 113-114.

[13] *Oklahoma State Capital*, April 12, 1905.

[14] Ibid., April 25, 1905.

[15] Ibid., April 26, 1905.

[16] *Guthrie Daily Leader*, January 13, 1904; *Oklahoma State Capital*, June 9, 1905.

[17] *Shawnee News*, September 23, 1905.

[18] *Daily Oklahoman*, November 23, 1905.

[19] Ibid.

[20] Ibid.

[21] Nancy Samuelson, *Shoot from the Lip*, Shooting Star Press, Eastford, Conn., 1998, pp. 88-89.

[22] *Oklahoma State Capital*, February 6, 1906.

[23] *Oklahoma State Register*, February 22, 1906.

[24] John Morris, et al, *Historical Atlas of Oklahoma*, University of Oklahoma Press, Norman, 1976, p. 58.

[25] *Guthrie Daily Leader*, October 18, 19, 1906.

[26] Glenn Shirley, *West of Hell's Fringe*, University of Oklahoma Press, Norman, 1978, p. 421.

[27] Nancy Samuelson, *Shoot from the Lip,* op. cit., pp. 89-91.

[28] *Guthrie Daily Leader*, December 8, 1910.

Chapter 14
A Lawman on the Trail Again

[1] *Daily Oklahoman*, August 27, 1907.

[2] *Guthrie Dailer Leader*, September 14, 1907; *Kingman Leader-Courier*, September 19, 1907. The 1907 Guthrie Directory shows the Millers living at 407 E. Oklahoma Avenue, but they had apparently moved to the Osage Boarding House at 117 ½ West Harrison by the time Richard died.

[3] Kent Ruth, et al, *Oklahoma: A Guide to the Sooner State*, University of Oklahoma Press, Norman, 1957, p. 381; George H. Shirk, *Oklahoma Place Names*, University of Oklahoma Press, Norman, 1987, p. 251.

[4] *Waurika News*, February 7, 1908.

[5] *History of Jefferson County Oklahoma*, Oklahoma Department of Library Archives, Norman, OK.

[6] *Kingfisher Times*, March 14, 1940.

[7] *Kingfisher Free Press*, March 18, 1940.

[8] *El Reno American,* September 19, 1908; January 1, February 1, 1909.

[9] *Oklahoma State Register*, February 8, 1906; *El Reno Democrat*, December 16, 1909; *Rock Island Lines Station Book*, February 1, 1910.

[10] *Kingfisher Times*, March 14, 1940.

[11] Ibid.

[12] *El Reno Democrat*, December 16, 1909.

[13] Oklahoma State Census, 1910; *Kingfisher Weekly Star*, February 29, March 7, 1912.

[14] *Kingfisher Weekly Star*, August 5, 12, 1912.

[15] *Kingfisher Weekly Star*, March 7, 1912; *Kingfisher Weekly Free Press*, August 1, 1918.

[16] *Kingfisher Weekly Free Press*, June 26, 1917; Kingfisher, Kingfisher County, Okla., 1920 Census; City of Kingfisher, Oklahoma, Minutes Record, November 10, 1919, p. 1, December 22, 1919, p. 7; February 21, 1920, p. 32; *Kingfisher Free Press*, May 26, 1920.

[17] Kingfisher, Kingfisher County, Divorce Petition, filed November 17, 1921, granted December 21, 1921.

[18] John W. Morris, *Cities of Oklahoma*, Oklahoma Historical Society, Oklahoma City, 1979, p. 138.

[19] *Daily Oklahoman*, March 10, 1940.

[20] *Oklahoma City Times*, November 3, 1924; *The Ardmore Statesman*, November 16, 1924. Lynn's first name is variously spelled "Wiley" and "Wylie."

21 Nancy Samuelson, *Shoot from the Lip*, Shooting Star Press, Eastford, Conn., 1998, pp. 121-124. Following his acquittal, Lynn resigned as a federal agent. In 1932, Wiley Lynn and a man named Crockett Long killed each other in a grudge gunfight in Madill, Oklahoma.

22 *Oklahoma City Times*, November 3, 1924. The timing of their coming to Oklahoma together is unclear since Fossett had earlier stated he rode to Kingfisher for the "opening" from his home in Kingman, Kansas (*Kingfisher Times*, April 15, 1926). The two men may have been in Dodge City together between the time Fossett left the railroad construction business at Memphis, Tennessee, in 1888, and the April 1889 opening (*Caldwell Journal,* January 26, 1888).

23 *Oklahoma City Times*, November 3, 1924.

Chapter 15
The Peaceful End to a Rough and Tumble Career

1 *Kingfisher Times*, March 4, 1926.

2 *Kingfisher Times*, December 2, 1926; State of Oklahoma, Canadian County, Marriage License, November 27, 1926; *Kingfisher Free Press*, March 19, 1903. M. A. Ball's livery business went bankrupt in 1903. Fossett was listed as trustee of the bankruptcy sale.

3 *Kingfisher Times*, August 8, 1928; Kingfisher City Cemetery Records, Mary M. Ball, 1857-1928. Mary was buried in a plot, previously purchased by her first husband, with a marker bearing the "Ball" name.

4 *Kingfisher Times*, April 21, 1927.

5 Genevieve Moss, "C. P. 'Doc' Wickmiller," *Chronicles of Oklahoma*, Summer 1985, Vol. LXIII, No. 2, p. 202.

6 Fred Smith Standley, "The Oklahoma Historical Society, 1893-1943," M.A. Thesis, University of Oklahoma, 1986, pp. 25-32. The Oklahoma Historical Society was moved to Norman, Oklahoma, in 1902 and later to Oklahoma City.

7 Albert Stehno, private collection of CSCPA attendance rolls, meeting records and by-laws.

8 Letter from William D. Fossett to H. S. Tennant, Oklahoma State Highway Commission, May 9, 1933. Robert Klemme of Enid performed the most recent marking of the Chisholm Trail. From November 1990 to September 1997, Klemme, bearing most of the expense and work himself, used an 1871 government survey map to set concrete markers every mile from the Red River to the Oklahoma-Kansas border.

[9] *Kingfisher Times*, June 6, 1934; March 14, 1940.

[10] *Kingfisher Free Press*, March 11, 1940.

[11] T.A. McNeal, *When Kansas Was Young*, Capper Publications, Topeka, 1940, pp. 206-207.

[12] The Kingfisher Study Club, *Echoes of Eighty-Nine*, 1939, p. 113.

[13] *Kingfisher Times*, March 13, 1940. Chris Madsen also "died in bed" in 1944.

[14] *Guthrie Daily Leader*, April 11, 1899.

[15] *Oklahoma Leader*, February 15, 1906.

[16] *Daily Oklahoman*, March 10, 1940.

[17] *Kingfisher Times*, March 14, 1940.

[18] *Kingfisher Free Press*, March 18, 1940.

[19] *Oklahoma State Register*, February 22, 1906.

Epilogue

[1] *Kingman Leader-Courier,* September 19, 1907; State of Oklahoma, Funeral Record and Standard Certificate of Death, Laura Fossett, January 20, 1950.

[2] *Tulsa World*, September 7, 1952; State of Oklahoma, Department of Health, Death Certificate for Lewis D. Fossett, No. 013321, October 15, 1952.

[3] Letter to the author from Deborah Klaver Durr, March 21, 2002.

[4] Ibid.

[5] Ibid.; Mrs. C.E. Goodrich (Anna Leah Fossett), "The Fossetts in America," genealogy, 1974.

[6] Letter to Paul D. Fossett, II, from Mrs. C. E. Goodrich, September 12, 1977.

Bibliography

Books

Abernathy, John. *A Son of the Frontier*. Privately published, 1935.

Alley, John. *City Beginnings in Oklahoma Territory*. Norman: University of Oklahoma Press, 1939.

Boecher, Lee. *Short Grass Country*. Privately published, 1968.

Butler, Ken. *Oklahoma Renegades*. Gretna, La.: Pelican Publishing Company, 1997.

Colcord, Charles, F. *The Autobiography of Charles Francis Colcord: 1859-1934*. Tulsa: 1970.

Collins, Hubert. *Warpath and Cattle Trail*. Niwot, Colo.: University Press of Colorado, 1928.

Croy, Homer. *Trigger Marshal, The Story of Chris Madsen*. NY: Duell, Sloan and Pearce, 1958.

Cutler, William G. *History of the State of Kansas*. Chicago: A.T. Andreas, 1883.

Dale, Edward Everett. *Cow Country*. Norman: University of Oklahoma Press, 1942.

Dary, David. *Cowboy Culture*. Lawrence, Kans.: University Press of Kansas, 1989.

Drago, Harry Sinclair. *Great American Cattle Trails*. NY: Bramhall House, 1965.

_____. *Outlaws on Horseback*. Lincoln: University of Nebraska Press, Bison Book Edition, 1998.

_____. *Wild, Wooly and Wicked*. NY: Clarkson N. Potter, Inc., 1960.

Dykstra, Robert R. *The Cattle Towns*. NY: Alfred A. Knopf, 1968.

Echoes of Eighty-Nine. Kingfisher, Okla.: The Kingfisher Study Club, 1939.

Edwards, John P. *Historical Atlas of Sumner County*. Philadelphia: 1883.

Encyclopedia of Oklahoma. St. Clair Shores, Mich.: Somerset Publishers, Inc., 1999.

Falk, Odie B. *Oklahoma: Land of the Fair God*. Northridge, Calif.: Windsor Publications, 1986.

Freeman, George D. *Midnight & Noonday,* Edited by Richard Lane. Norman: University of Oklahoma Press, 1984.

Gard, Wayne. *The Chisholm Trail*. Norman: University of Oklahoma Press, 1954.

Gittinger, Roy. *The Formation of the State of Oklahoma,1803-1906*. Norman: University of Oklahoma Press, 1939.

Guide Map of the Great Texas Cattle Trail from the Red River Crossing to the Old Reliable Kansas Pacific Railway. Kansas City: The Kansas Pacific Railway Company, 1874.

Haines, J. D. *Wiley G. Haines Frontier U.S. Deputy Marshal*. Austin: Eakin Press, 2002.

Handbook of Texas. Austin: The Texas State Historical Association, 1999.

Hanes, Bailey. *Bill Doolin: Outlaw O.T.* Norman: University of Oklahoma Press, 1968.

Hayes, William, Edward. *Iron Road to Empire, The History of the Rock Island Lines*. NY: Simmons-Boardman, 1953.

Hoig, Stan. *The Oklahoma Land Rush of 1889*. Oklahoma City: Oklahoma Historical Society, 1989.

Hurd, Fred. *A History of Kingman County: 1871-1969*. North Newton, Kans.: Mennonite Press, 1970.

James, Marquis. *The Cherokee Strip: A Tale of an Oklahoma Boyhood*. NY: Viking Press, 1945.

_____. *They Had Their Hour*. Indianapolis: The Bobbs-Merrill Company, 1926.

Jones, Mary Ellen. *The Nineteenth Century American Frontier*. Westport, Conn.: Greenwood Press, 1998.

Kingfisher Panorama. Kingfisher, Okla.: Kingfisher Times and Free Press, 1957.

Lentz, Lloyd C., III. *Guthrie, A History of the Capital City*. Guthrie: Thirty Seconds Press, 1999.

Littlefield, Daniel F., Jr. *Seminole Burning, A Story of Racial Vengeance*. Jackson, Miss.: University Press of Mississippi, 1996.

266

Bibliography

McNeal, T. A. *When Kansas Was Young*. Topeka: Capper Publications, 1940.

Mead, James R. *Hunting and Trading on the Great Plains*. Norman: University of Oklahoma Press, 1986.

Meeks, Beth Thomas, with Bonnie Speer. *Heck Thomas, My Papa*. Norman: Levite of Apache, 1988.

Miller, Nyle H., and Joseph W. Snell. *The Great Gunfighters of Kansas Cowtowns, 1867-1886*. Lincoln & London: University of Nebraska Press, 1963.

Morris, John W. *Cities of Oklahoma*. Oklahoma City: Oklahoma Historical Society, 1979.

Morris, John, et al. *Historical Atlas of Oklahoma*. Norman: University of Oklahoma Press, 1976.

Nash, Jay Robert. *Encyclopedia of Western Lawmen and Outlaws*. NY: Da Capo Press, Inc., 1994.

'Neath August Sun-1901, Second Edition. Lawton: Lawton Business and Professional Women's Club, 1955.

Nelson, Oliver. *The Cowman's Southwest; Being the Reminiscences of Oliver Nelson; Freighter, Camp Cook, Cowboy, Frontiersman in Kansas, Indian Territory, Texas, and Oklahoma, 1878-1889*, Edited by Angie Debo. Lincoln: University of Nebraska Press, 1986.

Nix, E. D. *Oklahombres*. Lincoln: University of Nebraska Press, 1993.

Pioneers of Kingfisher County: 1889-1976. Kingfisher, Okla.: Kingfisher Bicentennial Committee, 1976.

Portrait and Biographical Record of Oklahoma. Chicago: Chapman Publishing, 1901.

Preece, Harold. *The Dalton Gang*. NY: Hastings House, 1963.

Rainey, George. *The Cherokee Strip*. Enid: 1925.

Rainey, Mrs. George. *In Memory: Cherokee Strip Brands*. Enid: 1949.

Records, Laban S. *Cherokee Outlet Cowboy*, Edited by Ellen Jayne Maris Wheeler. Norman: University of Oklahoma Press, 1995.

Ridings, Sam P. *The Chisholm Trail*. Guthrie: Co-operative Publishing Company, 1936.

Rock Island Lines Station Book, Issued February 1, 1910, No. 58.

Roosevelt, Theodore. *Outdoor Pastimes of an American Hunter*. NY: Charles Scribner & Sons, 1905.

Ruth, Kent. *Oklahoma: A Guide to the Sooner State*. Norman: University of Oklahoma Press, 1957.

Samuelson, Nancy B. *Shoot from the Lip*. Eastford, Conn.: Shooting Star Press, 1998.

_____. *The Dalton Gang Story*. Eastford, Conn.: Shooting Star Press, 1992.

Sanders, Gwendoline, and Paul. *The Sumner County Story*. North Newton, Kans.: The Mennonite Press, 1967.

Shirk, George H. *Oklahoma Place Names*. Norman: University of Oklahoma Press, 1987.

Shirley, Glenn. *Desperado from Cowboy Flat*. Stillwater: Barbed Wire Press, 1997.

_____. *Guardian of the Law*. Austin: Eakin Press, 1988.

_____. *Heck Thomas: Frontier Marshal*. NY: Chilton Co., 1962.

_____. *They Outrobbed Them All*. Stillwater: Barbed Wire Press, 1992.

_____. *West of Hell's Fringe*. Norman: University of Oklahoma Press, 1978.

Standard Atlas of Kingfisher County. Chicago: George A. Ogle & Company, 1906.

Tanton, Ralph E. *Early Legends Along Osage Creek*. Medford, Okla.: Grant County Historical Society, 1975.

_____. *Historical Tales of the Cherokee Strip and the Rhubarb Farm*. Freeman, S.D.: Pine Hill Press, 1982.

Wellman, Paul I. *A Dynasty of Western Outlaws*. Garden City: Doubleday & Co., 1961.

White, Richard. *It's Your Misfortune and None of My Own: History of the American West*. Norman: University of Oklahoma Press, 1991.

Articles

Burchardt, Bill. "The Glass Mountains." *Oklahoma Today*, Winter, 1970-71, Vol. XXI, No. I.

Bibliography

Burton, Art. "Women of the Shooting Iron." *Oklahombres Journal*, Winter 1996, Vol. VII, No. 2.

Chapman, Berlin B. "The Legal Sooners of 1889 in Oklahoma." *Chronicles of Oklahoma*, 1957-1958, Vol. XXXV, No. 4.

Colcord, Charles F. "Reminiscences of Charles F. Colcord." *Chronicles of Oklahoma*, March 1934, Vol. XII. .

Cordry, Dee. "The Last of the Doolin Gang, Little Dick West." *Oklahombres Journal*, Spring 1998, Vol. IX, No. 3.

Fulbright, Jim. "W.D. 'Bill' Fossett, Pioneer & Lawman." *Oklahombres Journal*, Fall 2001, Vol. XII, No. 2.

Goodrich, Anna Fossett. "Frank J. Fossett." *Journal of the Cherokee Strip*, September 1977.

Koch, Michael. "Zip" Wyatt: The Cherokee Strip Outlaw." *Oklahombres Journal*, Spring 1996, Vol. VII, No. 3.

"Lawton: A Child of the Prairie." *Museum of the Great Plains*, Lawton, Okla., 2001.

Madsen, Chris, "Fourscore Years a Fighter." *Daily Oklahoman*, 1935-36.

Manigold, Burt, and Joseph Rosenberger. "Last of the Gunfighters." *Golden West Magazine*, May 1968.

Martin, Rebecca. "Lawbreaker, Lawbreaker." *A Moment in Time*, Kansas State Historical Society, September 1995.

Meade, J. M. "An Internal History of the Atchison, Topeka and Santa Fe Railway, 1916 to 1919." *Meade's Manual*, circa 1912.

Moss, Genevieve. "C. P. 'Doc' Wickmiller." *Chronicles of Oklahoma*, Summer 1985, Vol. LXIII, No. 2.

Richards, Albert. "History of Sumner County." *Historical Atlas of Sumner County*, Philadelphia, 1883.

Roberts, Gary, L. "Introduction." *Oklahombres* by E.D. Nix, Bison Press Edition, 1993.

Samuelson, Nancy B. "Some Notes on Oklahoma's Female Marshals." *Quarterly for the National Association of Outlaw and Lawman History*, July-September 1998, Vol. XXII, No. 3.

Seaver, W. G. "Railroad Skirmishes." *Railroad Man's Magazine*, Vol I, No. 1, New York, October 1906.

"The Blizzard of 1886." *A Kansas Portrait*, Kansas State Historical Society, 2001.

Whipple, Right Reverend Henry B. "Light & Shadow of a Long Episcopate, the Reminisces and Recollections of the Right Reverend Henry B. Whipple, Bishop of Minnesota, 1902." Minnesota Historical Society, Timepieces, The Dakota Conflict, 2001.

Unpublished Materials and Letters

Bristow, Neil Allen. "Colcord and Bristow Family Genealogy," 2001.

Brownlee, Emory D. "Why is Kingfisher?" An Address to the Eighty-Niner Celebration, Kingfisher, Okla., 1902.

Cheatum, Anita. An Address to the Kansas State Senate, January 23, 1996.

Daniels, C. C. "Oklahoma: Land of the Fair God," unpublished manuscript, 1947.

Durr, Deborah. Letter to the author regarding family genealogy, Kingman, Kans., April 12, 2002.

Fiegel, Melvin. "The Founding and Early Development of Kingfisher, Oklahoma," Thesis, Oklahoma State University, 1965.

Fossett, W. D. Letter to H.S. Tennant, Oklahoma State Highway Commission regarding location of Chisholm Trail, Kingfisher, Okla., May 9, 1933.

Fox, Harry. Letter from son of Rock Island Railroad Superintendent Harry P. Fox, about his father's experiences, to Preston Rishaw, Chester County, Pa., March 1958.

Goodrich, Mrs. C. E. (Anna Leah Fossett) Letter to Paul D. Fossett, II, September 12, 1977.

Goodrich, Mrs. C. E. (Anna Leah Fossett). "The Fossetts in America." Genealogy, 1974.

Kingman City Scrapbook, Kingman, Kansas, Carnegie Library, Vol. III.

Mitchell, Letha. "Chikaskia Township-Spivey Town," Kingman, Kansas, Carnegie Library, 1989.

Rock Island Technical Society. "A Brief Historical Overview of the Chicago, Rock Island & Pacific Railroad History." Rock Island Railroad, 1970.

Standley, Fred Smith. "The Oklahoma Historical Society, 1893-1943." M.A. Thesis, University of Oklahoma, 1986.

Collections

Barde, Frederick S. "A War Against the Railroad." 1897. Manuscript & Archives Division. Oklahoma Historical Society, Oklahoma City.

Barde, Frederick S. "Barde Collection." Manuscript & Archives Division. Oklahoma Historical Society, Oklahoma City.

Barnes, Louise S. "Summary of Indian-Pioneer History Project Interview with W. D. Fossett." November 18, 1937. Manuscript & Archives Division. Oklahoma Historical Society, Oklahoma City.

Byrd, Judge J. W. Indian-Pioneer History Project for Oklahoma. Interview by: Works Progress Administration, Vol. 90. Manuscript & Archives Division. Oklahoma Historical Society, Oklahoma City.

Callahan, F. J. Indian-Pioneer History Project for Oklahoma. Interview by: Works Progress Administration, March 14, 1938. Manuscript & Archives Division. Oklahoma Historical Society, Oklahoma City.

Durr, Deborah, Fossett and Miller Family Genealogy Files, Kingman, Kans.

Fossett, Eugene W. Fossett Family Geneaology Files, Venice Fla., May 2000.

Fossett, W. D. Indian-Pioneer History Project for Oklahoma. Interview by: Works Progress Administration, Aug. 11, 18, 1937. Manuscript & Archives Division. Oklahoma Historical Society, Oklahoma City.

Fossett, W. D. Files of Correspondence, 1902-1905. Western History Collection, Oklahoma University Library, Norman, Okla.

"History of Jefferson County Oklahoma." Oklahoma Department of Library Archives, Norman, Okla.

Stehno, Albert. Private Records Collection. Cherokee Strip Cowpunchers Association, Billings, Okla.

Documents, Records and Directories

Amherst Township, Fillmore County, Ohio, 1870 Census.

Canadian County, Oklahoma, Marriage License, November 27, 1926.

Colorado State Census, 1880, 1885.

Falls Township, Sumner County, Kansas, 1875 Census.

Guthrie, Oklahoma, Business and Residence Directory, Guthrie & Logan County, 1898, 1900-1907.

Homestead Act, Chapter LXXV, 37th Congressional Session II, 1862.

Kingfisher, Kingfisher County, Okla., County Court Case Record No. 2346, November 28, 1900.

Kingfisher, Kingfisher County, Okla., County Court Clerk Land Records, 1893 to 1931.

Kingfisher, Kingfisher County, Okla., Divorce Record, November 17, December 21, 1921.

Kingfisher, Kingfisher County, Okla., Patent Record, Book No. 1.

Kingfisher, Kingfisher County, Okla., 1920 Census.

Kingfisher, Okla., City Cemetery Records.

Kingfisher, Okla., City Minutes Record, November 10, December 22, 1919; February 21, 1920.

Kingman County, Kansas, Appearance Docket Book B, Case No. 494, March 1885.

Kingman County, Kansas, Register of Deeds, Numerical Index of Lands, Vol. 8.

Kingman County, Kansas, Register of Deeds records, April 8, 1884; March 29, 1886; May 24, 1886.

Kingman, Kansas, City Council Minutes, June 9, July 7, 18, 1884; October 6, 1884; July 1, 5, November 4, 1885; May 3, July 6, 1886.

Kingman, Kansas, City Directory, 1887.

Kingman, Kingman County, Kansas, 1885 Census.

Bibliography

McPherson County, Kansas, Marriage License, May 10, 1885.

Minnesota Adjutant General's Report of 1866: Personnel Roster of the Minnesota First Cavalry, 1863.

Oklahoma State Census, 1910, 1920.

Oklahoma State Department of Health, Death Certificate of Lewis D. Fossett, No. 013321, October 15, 1952.

Oklahoma State Department of Health, Delayed Certificate of Birth for Irene Madaline Miller, March 12, 1901.

Oklahoma State Department of Health, Funeral Record and Standard Certificate of Death of Laura Fossett, January 20, 1950.

Perry Township, Brown County, Ohio, 1860 Census.

Pueblo, Colorado, T. G. McCarthy Funeral Home and Roselawn Cemetery records, April 3, 1901.

Sedgwick County, Kansas, Marriage License, February 3, 1904.

Sumner County, Kansas, Register of Deeds, April 16, 1879, Vol. IX.

Sumner County, Kansas, 1880 Census.

Sumner County, Kansas, Register of Deeds, Book 2, p. 226, April 29, 1879.

U.S. Department of Justice, U.S. Marshal's Oath of Office, April 7, 1902.

U.S. District Court Expense Record, Form #270, March 31, 1901.

U.S. District Court Expense Record, Form #22, June 30, 1903.

U.S. Government General Pension Index, 1861-1934, Roll 312, Document 18, Deposition "C" by Isaac H. Fossett, September 26, 1900.

U.S. Government General Pension Index, 1861-1934, Roll 312, Document 16, Deposition "A" by Elizabeth Fossett.

U.S. Government Receiver's Office, Land Certificate No. 12035, Wichita, Kansas, April 14, 1880.

Newspapers

Anadarko Daily Democrat, May 23, 24, 1906.

Anadarko Tribune, July 4, 1902.

Ardmore State Herald, March 14, 1895.

273

Ardmore Statesman, November 16, 1924.

Arkansas (City, Kansas) *Republican*, April 10, 1886.

Belle Plaine News, April 17, September 4, 1886.

Caldwell Commercial, May 20, July 1, 8, 28, 1880; November 3, 1881; June 29, 1882.

Caldwell Journal, January 26, 1888.

Caldwell Messenger, May 10, 1971.

Caldwell Post, July 10, August 21, November 18, 27, December 4, 18, 1879; January 8, May 18, June 24, 1880; July 28, December 22, 1881.

Chandler Tribune, April 3, 1902.

Cherokee (Talequah, Oklahoma) *Advocate*, March 27, 1897.

Cherokee (Pond Creek, Oklahoma) *Sentinel,* April 12, 26, May 17, June 7, 20, 1894; April 20, 1895.

Chickasha Daily Express, March 14, July 6, 29, August 5, 7, 1901.

Clark County (Kansas) *Clipper*, October 23, 1930.

Cordell Beacon, January 3, 1902.

Daily Oklahoman, May 26, 1894; April 1, 1902; November 23, 1905; August 27, 1907; April 23, 1939; March 10, 1940.

El Reno American, September 19, 1908; January 1, February 1, 1909.

El Reno Democrat, December 16, 1909.

El Reno Eagle, April 8, 1895.

Enid Daily Wave, April 10, 13, May 5, July 13, 1894; October 3, 1895.

Enid Morning News, March 30, 1912.

Enid News & Eagle, March 3, 1993.

Enid Weekly Wave, August 8, 1895.

Guthrie Daily Leader, September 19, 1893; January 25, July 8, 1896; February 17, March 11, April 9, 1898, May 26, 1898; April 11, 1899; January 3, 1902; January 29, February 16 March 5, 7, 9, May 11, July 8, 17, 1903; January 2, 13, February 27, June 9, August 5, 1904; April 13, 1905; October 18, 19, 1906; September 14, 1907; December 8, 1910; April 14, 1963.

Hennessey Clipper, April 4, 6, 11, August 1, 8, 1895; March 21, 1940.

Bibliography

Hobart (Oklahoma) *News-Republican*, May 17, 1906.

Kansas City Sunday Times, January 12, 1882.

Kingfisher Daily World, March 26, 1891.

Kingfisher Free Press, June 9, September 1, 1892; June 1, 22, 1893; April 14, 18, June 17, August 1, 8, 15, 25, November 28, 1895; May 13, October 18, November 9, 11, 1897; May 16, 1898; January 18, June 7, 1900; May 30, June 13, 1901; January 16, April 3, October 8, 1902; March 12, 19, 1903; May 26, 1920; October 24, 1929; April 17, 1939; March 11, 18, 1940; April 18, 1949.

Kingfisher Reformer, March 24, 1904.

Kingfisher Times Weekly, September 8, 1892.

Kingfisher Times, April 4, 1895; April 3, 1902; January 7, March 4, April 15, December 2, 1926; April 21, 1927; August 8, 1928; October 17, 1929; June 6, 1934; March 13, 14, 1940.

Kingfisher Weekly Free Press, June 26, 1917; October 1, 1918.

Kingfisher Weekly Star, February 29, March 7, August 5, 12, 1912.

Kingman Courier, April 18, May 9, June 6, 13, 20, November 21, 1884; January 2, April 24, June 12, 19, July 24, 31, August 7, 14, September 11, 18, 25, October 9, 1885; January 8, 22, 29, April 23, March 12, June 11, September 10, 17, 24, October 8, December 31, 1886; January 7, May 13, September 22, December 1, 1887; March 15, 1940.

Kingman Journal, September 20, 1907.

Kingman Leader-Courier, September 19, 1907; April 14, 1981.

Kingman Mercury, August 2, 1882; December 6, 1883.

Kingman Morning Courier, January 1, 1887.

Larned Tiller & Toiler, June 1996.

Lawton Daily Democrat, August 6, 1901.

Lawton News-Republican, February 15, 1906.

McAlester News, February 27, 1902.

Muskogee Weekly Phoenix, November 19, 1891.

New World (Kingfisher, Oklahoma), May 18, 1889; April 4, 1891.

Norman Transcript, August 14, 1902.

North Enid Weekly Tribune, April 12, 1894.

Oklahoma City Times, November 3, 1924.

Oklahoma Daily Times-Journal, August 5, 1895; January 20, 24, 1896.

Oklahoma Leader, February 15, 1906.

Oklahoma State Capital, April 11, 12, 1894; August 26, 1896; June 10, October 13, November 8, 1897; April 8, 1898; May 2, September 14, 22, 1901; January 3, 5, November 8, 12, 1902; March 5, 1903; April 9, 12, June 9, 1905; February 6, 1906; November 11, 1987.

Oklahoma State Register, February 8, 22, 1906.

Perkins (Oklahoma) *Journal*, August 5, 1904.

Pond Creek Echo, April 13, June 23, 1894.

Pond Creek News, April 14, 1894.

Pond Creek Tribune, April 12, 1894.

Shawnee Herald, July 2, 12, 1902.

Shawnee News, September 23, 1905.

Southern Kansas Democrat, October 20, 1883; August 14, November 20, December 4, 1884; February 12, April 23, June 4, 1885.

Sumner County Press, June 17, 1875; January 6, June 1, July 6, 1876; February 28, 1878; December 22, 1881.

Tulsa World, September 7, 1952.

Watonga Republican, January 9, 1902.

Waurika News, February 7, 1908.

Weekly Oklahoma State Capital, November 8, 1902.

Wellington Monitor Free Press, April 11, 1895.

Wellington Monitor Free Press, April 11, September 18, 19, 1895.

Wichita Eagle, April 11, 1894; February 4, 1904; April 11, 1907.

Wichita Times, December 17, 1881.

Photo Credits

Index

G

Gallagher, ____(Rock Island engineer), 121
Gallagher, Pete, 21, 22
Garfield County, 88, 112, 133, 136, 200
Geary, O.T., 186, 187
Glasgow, Scotland, 4
Glass Mountains, 125, *128*, 129, 130, 138, 185
Glitsch, Carl, 211
Godown, H.S., 46
Goemmer, Sherry (Fieser), 223
Goodrich, Anna Leah (Fossett), 224
Grant County, O.T., 88, 93, 95, 112
Green, Donald Robertson "Cannonball," 51, 52, 53
Greensburg, Kansas, 52, 125
Greer County, 79
Greever Canyon, 130
Grimes, Joseph, 72, 155, 156, *157*, 159, 160, 162, *165*, 207, 219
Grimes, William, 76, 80, 122, 123, 141
Gulf, Colorado & Santa Fe Railway, 83
Guthrie Daily Capital, 152
Guthrie Daily Leader, 84, 141, 146, 186, 197, 203, 204
Guthrie, O.T., 79, 80, 83, 87, 94, 124, 125, 135, 139, 141, 142, 144, 145, 146, 150, 151, 152, 155, 156, 163, 167, 171, 177, 179, 180, *182*, 186, 187, 188, *190, 191, 192*, 194, 197, 199, 201-205, 209, 211, 216, 218, 219

H

Hagar, R.H., 105, 108, 110
Haines, Wiley G., 186-188
Harmon, Jake, 103, 104, 107, 108, 110, 112

Hancock, J.E., 73
Harper County, Kansas, 60
Harper, Kansas, 57, 60, 70
Harrison, Ark., 177
Harrison, Benjamin, 68, 79, 80
Hayes, William Edward, 86
Hays, Kansas, 16
Hennessey, O.T., 17-19, 52, 87, 91, 112, 119, 133, 134, 136, 163, 183-187
Hennessey, Pat, 17, 18, 19
Hicks, W.J., 89
Hildreth, Marion, 132
Hill, Doug, 35, 37, 40
Hitchcock, Ethan, 168
Hitt,____(Rock Island Gen. Manager), 133
Hobart, O.T., 178
Holder, Stephanie (Meilert), 223
Holt, Bill, 184
Homestead Act, 1, 68, 132
Homestead, O.T., 132
Horseman, William, 33
Houston, Luther "Lute," 174, 175, 177, 178
Hubbard, George E., 74
Hubbel, W.N., 34
Hudson, William Wesley (aka Fred & Little Wes), 6, 173-179
Hudson's Bay Company, 6
Hughes, Ben, 170, 171, 174, 178
Hughes, Bob, *109*, 113, 119, 174
Hughes, Jim, 170, 171, 174, 175, 178
Hughes, Mattie (Houston), 174
Humphrey, Lew, 102
Hunnewell, Kansas, 30
Hunt, C.B., 179
Hunt, Frank, 33, 34
Hutchinson, Kansas, 20, 44
Hutchinson-Medicine Lodge Trail, 44

Index

Laredo, Texas, 10
Laughlin's Bull Train, 12
Lawton Daily Democrat, 162
Lawton, O.T., 159, 160, 162, 163, 168, 169, 170
Leadville, Colorado, 22
Leahy, David, 216, 218
Leard, Frank, 147, 148
Leard, Julius, 147, 148
Leard, Mary, 147, 153
Leavenworth, Kansas, 28
Ledbetter, James F. "Bud," 144
Leland House Hotel, Caldwell, Kansas, 33
Lewis County, New York, 4
Lewis, Admire O., 76
Liggett, W.A., 47
Lisbon, O.T., 72, 74, 76
Little Beaver Creek, 186
Lockett, F.M. "Ed," 173-177
Logan County, O.T., 79, 134, 144, 183
Love, Tom, 35-39
Lowe, Marcus A., 115
Lynn, Wiley, 211, 212

M

Mack, James, 122
Madsen, Chris, 110, 113, 118, 119, 122, 137, 174, 175, 218
Majors, Henry, 186
Malaley, W.E., "Billy," 19, 115
Manigold, Elizabeth (Fossett),4, 7, 8
Mankato, Minnesota, 5
Mankin, "Comanche Bill," 36
Manning, C.H., 24, 43, 48
Manning, E.C., 45
Marland, Okla (see Bliss), 216
Marlow, I.T., 159, 160
Marshall, O.T., 134
Marshall, Texas, 209
Martin, Jim, 35, 37
Martin, Sam, 183-187

Martin, Will, 183-187
Matoon, Illinois, 24
Maud, O.T., 149, 151
McCartney, Jesse, 20, 21
McCoy, Joseph G., 15
McCracken, J.L., 171, 173, 177, 184
McDonald, Alva, 211, 219
McDonald, Bill, 197
McEllen, Joe, 108
McGeisey, Lincoln, 148, 152
McGuire, Bird S., 201, 202
McKinley, William, 80, 140, 167, 195
McKenzie, Dr. H.B., 137
McMartin, Colonel D.F., 69
McMechan, Thomas, 151
McPherson County, Kansas, 56
Mead, Edgar A., 53, 58, 63
Mead, James R., 85
Meade, Kansas, 81
Meagher, Mike, 33-39
Medford, Grant County, Okla., 95
Medicine Lodge Trail, 44
Medicine Lodge, Kansas, 40, 48
Meilert, Cary, 223
Memphis, Tennessee, 62, 65
Miles, John D., 19, 74
Miller Brothers' "101" Ranch, 216
Miller, Ben, 144
Miller, Fred, 54
Miller, Freeman E., 141
Miller, Irene Madaline, 154, 155, 206, 222 (see also Madaline Miller Klaver)
Miller, John, 170
Miller, Louisa, 222
Miller, Mary Frances "Mamie," 154, 155, 179, 188, 205, 206, 221, 222 (see also "Mamie" Fossett)
Miller, Minnie, 54, 222
Miller, Peter, 54, 146, 222
Miller, Richard Hugo, 54, 146, 147, 154, 155, 179, 180, 188, 205, 206, 221, 222
Milnee, Bert, 10

Index

S

T

The Author

Jim Fulbright is a professional pilot and former journalist whose awards include four Emmys for television news and documentary specials. He is the author of the history book, *Aviation in Tennessee*, and has written numerous articles on aviation and Western Americana.

He and his wife live in Goodlettsville, Tennessee. They have three children and three grandchildren.